ISSN 1020-5489

# THE STATE OF WORLD FISHERIES AND AQUACULTURE

## 2000

FAO Fisheries Department

**FOOD AND AGRICULTURE ORGANIZATION OF THE UNITED NATIONS**
**Rome, 2000**

Editing, design, graphics and desktop publishing:
**Editorial Group**
**FAO Information Division**

ISBN 92-5-104492-9

# FOREWORD

This is the third issue of *The State of World Fisheries and Aquaculture.* It follows the pattern set by the previous issues, published in 1996 and 1998. The purpose continues to be to provide policy-makers, civil society and those who derive their livelihood from the sector a comprehensive, objective and global view of capture fisheries and aquaculture, including associated policy issues.

The concerns of consumers and fishers, which are central to the state of world fisheries and aquaculture, are reflected in a number of topics examined in *The State of World Fisheries and Aquaculture 2000.* A discussion of current issues is complemented by summary reports on national and international activities undertaken to address them. Some issues are well known and figure prominently in the international debate – the issue of fish quality and safety, for instance, and that of genetically modified organisms and fisheries. Also discussed are two important issues that are much less known and understood: the first is fishers' safety; the second is the culture of fishing communities. It is not commonly known that fishing at sea is probably the most dangerous occupation in the world. *The State of World Fisheries and Aquaculture 2000* reports on this issue in the hope that a more widespread realization of this aspect of fisheries will lead to effective measures to improve fishers' safety. Recent developments in fisheries governance seem to lead to a larger role for fishers in fisheries management. However, for fishers to become effective partners in management, a better understanding of their communities' culture is essential. Highlights from a recently completed FAO study of this subject are included in this publication on the premise that reaching a better understanding of such cultures is a key to fisheries management and food security in most artisanal and small-scale fisheries.

Sustainable exploitation continues to be a desirable goal for all fisheries and aquaculture operations. This year, we report on some aspects of the progress made by the international fisheries community towards achieving this goal. Summary information is provided on the state of fisheries management, and several factors to be considered in efforts to improve management are discussed, for example: i) property rights – seen as a means for defining and specifying the entitlements, privileges and responsibilities created by different types of fisheries management regimes; ii) the role of indicators of sustainable development and their integration with the precautionary approach, as the use of such indicators is set to become a practice leading towards an ecosystems framework for management; iii) a plausible approach for dealing with illegal, unreported and unregulated fishing; and iv) ecolabelling, the basic principles of which are described, together with the somewhat controversial standing of this practice and its potential contribution to fisheries management.

As in the past, *The State of World Fisheries and Aquaculture 2000* begins by reviewing recent developments in the status of resources, production from capture fisheries and aquaculture, utilization and trade. Recent advances in fishing technology are also covered. This information is complemented by a report – in Part 3 – on the economic viability of selected commercial fishing fleets. A general outlook is provided in Part 4, which examines recent trends and their possible impact on the nature and character of the fishing industry, as well as on the level and distribution of future fish consumption.

It is my hope that *The State of World Fisheries and Aquaculture 2000* will generate awareness of the increasing global interaction inherent in the sector. In turn, this greater awareness should stimulate global, regional and national efforts to improve responsible practices and promote sustainability in fisheries and aquaculture.

**Ichiro Nomura**
Assistant Director-General
FAO Fisheries Department

# CONTENTS

# BOXES

# TABLES

# FIGURES

# ACKNOWLEDGEMENTS

*The State of World Fisheries and Aquaculture 2000* was prepared by FAO Fisheries Department staff, led by a team comprising U. Wijkstrom, A. Gumy and R. Grainger. General direction was provided by the department's management staff, including: L. Ababouch; J. Csirke; S.M. Garcia; J. Jiansan; Z. Karnicki; I. Nomura; B. Satia; J. Valdemarsen; and G. Valdimarsson.

The preparation of Part 1, World review of fisheries and aquaculture, was the overall editorial responsibility of P. Medley and R. Grainger, who coordinated the contributions made by R. Grainger (production, capture fisheries); J. Csirke (resources); P. Medley (ecosystems, management); I. Orzsesko (management information); A. Smith (fishing vessels); J. Valdemarsen (fishing technology); R. Subasinghe (aquaculture); D.M. Bartley (inland fisheries); A. Crispoldi (consumption); and S. Vannuccini (trade).

Contributors to Part 2, Selected issues facing fishers and aquaculturists, included: J. Turner (fishers' safety); H.M. Lupin (fish quality and safety); R. Metzner, who is with Fisheries Western Australia (property rights and fisheries management); D. Doulman (illegal, unreported and unregulated fishing); S.M. Garcia (indicators of sustainable development and the precautionary approach in marine capture fisheries); P. Medley (monitoring the impact of fishing on the marine ecosystems); D.M. Bartley (genetically modified organisms and fisheries); and R. Willman (ecolabelling in fisheries management).

Contributors to Part 3, Highlights of special FAO studies, included: J.R. McGoodwin (understanding the cultures of fishing communities: a key to fisheries management and food security); U. Tietze (economic viability of marine capture fisheries); and S. Garcia and J. de Leiva Moreno (trends in world fisheries and their resources).

Part 4, Outlook, was written by U. Wijkstrom.

Part 5, Fisheries activities of country groupings, was written by A. Gumy.

Several other staff members as well as non-FAO authors have contributed texts on specific issues, and they are cited in the relevant boxes throughout the publication. Information of relevance for all five parts has been provided by FAO staff in the Regional and Subregional Offices.

The Editorial Group of the FAO Information Division was responsible for the editing, design and production of *The State of World Fisheries and Aquaculture 2000*.

# GLOSSARY

**ACFR**
Advisory Committee on Fisheries
Research (FAO)

**ACP**
African, Caribbean and Pacific Group of
States (EU)

**AFFP**
Arab Federation of Fish Producers

**AIS**
automatic identification system

**AMAF**
Asian Ministers of Agriculture and
Fisheries (ASEAN)

**APFIC**
Asia-Pacific Fisheries Commission

**ASEAN**
Association of Southeast Asian Nations

**ASFA**
Aquatic Sciences and Fisheries
Abstracts

**CAC**
Codex Alimentarius Commission

**CAP**
Common Agricultural Policy (EC)

**CARICOM**
Caribbean Community and Common
Market

**CCAMLR**
Commission for the Conservation of
Antarctic Marine Living Resources

**CCSBT**
Commission for the Conservation of
Southern Bluefin Tuna

**CDC**
Centers for Disease Control and
Prevention (USA)

**CDQ**
community development quota

**CECAF**
Fishery Committee for the Eastern
Central Atlantic

**CEMARE**
Centre for the Economics and
Management of Aquatic Resources (UK)

**CFP**
Common Fisheries Policy (EC)

**CFRAMP**
CARICOM Fisheries Resource
Assessment and Management Program

**CIDA**
Canadian International Development
Agency

**CIS**
Commonwealth of Independent States

**COFI**
Committee on Fisheries (FAO)

**COMESA**
Common Market for Eastern and
Southern Africa

**CPUE**
catch per unit effort

**CSD**
Commission on Sustainable
Development (UN)

**DANIDA**
Danish International Development Agency

**DWFN**
Distant Water Fishing Nations

**EC**
European Community

**ECOWAS**
Economic Community of West African
States

**EEC**
European Economic Community
(superseded by EC)

**EEZ**
exclusive economic zone

**EU**
European Union

**FAD**
fish attraction device

**FCA**
fisheries cooperative association

**FFA**
South Pacific Forum Fisheries Agency

**FIFG**
Financial Instrument for Fisheries
Guidance (EC)

**FIGIS**
Fisheries Global Information System

**GAA**
Global Aquaculture Alliance

**GFCM**
General Fisheries Commission for the
Mediterranean

**GIS**
geographic information system

**GMDSS**
Global Maritime Distress Safety System

**GMO**
genetically modified organism

**GPS**
global positioning system

**GRT**
gross registered ton

**GT**
gross tonnage, or tonnage (abbrev.)

**HACCP**
Hazard Analysis and Critical Control
Point (system)

**HP**
horsepower

**IASR**
Icelandic Association for Search and
Rescue

**IBSFC**
International Baltic Sea Fishery
Commission

**ICCAT**
International Commission for the
Conservation of Atlantic Tunas

**ICES**
International Council for the Exploration
of the Sea

**ICLARM**
International Centre for Living Aquatic
Resources Management

**IFPRI**
International Food Policy Research Institute

**IFQ**
individual fishing quota

**ILO**
International Labour Organization

**IMO**
International Maritime Organization

**IOTC**
Indian Ocean Tuna Commission

**IPHC**
International Pacific Halibut Commission

**IPTP**
Indo-Pacific Tuna Development and
Management Programme

**IQ**
individual quota

**ISO**
International Organization for
Standardization

**ITE**
individual transferable effort

**ITLOS**
International Tribunal for the Law of the
Sea

**ITQ**
individual transferable quota

**ITSQ**
individual transferable share quota

**IUCN**
World Conservation Union

**IUU**
illegal, unreported and unregulated (fishing)

**IVQ**
individual vessel quota

**IWC**
International Whaling Commission

**LAES**
Latin American Economic System

**LIFDC**
low-income food-deficit country

**LMIS**
Lloyd's Maritime Information Services

**LMO**
living modified organism

**MAC**
Marine Aquarium Council

**MAGP**
Multi-Annual Guidance Programme (EC)

**MCS**
monitoring, control and surveillance

**MHLC**
Multilateral High-Level Conference on the Conservation and Management of Highly Migratory Fish Stocks in the Central and Western Pacific

**MLTAY**
maximum long-term average yield

**MSC**
Marine Stewardship Council (WWF)

**MSY**
maximum sustainable yield

**NACA**
Network of Aquaculture Centres in Asia-Pacific

**NAFO**
Northwest Atlantic Fisheries Organization

**NAFTA**
North American Free Trade Agreement

**NASCO**
North Atlantic Salmon Conservation Organization

**NCM**
Nordic Council of Ministers

**NEAFC**
Northeast Atlantic Fisheries Commission

**NGO**
non-governmental organization

**OECD**
Organisation for Economic Co-operation and Development

**OLDEPESCA**
Latin American Organization for Fisheries Development

**PSR**
pressure-state-response (framework)

**QMP**
Quality Management Programme (Canada)

**RFS**
Responsible Fisheries Society (USA)

**SAARC**
South Asian Association for Regional Cooperation

**SADC**
Southern African Development Community

**SCRS**
Standing Committee on Research and Statistics (ICCAT)

**SCU**
Sector Coordinating Unit (SADC)

**SEAFDEC**
Southeast Asian Fisheries Development Centre

**SEAFO**
Southeast Atlantic Fisheries Organization

**SPF**
South Pacific Forum

**STCW-F**
Convention for the Standards of Training,
Certification and Watchkeeping for
Fishing Vessel Personnel

**SURFS**
stock use rights in fisheries

**TAC**
total allowable catch

**TRIPS**
(Agreement on) Trade-Related
Aspects of Intellectual Property
Rights (WTO)

**TURFS**
territorial use rights in fisheries

**UNCED**
United Nations Conference on
Environment and Development

**UNCLOS**
United Nations Conference on the Law
of the Sea

**UNDP**
United Nations Development
Programme

**USDA**
United States Department of Agriculture

**USFDA**
United States Food and Drug
Administration

**VMS**
Vessel Monitoring System

**WECAFC**
Western Central Atlantic Fisheries
Commission

**WHO**
World Health Organization

**WRI**
World Resources Institute

**WTO**
World Trade Organization

**WWF**
World Wide Fund for Nature

# PART 1
# World review of fisheries and aquaculture

# World review of fisheries and aquaculture

**OVERVIEW**
Despite fluctuations in supply and demand, caused by the changing state of fisheries resources, the economic climate and environmental conditions, fisheries and aquaculture remain very important as a source of food, employment and revenue in many countries and communities.

Reported global capture fisheries and aquaculture production contracted from a figure of 122 million tonnes in 1997 to 117 million tonnes in 1998. This was mainly owing to the effects of the climate anomaly, El Niño, on some major marine capture fisheries (Figure 1, p. 4 and Table 1, p. 6). However, production recovered in 1999, for which the preliminary estimate is about 125 million tonnes. The production increase of 20 million tonnes over the last decade was mainly due to aquaculture, as capture fisheries production remained relatively stable.

For the two decades following 1950, world marine and inland capture fisheries production increased on average by as much as 6 percent per year, trebling from 18 million tonnes in 1950 to 56 million tonnes in 1969. During the 1970s and 1980s, the average rate of increase declined to 2 percent per year, falling to almost zero in the 1990s. This levelling off of the total catch follows the general trend of most of the world's fishing areas, which have apparently reached their maximum potential for capture fisheries production, with the majority of stocks being fully exploited. It is therefore very unlikely that substantial increases in total catch will be obtained. In contrast, growth in aquaculture production has shown the opposite tendency. Starting from an insignificant total production, inland and marine aquaculture production grew by about 5 percent per year between 1950 and 1969 and by about 8 percent per year during the 1970s and 1980s, and it has increased further to 10 percent per year since 1990.

The global patterns of fish production owe much to the activities of China, which reports production in weight that accounts for 32 percent of the world total. Other major producer countries are Japan, India, the United States, the Russian Federation and Indonesia.

When China is excluded, however, the production of fish used as food for humans has remained relatively stable (Figure 2), but the production of fish destined for animal feed has decreased in recent years – the decline registered in 1998 was largely due to the El Niño effect, particularly on the anchoveta fishery which supplies a significant proportion of the fish used for fishmeal and fish oil. However, the event had much less impact on the supply of fish for food, which declined only slightly to 11.8 kg per capita. Outside China, the world's population has been increasing more quickly than total fish production and the per capita fish supply has declined since the mid-1980s.

In contrast, China has reported increases in fish production and shows little sign of slowing growth (Figure 3). Most of the production is used domestically and for human consumption, but there has also been a recent expansion in the production of feed. There has been a major growth of aquaculture, which now dominates China's production, although capture fisheries have also seen increases. Per capita fish supply, based on reported production, has increased dramatically over the last 20 years, indicating the growing importance of fish as food. This increased supply has been helped by China's slowing population growth.

Employment in the primary capture fisheries and aquaculture production sectors in 1998 is estimated to have been about 36 million people, comprising about 15 million full-time, 13 million part-time and 8 million occasional workers. For the first time, there is an indication that growth in employment in the primary sectors of fisheries and aquaculture has ceased (Figure 4). Employment in inland and marine aquaculture has been increasing, and is now estimated to account for about 25 percent of the total. Marine capture fisheries account for about 60 percent and inland capture fisheries for the remaining 15 percent.

International trade in fishery commodities fell back from a peak of US$53.5 billion dollars (f.o.b.) in 1997 to US$51.3 billion in 1998. This is probably the result of a combination of factors, including a recession in East Asia which weakened demand,

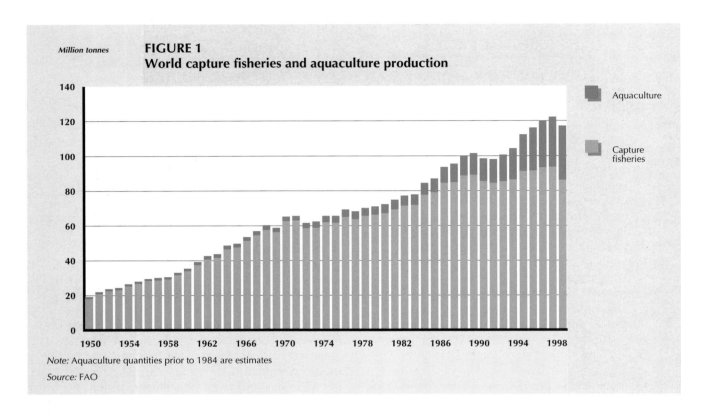

**Million tonnes**

**FIGURE 1**
**World capture fisheries and aquaculture production**

Aquaculture

Capture fisheries

*Note:* Aquaculture quantities prior to 1984 are estimates

*Source:* FAO

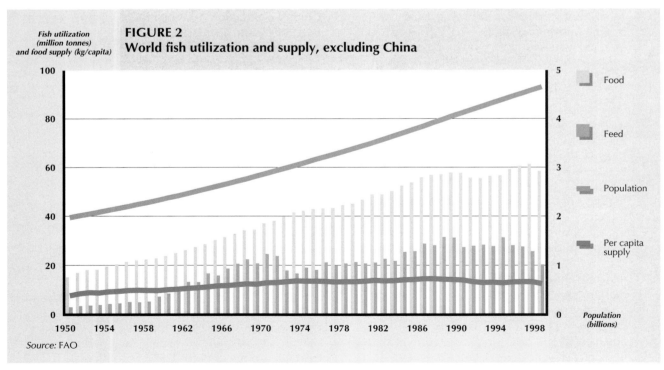

**Fish utilization (million tonnes) and food supply (kg/capita)**

**FIGURE 2**
**World fish utilization and supply, excluding China**

Food

Feed

Population

Per capita supply

*Population (billions)*

*Source:* FAO

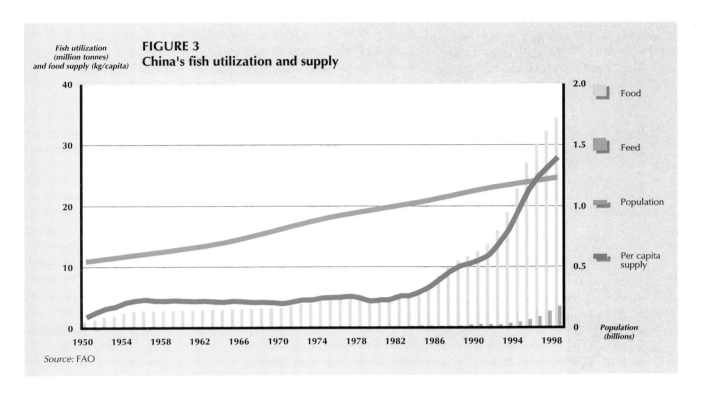

Fish utilization
(million tonnes)
and food supply (kg/capita)

**FIGURE 3**
**China's fish utilization and supply**

☐ Food

■ Feed

▬ Population

■ Per capita supply

Population
(billions)

*Source:* FAO

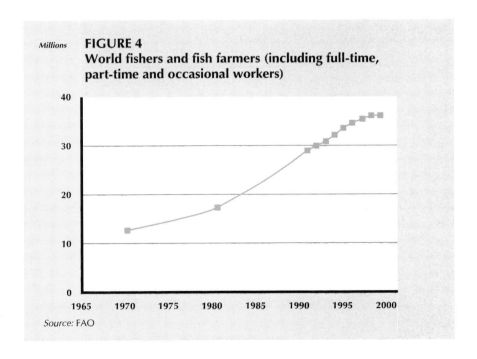

Millions

**FIGURE 4**
**World fishers and fish farmers (including full-time, part-time and occasional workers)**

*Source:* FAO

particularly in Japan, and lower fishmeal production and trade resulting from decreased catches of anchoveta. Preliminary 1999 data indicate a 4 percent growth in the value of world fishery trade (US$53.4 billion). However, there are no indications of increased capture fisheries production in the long term, so any long-term rise in the value of exports is likely to depend on increased aquaculture production or product prices. Developing countries registered a net fishery trade surplus of US$16.8 billion, slightly down from the 1997 level of US$17.3 billion.

## CAPTURE FISHERIES PRODUCTION
**Total capture fisheries production** in 1998 amounted to 86 million tonnes, a noticeable decline from the maximum of about 93 million tonnes recorded in 1996 and 1997, although there was a considerable recovery to an estimated 92 million tonnes in 1999. In 1998, China, Japan, the United States, the Russian Federation, Peru, Indonesia, Chile and India (in that order) were the top producing countries, together accounting for more than half of total capture fisheries production by weight for 1998 (Figure 5). Although in decline, marine capture fisheries continue to account for more than 90

percent of world capture fisheries production. The remainder comes from inland water fisheries, which have increased their output by almost 0.5 million tonnes per year since 1994.

**World marine capture fisheries production** dropped to 78 million tonnes in 1998 (Table 1), representing a 9 percent decline with respect to the all-time production highs of about 86 million tonnes in 1996 and 1997. The decline appears to have been caused essentially by climatic conditions. However, it does not affect the previously reported slowdown in the rate of increase of marine catches for the last decade. The estimated first sale value of the landings also decreased, from about US$81 billion in 1996 and 1997 to US$76 billion in 1998.

Most of the decline in the world's marine fisheries landings in 1998 can be attributed to changes in the Southeast Pacific, which was severely affected by the El Niño event in 1997-1998. Total capture fisheries production from this area dropped from 17.1 million tonnes in 1996 to 14.4 million tonnes in 1997, decreasing even more dramatically to 8 million tonnes in 1998. These figures represent annual declines of 15 and 44 percent,

TABLE 1

### World fisheries production and utilization

| | 1994 | 1995 | 1996 | 1997 | 1998 | 1999[1] |
|---|---|---|---|---|---|---|
| | | | (million tonnes) | | | |
| **PRODUCTION** | | | | | | |
| INLAND | | | | | | |
| Capture | 6.7 | 7.2 | 7.4 | 7.5 | 8.0 | 8.2 |
| Aquaculture | 12.1 | 14.1 | 16.0 | 17.6 | 18.7 | 19.8 |
| **Total inland** | **18.8** | **21.4** | **23.4** | **25.1** | **26.7** | 28.0 |
| | | | | | | |
| MARINE | | | | | | |
| Capture | 84.7 | 84.3 | 86.0 | 86.1 | 78.3 | 84.1 |
| Aquaculture | 8.7 | 10.5 | 10.9 | 11.2 | 12.1 | 13.1 |
| **Total marine** | **93.4** | **94.8** | **96.9** | **97.3** | **90.4** | 97.2 |
| | | | | | | |
| Total capture | 91.4 | 91.6 | 93.5 | 93.6 | 86.3 | 92.3 |
| Total aquaculture | 20.8 | 24.6 | 26.8 | 28.8 | 30.9 | 32.9 |
| **Total world fisheries** | **112.3** | **116.1** | **120.3** | **122.4** | **117.2** | **125.2** |
| | | | | | | |
| **UTILIZATION** | | | | | | |
| Human consumption | 79.8 | 86.5 | 90.7 | 93.9 | 93.3 | 92.6 |
| Reduction to fishmeal and oil | 32.5 | 29.6 | 29.6 | 28.5 | 23.9 | 30.4 |
| Population (billions) | 5.6 | 5.7 | 5.7 | 5.8 | 5.9 | 6.0 |
| Per capita food fish supply (kg) | 14.3 | 15.3 | 15.8 | 16.1 | 15.8 | 15.4 |

[1]Preliminary estimate.

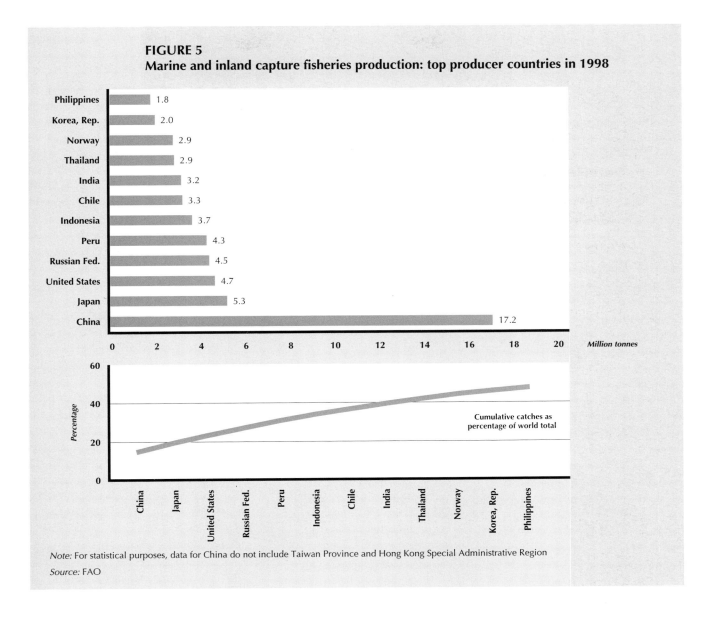

**FIGURE 5**
**Marine and inland capture fisheries production: top producer countries in 1998**

*Note:* For statistical purposes, data for China do not include Taiwan Province and Hong Kong Special Administrative Region

*Source:* FAO

respectively, occurring over two consecutive years in one of the most important fishing areas of the world. Apart from the Southeast Atlantic, the Southwest Pacific and the Western Central Pacific, which have shown positive trends in catches in recent years, all of the world's major fishing areas showed minor changes or declines in landings.

The Northwest Pacific had the largest reported landings in 1998, followed by the Northeast Atlantic and the Western Central Pacific (Figure 6). Typically, high landings are dependent on one or two productive stocks, such as Alaska pollock and Japanese anchovy in the Northwest Pacific, Atlantic herring in the Northeast Atlantic and skipjack and yellowfin tunas in the Western Central Pacific. The dependence of some areas on the

production of a few species is illustrated by the low ranking of the Southeast Pacific, which was the result of the 1998 El Niño event. This area would usually rank second after the Northwest Pacific.

Alaska pollock from the North Pacific had the highest landings in 1998 (Figure 7a). This, too, is unusual, as anchoveta landings generally exceed this quantity and those of Chilean jack mackerel equal it. However, the fisheries for both these species were severely affected in 1998. Alaska pollock catches have fallen by 0.5 million tonnes since 1996, continuing a general decline in production since the mid-1980s, when landings exceeded 6 million tonnes.

The Western Central Pacific shows an overall trend of increasing production, with no

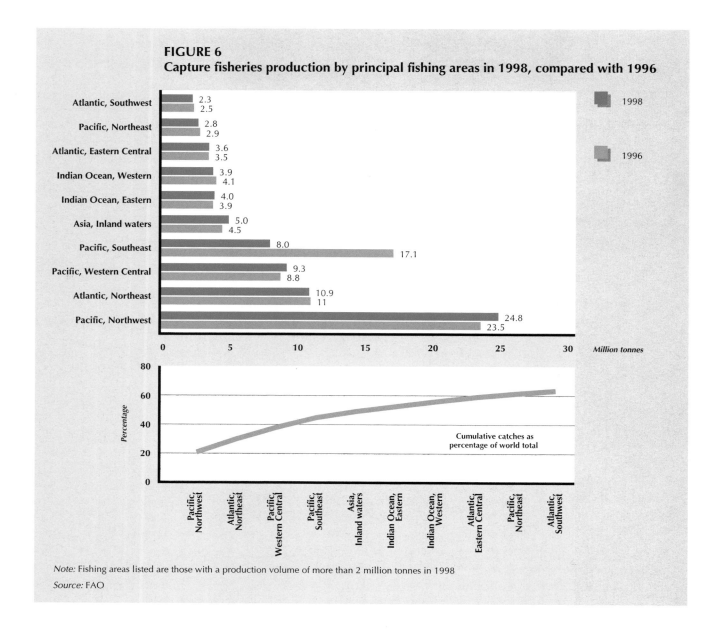

**FIGURE 6**
**Capture fisheries production by principal fishing areas in 1998, compared with 1996**

Note: Fishing areas listed are those with a production volume of more than 2 million tonnes in 1998

Source: FAO

evidence of levelling off in the near future. This overall trend depends not only on the major tuna stocks but also on very wide categories of marine fish, which makes it difficult to assess the underlying trends of different species and stocks. In contrast to these two regions, production in the Northeast Atlantic has remained stable at around 11 million tonnes since the mid-1970s (Figure 7b), although the biomass of cod stocks is currently at a very low level.

It is worth noting that production from the Northwest Pacific has shown a constant overall increase since 1950. However, since 1992, this has continued only because China's reported increases in production have more than made up for combined declines of

all the other countries in the area (Figure 8).

Major fluctuations have been recorded for some individual species over the last three years. Of particular relevance are the increases in landings between 1997 and 1998 for some of the 30 highest-producing species, such as Patagonian grenadiers (up by 285 percent), blue whiting (up by 67 percent), Japanese Spanish mackerel (up by 51 percent), South American pilchard (up by 30 percent) and Japanese anchovy (up by 26 percent). However, overall, the increases in production of some species have been outweighed by the production declines for others, particularly those of major high-producing species, such as anchoveta (down by 78 percent), Chilean jack mackerel (down by 44 percent), capelin (down

## FIGURE 7a
## Capture fisheries production: top species in 1998, compared with 1996

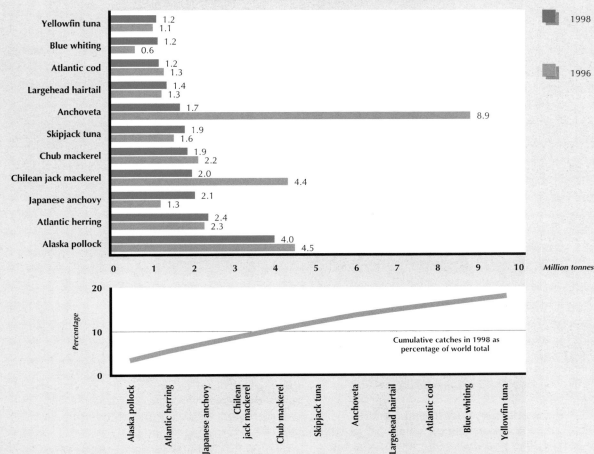

Note: Species listed are those with a production volume of more than 1 million tonnes in 1998

## FIGURE 7b
## Fisheries production trends in selected major fishing areas

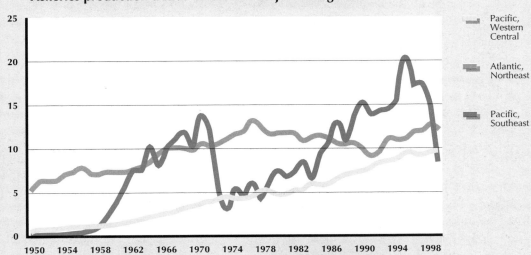

Source: FAO

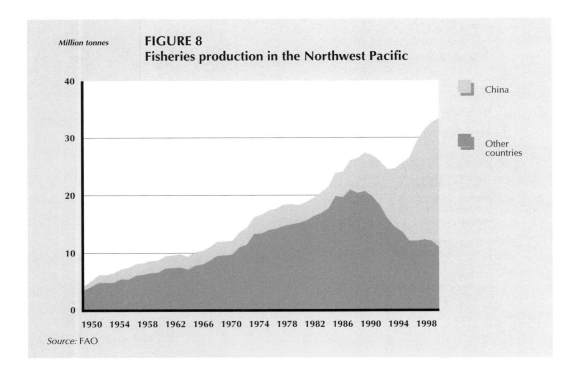

*Million tonnes*

**FIGURE 8**
**Fisheries production in the Northwest Pacific**

China

Other countries

*Source:* FAO

by 38 percent), Japanese flying squid (down by 37 percent), Argentine shortfin squid (down by 33 percent), Atlantic horse mackerel (down by 22 percent) and chub mackerel (down by 21 percent).

In 1998, production from inland capture fisheries was 8 milion tonnes, which represents a 6 percent increase over 1997 levels. The top ten countries with regard to inland fisheries production are listed in Table 2. These countries account for 65 percent of the world's total inland catch. More than 90 percent of this production in 1998 came from developing countries, and only 3.5 percent from industrial countries.

Much of the information on harvests of inland fisheries is not broken down by individual species. Some 46 percent of the catch comprises freshwater fish that are not identified by species, while unidentified crustaceans and molluscs contribute 7.6 and 7 percent, respectively, to production. Overall, 80 percent of the catch in inland waters is not identified by species.

## THE STATUS OF FISHERIES RESOURCES

Although the situation regarding some of the highest-producing stocks has worsened, global exploitation of the main marine fish stocks for which assessment information is available continues to follow the general trend observed in previous years. Overall, the number of underexploited and moderately exploited fisheries resources continues to decline slightly and, as fishing pressure increases, the number of fully exploited stocks remains relatively stable while the number of overexploited, depleted and recovering stocks is increasing slightly.

Among the major marine fish stocks or groups of stocks for which information is available, an estimated 25 to 27 percent are underexploited or moderately exploited and thus represent the main potential source for expansion of total capture fisheries production. About 47 to 50 percent of stocks are fully exploited and are, therefore, producing catches that have either reached or are very close to their maximum limits, with no room expected for further expansion. Another 15 to 18 percent are overexploited and have no potential for further increase. Moreover, there is an increasing likelihood that catches from these stocks will decrease if remedial action is not taken to reduce or revert overfishing conditions. Only then will sustained higher catches be possible. The remaining 9 to 10 percent of stocks have been depleted or are recovering from depletion. As they are less productive than usual, depleted and recovering stocks tend to have ample potential for recuperation that is commensurate with their pre-depletion catch levels. Realizing this potential, however, can be a major undertaking and usually implies the adoption of drastic management measures in order to revert uncontrolled and excessive fishing pressure as well as any other condition that could have contributed to the stock's overexploitation or depletion.

Total catches from the Northwest and the Southeast Atlantic are levelling off after reaching their maximum levels a decade or two ago. In the Eastern Central Atlantic and the Northwest Pacific, total catches are increasing again, after a short decline following their maximum production levels of a decade ago. Most of these changes result from increases in landings of small pelagics. In the Northeast Atlantic, the Western Central Atlantic, the Northeast Pacific, the Mediterranean and Black Sea, the Eastern Central Pacific and the Southwest Pacific, annual catches have stabilized or are declining slightly, having reached their maximum potentials a few years ago. In the Southwest Atlantic and the Southeast Pacific, total annual catches have declined sharply only a few years after reaching their all-time highs. These two areas have been seriously affected by the decline, and in some cases the serious depletion, of important stocks. Among such stocks are Argentine shortfin squid and Argentine hake in the Southwest Atlantic and anchoveta and horse mackerel in the Southeast Pacific.

The areas where total catches are still tending to grow, and where – at least in principle – there is the highest potential for

TABLE 2

| Top ten countries in inland fisheries production | | |
|---|---|---|
| Country | Production in 1998 | Percentage of world production |
| | (tonnes) | (65% for top ten countries) |
| China | 2 280 000 | 28.5 |
| India | 650 000 | 8.1 |
| Bangladesh | 538 000 | 6.7 |
| Indonesia | 315 000 | 3.9 |
| Tanzania, United Rep. | 300 000 | 3.7 |
| Russian Federation | 271 000 | 3.4 |
| Egypt | 253 000 | 3.2 |
| Uganda | 220 000 | 2.8 |
| Thailand | 191 000 | 2.4 |
| Brazil | 180 000 | 2.3 |

TABLE 3

| Inland fisheries production by economic class | | |
|---|---|---|
| Economic class | Production in 1998 | Percentage of world production |
| | (tonnes) | |
| Developing countries or areas | 7 347 000 | 91.8 |
| Economies in transition | 370 000 | 4.6 |
| Industrial countries | 284 000 | 3.6 |
| **Total** | **8 003 000** | |

production increases, are the Eastern and Western Indian Ocean and the Western Central Pacific. These areas tend to have a lower incidence of fully exploited, overexploited, depleted or recovering fish stocks, and a prevalence of underexploited or moderately exploited stocks, although they also have the highest incidence of stocks whose state of exploitation is unknown or uncertain and for which overall production estimates are consequently less reliable.

Inland aquatic resources continue to be under pressure from loss or degradation of habitat and overfishing. Freshwater species are reported to be the most threatened group of vertebrates harvested by humans; however, accurate data are difficult to collect. In areas where studies have been carried out, about 20 percent of freshwater species are threatened, endangered or extinct.[1] Inland fisheries statistics reflect the poor state of information on many inland fisheries resources; only three of the top ten taxa in terms of production are identified by species, and these three account for less than 8 percent of total production. As has already been noted,[2] in many areas, the actual yield from inland fisheries may be several times higher than reported, but work is under way to correct this situation. The Mekong River Commission has revised its unofficial estimates of fisheries production from the Mekong basin, increasing them from approximately 300 000 to 1.2 million tonnes by including family and small-scale fishers whose catches were previously not counted. It is

[1] M. Bruton. 1995. Have fishes had their chips? The dilemma of threatened fishes. *Environmental Biology of Fishes,* 43: 1-27; and World Resources Institute at www.wri.org/wri/wr2000/index.html/.

[2] FAO. 1999. Fisheries Circular No. 942. Rome.

extremely difficult to assess the state of inland fisheries resources when reporting does not include all the sectors of the fishery and when the catch is not broken down by species.

## THE STATUS OF THE ECOSYSTEMS

In addition to the concerns expressed about individual stocks, there is increasing interest in ecosystems and the impact that fishing may be having on their structure and function. There is a shortage of general information on the relationship between the state of marine ecosystems and fishing. Broad indicators of change are available from data on capture fisheries production in the major fishing areas but it is usually difficult to separate changes in exploitation patterns from changes in the underlying ecosystem.

The trend has been for the variety of resources being exploited to increase, probably reflecting the reaching of production limits for major stocks and an expansion of markets for a wider range of fishery products. Indicators regarding the ecologies in which fisheries can develop suggest that the ecosystems in most areas are close to full exploitation. The Eastern Indian Ocean and the Western Central Pacific are the only areas showing little sign of stress, and hence the potential for continued development of resources.

The Northeast Atlantic has followed a trend of declining catches together with a shift towards landings of fish from lower levels in the food web, which may indicate an underlying ecological change (see Monitoring the impact of fishing on marine ecosystems, Part 2, p. 65). The indices that were developed to monitor such change suggest that ecosystems may be shifting away from the unexploited state, giving cause for concern that continued heavy fishing may lead to more widespread changes.

Rivers, lakes and wetlands account for less than 1 percent of the global surface area, but yield at least 8 percent of global fisheries production. However, these productive ecosystems are under pressure from the needs of a growing human population. The World Resources Institute (WRI)[3] reported that half of the world's wetlands were lost in the last century and that dams, diversions and canals fragment almost 60 percent of the world's

largest rivers. Per capita water consumption increased by 50 percent between 1950 and 1990, and human use of available water resources is expected to increase from its current level of about 54 percent to more than 70 percent by 2025.[4] Although inland water ecosystems have improved in some areas of North America and Europe, their condition is continuing to deteriorate in much of the world.

## THE STATUS OF THE FISHING FLEET
### Large fishing vessels

Since the last issue of *The State of World Fisheries and Aquaculture* (1998), 1 124 fishing vessels have been added to Lloyd's database of vessels over 100 tons,[5] 548 of which were built in the period 1997-1999. The remainder were built earlier and their inclusion in the database represents an improvement in its coverage rather than a real increase in the fleet. The trends are similar to those identified in 1998, with decreased numbers of vessels in developed countries' fishing fleets and increased numbers in some developing countries. Late reporting is still a problem so, although the data should refer to 1998 and 1999, it is more practical to consider the period as mid-1997 to mid-1999. There were 955 deletions from the database, but this is probably an underestimate as some of the vessels scrapped were of unknown flag. The estimated decrease in the fleet (i.e. the vessels removed from the database minus the vessels built in 1998-1999) is 407 vessels, giving a total of 23 014 vessels at the end of 1999.

The United States shows an increase of roughly 10 percent, mainly because about 300 vessels that should have been in the 1997 and earlier databases were added in 1998-1999. In fact, the United States fleet really decreased by 26 vessels. Belize showed an increase in flagged fishing vessels from 158 to 427. New vessels and flagging in from other countries contributed to this increase. The Panama fleet decreased from its maximum of 574 vessels in 1994 to 226 in 1999. The recent decrease followed efforts by the International Commission for the Conservation of Atlantic Tunas (ICCAT) to control the activities of the

[3] World Resources Institute at www.wri.org/wri/wr2000/freshwater.html/.

[4] S.L. Postel *et al.* 1996. Human appropriation of renewable freshwater. *Science,* 271.

[5] Figures are as of January 2000 and refer to gross tonnage (GT). Information drawn from Lloyd's Register of Shipping is provided under exclusive licence by Lloyd's Maritime Information Services (LMIS).

high seas tuna fleet. The Philippines increased its fleet from 367 to 436 (16 percent) by building new vessels and flagging in. The Cuba fleet decreased from 113 to 49 through the scrapping of a fleet of vessels built mainly in the 1960s.

Some countries prepared fishing capacity reduction plans according to the International Plan of Action for the Management of Fishing Capacity.

### New vessels built

The database records 548 new vessels built in the two-year period since the previous study reported in *The State of World Fisheries and Aquaculture 1998*, including 171 vessels built in 1997 but reported late, 243 in 1998 and 134 in 1999 (this will probably increase owing to late reporting). Five countries made up 58 percent of this total: the United States (75 vessels), Belize (47), Spain (99), Norway (43) and Japan (56). The other countries of the European Community (EC) account for a further 82 vessels, bringing their contribution up to 73 percent of the total. The significant number of new vessels built under the Belize flag means that 15 percent of the total new buildings are recorded in open registers. Despite the number of vessels built during the two-year period, the United States, Japan and Spain achieved reductions in their national fleets by scrapping and flagging out.

The decrease in building since the early 1990s is significant, not only in terms of numbers, but also in terms of average and aggregate tonnage. In the period 1991-1993, 2 126 vessels were built, with an aggregate tonnage of 990 000 tons. In the period 1997-1999, 1 127 fishing vessels were built with an aggregate tonnage of 418 000 tons. The average tonnage dropped from 465 to 370 tons, although this decrease is highly likely to be an underestimate because there was also a change in the unit of measurement during this period from gross registered tonnage (GRT) to gross tonnage (GT).

### Scrapping and loss

Some 955 vessels were removed from the database in the two-year period, i.e. fewer than were predicted in *The State of World Fisheries and Aquaculture 1998*. However, there has been a substantial increase in the number of vessels changing their flags to "unknown"; from six in 1994, to 694 in 1997 and 931 in 1999. The average age of these vessels is 27 years, so it is likely that most are intended to be scrapped. Nevertheless, the share of vessels over 40 years of age is slightly more than 1 percent of the total. The average age of vessels scrapped or lost was 30.6 years compared with 27.3 two years ago, and the average age of the fleet was 21.3 years, against 22.1 years two years ago. The average age decreased because, although very few new vessels were built, some very old vessels were removed from the fleet.

### Reflagging

During the two-year period, 1 216 vessels were reflagged. The most significant reflagging was to the Belize flag (182), which also acquired a large number of new vessels (47). The number of fishing vessels under the Belize flag increased from 211 to 427. Honduras, St Vincent, Vanuatu and Cyprus slightly increased the numbers of vessels registered in their open registers. On the other hand, following ICCAT measures for improved flag state responsibility, Panama showed a significant decrease, from 321 to 226 vessels. Registration and reflagging of fishing vessels are described in Box 1.

## FISHING TECHNOLOGY DEVELOPMENT

Fishing technologies evolve in response to a wide variety of factors. Demand-driven developments are particularly important. Another, and probably even more prominent factor, is development resulting from general technical innovations in disciplines that are not always directly related to fisheries. The following recent developments will probably have a significant impact on fisheries in the future.

### Limiting the environmental impact of fishing

The impact of fishing on the environment is a global issue of growing concern. Various gears and fishing methods have attracted attention for their potential impact on the environment. Concerns are mostly related to gear selectivity and habitat damage, the major issues being:

- trawls are non-selective and can take considerable by-catch, which is often discarded. In addition, trawls sometimes interact with the bottom, leading to irreversible modifications to bottom ecosystems.
- purse seines can catch mammals and juvenile fish.
- longlines and gillnets catch seabirds and lost gillnets can continue to catch and kill fish unintentionally.

*BOX 1*
## Registration and reflagging of fishing vessels

To avoid duplication in administration, it is common practice for most states to include large fishing vessels on their shipping registers as a separate class of vessel. It is less important for states to include smaller vessels that fish within their national jurisdiction on the register, although many have made registration compulsory.

Increasingly, shipping and fishing regulations require vessels to carry national certificates of registry, particularly on the high seas and in waters under the jurisdiction of another state. This requirement is summarized as follows in the UN Convention on the Law of the Sea, Part VII, High Seas:

### Article 91
### Nationality of ships
1. Every State shall fix the conditions for the grant of its nationality to ships, for the registration of ships in its territory, and for the right to fly its flag. Ships have the nationality of the State whose flag they are entitled to fly. There must exist a genuine link between the State and the ship.
2. Every State shall issue to ships which it has granted the right to fly its flag documents to that effect.

The international standards for the registration of ships have been codified in the UN Convention on the Conditions for the Registration of Ships (1986). Although this Convention is not yet in force and exempts fishing vessels, it clearly describes the procedures to be followed in order to avoid any misuse or fraudulent practice associated with registration. For instance, it describes the procedures to be followed in bare-boat chartering when the vessel is subject to dual registry.

The issue of "open registers" stems from the stipulation quoted above: "There must exist a genuine link between the State and the ship". While many states have implemented regulations and requirements to establish such a genuine link for registration, there have been no agreed international criteria for what constitutes a "genuine link". Regulations usually establish linkages through nationality of ownership and/or of the crew. It then becomes a question of the degree of linkage, described in vaguely defined terms – in decreasing degree of linkage – as "genuine national registers", "offshore registers", "open registers" and "flag of convenience registers".

Owners choose to register their fishing vessels under foreign flags for a variety of reasons. Similar patterns of registration in the trading and fishing fleets would suggest that a major reason for registering under a particular flag may be to avoid taxation. Some countries with open registers are also well-known offshore tax havens. However, increasingly, the reflagging of fishing vessels in particular fisheries has been directly associated with the avoidance of fisheries management measures, and the share of large fishing vessels registered in open registers has increased to around 6 percent of the global total.

*Source:* A. Smith, FAO Fisheries Department.

Much has been done recently to address such problems, and gear and techniques are being modified to reduce the possible impacts. The selective performance of trawl gear is being improved continuously and selective grids have, to a large extent, eliminated the by-catch of fish in the northern shrimp fisheries. Selective grids and square meshes are used in several trawl fisheries to reduce the capture of small-sized individuals. Technologies that depend on behaviour differences between shrimp and fish are increasingly being introduced in tropical shrimp fisheries, resulting in reduced fish by-catches. Another prevailing tendency in tropical shrimp fisheries is an increase in landings of fish by-catches.

The impact of trawling on the bottom habitat is being investigated in many countries. Except for the obvious damage caused to coral reefs by large trawlers, for example in some areas off the coast of Norway, little is known about the long-term effects. In 1999, Norway introduced non-trawling areas where the risk of damage to deep-water coral reefs was high.

One widespread practice is to encircle drifting objects – fish attraction devices (FADs) – with purse seines when fishing for tuna. FADs often attract many small fish, and the capture of small tunas and other fish species around FADs are now considered a major problem in some purse seine fisheries. No way of mitigating this problem has yet been found, apart from reducing the use of such practices. One possible solution now being investigated is to insert selective devices made from panels of larger meshes or sorting grids into the purse seine.

A number of measures can be adopted to reduce the incidental catch of seabirds by longlines, including attaching extra weight to the line while setting; setting during darkness; and the use of scaring devices when setting longline gear. Such mitigation techniques are being introduced in several longline fisheries, either as part of national regulations or through voluntary adoption by fishers who recognize the benefits of not having bait stolen from their hooks by seabirds. The International Plan of Action for Reducing Incidental Catch of Seabirds in Longline Fisheries adopted by FAO's members in 1999 will most likely accelerate the implementation of measures to reduce seabird by-catch in longline fisheries.

### New fibres

Since the introduction of such synthetic fibres as polyamide, polyester and polypropylene to fishing gear in the 1950s, there were no major introductions of new fibres in fishing gear until the arrival of Dynema fibre – a polyethylene of ultra-high molecular weight. The fishing industry now has a material that might have a significant impact on the catching performance of fishing gear. The basic property of Dynema fibre is that it has a density of slightly less than 1, which makes it float in water. Its tensile strength on a diameter basis exceeds that of steel by 50 to 100 percent and that of polyamide (nylon) by 300 to 400 percent. Another feature of Dynema is its low elongation compared with other synthetic fibres, which makes it nearly as inelastic as steel.

At present, the fibre is relatively expensive and its application is therefore limited. However, there are several signs of increased use, particularly in pelagic trawls, where thinner twine results in reduced towing resistance and can therefore be used to save fuel (by using a similar-sized trawl) or, when the trawl size is increased, improves the catching efficiency of the vessel compared with others of its size. This latter feature is used to develop viable trawl fisheries on scattered fish concentrations, which require large trawl mouth areas. Other fisheries for which the fibre might make profitable improvements are those aimed at smaller individuals, such as small crustaceans and mesopelagic fish, which require large volumes of water to be filtered.

### Multirig trawling

The towing of two or more trawls simultaneously was, until recently, only practised by outrigger shrimp trawlers. Thousands of such trawlers fish penaeid shrimps in tropical waters. Towards the end of the 1990s, multirig trawling was successfully introduced into fisheries of such species as nephrops, deepwater shrimp and, to some extent, flatfishes. Particularly in Iceland and Norway, large trawlers equipped for towing two trawls have been built for harvesting deepwater shrimp. The catching efficiency of vessels using multirig trawls increases by 50 to 100 percent, clearly indicating an expanded capacity to exploit shrimp resources. Multirig trawling is now widely used in the North Sea nephrops fishery and is increasingly replacing single-otter trawling. An important innovation that facilitates the operation of twin trawls is the symmetry sensor, which monitors the two trawls during towing.

## Electronic aids for navigation and fishing

In the last few years, the introduction of satellite communications, which are replacing medium-frequency radios, has had a great impact on skippers' ability to manage all aspects of the fishing operation. The new equipment is controlled by microprocessors, including an inbuilt global positioning system (GPS) module. Some of the better known applications of satellite communications equipment include the Global Maritime Distress Safety System (GMDSS) or the Vessel Monitoring System (VMS). When the GMDSS is activated, a distress message is sent by pushing a button. An electronic message, which includes the identity of the vessel and its position, is sent to all other vessels and radio stations in the immediate area. The crew of the vessel can then concentrate on the emergency, secure in the knowledge that the distress message will be effective. The message activates alarms on the other vessels and allows them to go straight to the emergency without having to search for it.

VMS is used by fisheries management authorities to observe the positions of vessels. At predetermined intervals, the satellite communications system automatically sends a message, containing the identity and position of each vessel to the fisheries monitoring centre. The sequence of positions of an individual vessel can be stored and subsequently displayed on a monitor, to give an indication of that vessel's activities. If the vessel is considered to be acting suspiciously, a patrol craft can be sent directly to investigate further.

VMS is playing an increasingly important role in monitoring, control and surveillance (MCS), and it makes such activities more cost-effective. The EC's implementation of the VMS scheme for most of its fishing vessels over 24 m will bring the total number of vessels reporting their identity and position to fisheries management authorities using VMS technology to around 8 000 worldwide.

Satellite surveillance of fishing vessels is becoming a tool for MCS. Longline vessels are particularly easy to locate by microwave sensors because they carry radar reflectors on their buoys. The complementary information from VMS and satellite surveillance will make it possible to locate non-compliant vessels, which are more likely to be involved in illegal fishing. Satellite surveillance could be implemented far more quickly than VMS has

been because it is completely independent of the vessel and does not rely on cooperation.

The integration of three separate modules of equipment into one unit (i.e. computer, GPS and a satellite communications system) is expected to increase efficiency. Electronic fishing logbooks are being tested, and will make it possible to send information, at predetermined intervals or on demand, through a satellite link to the fisheries management authorities. The information can also be sent to fish markets, resulting in a quicker, more efficient sales process and a better quality of product because of minimal handling. Even fish stock assessment and fisheries management will benefit from the almost real-time reporting of fish catches and more detailed information on where the fish are caught. One fishery in Australia is already being managed by these means. Attaching video cameras with a wide enough band to the satellite communications systems allows the transmission of video images. This could be used to assist in treating injured or sick personnel on fishing vessels. The repair of equipment such as engines, winches or electronic equipment, which normally requires the intervention of specialized engineers, can also be undertaken following advice given over the satellite link. This would avoid the costly and time-consuming travel that is currently needed for specialized engineers.

The most up-to-date navigation equipment, GPS, now has an accuracy of +/-10 m because the satellite signal is no longer artificially degraded. However, the size of other pieces of equipment and their dependence on microprocessors mean that they can be linked together to become more interactive. Monitors are already being used to provide displays or readouts from multiple pieces of equipment. Monitors can also overlay the information obtained from radar, sonar and navigation equipment.

These developments may lead to some of this new equipment becoming a legal requirement for larger vessels over 300 tons within the next decade. An example is voyage data recorders, which are similar to the flight recorders carried on aircraft. The use of an automatic identification system (AIS) will also become mandatory in busy sea lanes for this size of fishing vessel. AIS uses automatic interrogation by satellite communication, so that the name, type and size of the ship, along with details of its course and speed, can be displayed on the radar in the traffic control centre. This is potentially useful for fisheries patrol vessels when they are passing through areas with a high density of fishing vessels because it would obviate the necessity of boarding and checking the licences of each fishing vessel.

## FISHERIES POLICY AND MANAGEMENT[6]
### Objectives
Most countries have similar management objectives, although the emphasis differs between developed and developing nations. Developed countries are usually faced with fully or overexploited stocks, so their management objectives concentrate on stock rebuilding and capacity reduction, although most countries also have significant aims regarding markets and social conflict. The most urgent objective is to scale fleet sizes so that they become commensurate with sustainable exploitation of the resources. Management plans also increasingly recognize the need for a policy that integrates fisheries with management of the coastal zone or inland waters.

In contrast, developing countries tend to concentrate on fisheries development in terms of new resources and technology. Although it is recognized that some stocks are overfished, objectives are concentrated more on enhancing and diversifying fisheries rather than on limiting fishing efforts. This is perhaps because the underlying concern for many countries is the relatively important role fisheries play in employment and food security for some of their poorest people. More specific aims include building infrastructure (particularly for processing to reduce post-harvest losses and increase the value added); fishery enhancement, through restocking; and reducing social conflicts, not only among different fishing groups but also between fisheries and other sectors.

### The current state of management
Fisheries management is widely considered to be ineffective because of the poor state of many important fish stocks. However, in many respects, management has improved a great deal over recent years. Policies and objectives appear more realistic, concentrating more on management and less on development, and

making the best social use of resources. Explicit recognition of risk and consideration of longer-term production, for example in the adoption of the precautionary approach (see Indicators of sustainable development and the precautionary approach in marine capture fisheries, Part 2, p. 60), are increasingly reflected in decision-making, and there has been growing recognition of the need to protect the ecosystem as well as individual stocks, through measures that include the provision of marine reserves. Technical innovations for improving management advice have been developed rapidly, but implementation has been slow because of the short-term economic and political consequences. As a result, the rate of real change in management has been slow, and it is debatable whether improvements have kept pace with the increasing pressures on resources. Nevertheless, there are situations where management has improved and clear benefits are apparent. Some countries have reported the successful implementation of property rights schemes for fisheries (see Property rights and fisheries management, Part 2, p. 52).

It is becoming increasingly clear that effective fisheries management, at both the policy-making and the implementation stages, depends critically on consensus and participation that utilize objective and reliable reporting of fishery status and trends (see Box 2).

### Administration
The FAO Code of Conduct for Responsible Fisheries[7] is being used as a foundation on which to base fisheries policy and management. Together with the guidelines for its implementation, the Code contains a broad set of principles and methods for developing and managing fisheries and aquaculture. It is widely recognized by governments and non-governmental organizations (NGOs) as setting the aims for sustainable fisheries over the next few decades and as a basis for national legislation as well as industry-supported Codes of Conduct.

Some countries have no officially approved fisheries management policy. While such an approach appears to leave fisheries

---

[6] This section is based on information provided to the FAO Fisheries Department by member countries. Most of it was obtained over the last two years.

[7] Adopted by the 28th Session of the FAO Conference in October 1995, the Code of Conduct for Responsible Fisheries is referred to throughout this publication as "the Code".

management with a free licence, the result is often a lack of transparency and effectiveness. The problem arises in both developed and developing countries and leads to management authorities having poor accountability to the fisheries sector and the public. It is being addressed specifically through extensive consultation procedures among stakeholders (e.g. in Australia and New Zealand), and by emphasis on comanagement systems in many countries. Participatory approaches, where fishing communities are involved in the

---

*BOX 2*
## Objective and reliable fishery status and trends reporting

Sustainable fisheries and aquaculture require informed decisions and actions at all levels, from policy-makers to individual fishers, as well as environmentalists – who are increasingly concerned about fisheries – consumers and the public. Decision-making based on the best scientific evidence requires reliable, relevant and timely information. There are growing demands for objective, unbiased, peer-reviewed and transparent information on the status and trends of fisheries and fisheries resources as a basis for policy-making and fisheries management. The driving forces behind such demands include increasing recognition that overfishing is pervasive and effective management often lacking; the widespread adoption of the precautionary approach to fisheries management as embodied in the United Nations Fish Stocks Agreement[1] and the FAO Code of Conduct for Responsible Fisheries; ecolabelling issues; and concerns about rare or endangered species and the environment.

Status and trends reporting has become an issue because of the risk of misinformation. A study by the University of Washington[2] evaluated the validity of 14 statements commonly made about the state of marine fisheries resources and found that ten of these were unsupportable or questionable, whereas only four were supportable. (Most of the supportable statements and only a few of the unsupportable ones were attributed to FAO.) Irrespective of whether such inaccurate information is generated deliberately to promote a specific cause or inadvertently through ignorance, it can have a major impact on public opinion and policy-making that may not be in the best interests of either sustainable use of fisheries resources or the conservation of aquatic ecosystems.

FAO is addressing this issue by proposing the improvement of fishery status and trends reporting using a multifaceted approach as outlined by the FAO Advisory Committee on Fisheries Research (ACFR). ACFR has proposed that this could be facilitated by an international plan of action on fishery status and trends reporting, which states would adopt through FAO's Committee on Fisheries (COFI). As envisaged, the plan of action would be a voluntary instrument that would specify actions and procedures to be undertaken by states, both individually and through regional fishery bodies or arrangements, and by FAO to improve fishery status and trends reporting. The plan of action could be built around the following principles:

*Sustainability and security.* States would demonstrate their commitment to sustainable development of fisheries resources and fisheries by providing, *inter alia*, the best information possible on the status and trends of fisheries within their jurisdictions and in other areas in which they participate.

*Best scientific evidence.* States would seek to improve their collection, compilation and dissemination of the best scientific evidence available on the nature and conduct of fisheries, including environmental and socio-economic information, in conformity with the United Nations Conference on the Law of the Sea (UNCLOS).

*Participation and cooperation.* States would adopt mechanisms for inclusion of all relevant participants in the preparation, analysis and presentation of fisheries information, including fishers, government and NGOs. States would cooperate with other states in developing and maintaining such information either directly or through regional fishery bodies or arrangements, as appropriate.

*Objectivity and transparency.* States would individually, and through regional fishery bodies and FAO, prepare and disseminate fisheries information in an objective manner, taking into account the best scientific evidence available (including uncertainty), the precautionary approach and national and international obligations related to it, and applying quality

planning, implementation and evaluation of management systems, are widely supported, at least in principle.

### Fishing controls
Total allowable catches (TACs) are probably the most common fisheries management tool, at least for major fisheries and those in the Northern Hemisphere. There is a growing recognition of the need to control capacity, including fleet sizes, in order to protect stocks and improve economic performance. Gear

criteria and quality assurance protocols. The plan of action would be implemented in a transparent manner in conformity with Article 6.13 of the Code.

A mechanism to collate and exchange fisheries information, including status and trends reports is under development at FAO, and it could serve as the key vehicle for implementation of the plan of action. FAO is making a major effort to develop a Fisheries Global Information System (FIGIS), which will facilitate the exchange of fisheries information from a wide variety of domains such as fisheries statistics, exploited species, fisheries resources and stocks, the fisheries themselves, fishing methods, fishing fleets, fish processing and food safety, fish marketing and trade, species introductions and fish diseases. The information architecture will be designed so that the complex system can be presented in a simplified way through logical navigation channels. FIGIS will not be just a dissemination system, but also a means for partners to contribute information. The information will be exchanged according to arrangements specified in partnership agreements involving FAO, regional fishery bodies and national centres of excellence, and using agreed protocols. Thus, the main novelty will be the more systematic and transparent assembly and synthesis of information from national to regional and then to global scales, with users having the possibility of accessing a much more comprehensive range of information. Another main focus and beneficiary of this approach will be the synthesis of the global state of marine fisheries resources.

FAO has a major responsibility to support capacity building in developing countries, thereby allowing users to access, utilize and contribute to fisheries information and knowledge systems, including FIGIS. For example, the Aquatic Sciences and Fisheries Abstracts (ASFA) bibliographic database may be linked to FIGIS, and work is under way to provide low-income food-deficit countries (LIFDCs) with access to ASFA as well as to ensure more input to the database from those countries. Communication

between FIGIS and FAO regional information systems, such as those for Mediterranean capture fisheries and aquaculture or a geographic information system (GIS) project for the West African coast, will be given precedence during the early phases of the FIGIS initiative. Likewise, software for the collection and processing of fisheries statistics has been implemented in many developing countries to improve the quality of national statistics and facilitate their exchange at the regional and global levels.

---

[1] Agreement for the Implementation of the Provisions of the United Nations Convention on the Law of the Sea of 10 December 1982 Relating to the Conservation and Management of Straddling Fish Stocks and Highly Migratory Fish Stocks.

[2] D.L. Alverson and K. Dunlop. 1998. *Status of world marine fish stocks*. University of Washington School of Fisheries, United States.

*Source:* R. Grainger, FAO Fisheries Department.

controls are also a common conservation measure and include the prohibition of destructive methods such as fish poisons and dynamite, the introduction of gears that reduce by-catch, such as turtle excluder devices and mesh size restrictions.

There is also concern about gears that have attracted criticism from environmentalists, such as drift nets, longlines and demersal trawls, and such gears are likely to be more selectively used. Many countries have a policy of developing fishery enhancement through restocking heavily fished resources, thereby avoiding the need to rebuild stocks through reductions in fishing. This is done particularly in inland fisheries, where enhancement, rehabilitation of habitat and reduction of pollution are major aims, alongside the reduction of fishing in order to conserve resources.

Fishing capacity control and reduction is a feature of many countries' policies. Approaches include licensing, buy-back schemes or individual transferable quotas (see Property rights and fisheries management, Part 2, p. 52). Reducing the access of other countries is also seen as a useful method of conserving resources, and is often adopted before controls and limits are imposed on the national effort capacity. Diversifying fisheries by encouraging vessels to exploit underutilized resources where these are available is seen as the best alternative to fleet reduction, even though such resources are very scarce and, without control of the fishing effort, cannot be exploited sustainably.

Conflicts among user groups are resolved through zoning, stock enhancement, public education, better enforcement of legislation and, too rarely, resource allocation and control of access. A common problem is conflict between industrial and artisanal fleets. The artisanal sector is particularly vulnerable as it often depends on set gears that are incompatible with towed gears, such as industrial trawls. The solution is often clear – i.e. introduce zones that separate the gears (particularly when stocks do not move) – but enforcement may be difficult.

### Social and economic development
Improved post-harvest processing is seen as a way of developing the fishing industry without increasing harvests. As well as reducing losses through poor handling, improved processing can raise the value added of fish products and establish uses for otherwise discarded catch.

Food safety remains important and has become increasingly stringent for exported products; in many cases Hazard Analysis and Critical Control Point (HACCP) procedures must be applied by processors. The distribution of marine fish to inland areas, distant from the coast, appears to be a problem for many of the countries that depend on capture fisheries and have poor infrastructure. This is often a reason for developing freshwater aquaculture closer to markets.

For low-income food-deficit countries (LIFDCs), food security, employment, poverty alleviation and equitable access to resources are seen as priority concerns. Women and economically disadvantaged groups are identified in many management plans for special consideration in the provision of finance and training.

Budget and general resource constraints are seen as a significant problem for management. While there is a general shortage of human and financial resources for fisheries management in developing countries, other countries are concentrating on methods to cover management costs from resource revenue.

### Regional and global management
Regional cooperation has many other benefits in addition to cost savings. Many fishery policies explicitly concern themselves with the need to harmonize management measures among and even (in the larger ones) within countries. Benefits stem mainly from improved MCS, which is one of the most expensive aspects of management. Regional cooperation can greatly reduce these costs. The sharing of information and technical expertise, as well as the joint management of shared stocks, are also of increasing interest to multilateral cooperation. To support these there is a need to strengthen regional fisheries management organizations and make them more efficient (see Box 3 for examples of activities in regional fishery bodies).

Although there has been a general decline in distant-water fishing, some developing countries still rely on long-range fleets, usually from developed countries, to exploit their offshore resources. Because of the need to share information on foreign fleets, regional management is particularly valuable in dealing with fisheries that have a large foreign component.

However, regional bodies improve the cooperation between states even when distant-water fishing is in decline. Regional fisheries management bodies have an important role to play in combating illegal, unreported and unregulated (IUU) fishing (see the section on IUU fishing, Part 2, p. 57).

## Inland fisheries management

Management of inland fisheries is constrained by the same factors that make accurate data collection difficult: the diverse and diffuse nature of the fisheries; incomplete or inaccurate reporting; and competition for water resources from other sectors such as agriculture and energy production. In efforts to rebuild fisheries or to add value to the catch of certain water bodies,

---

*BOX 3*
**Regional fishery bodies:
IOTC and NEAFC**

***Indian Ocean Tuna Commission***
The Atlantic and the Eastern Pacific Oceans have had tuna management bodies for several decades. Discussions leading to the creation of the Indian Ocean Tuna Commission (IOTC) started in 1986. The agreement establishing IOTC entered into force with the accession of the tenth member in 1996. This body was established under Article XIV of the FAO Constitution and now has 18 members, including the EC and 17 states. Membership is open to coastal countries of the Indian Ocean as well as non-riparian countries that are fishing for tuna in this ocean. The commission's objective is the optimum utilization of 16 species of tuna and tuna-like fishes in its area of competence, which is defined as the Indian Ocean and adjacent seas. This commission is the first of its kind in FAO, as it has management powers and is funded totally from member party contributions.

Initially, tuna catches in this area were half those of the Atlantic or the Eastern Pacific Oceans, but they have increased rapidly and now account for more than a quarter of world tuna landings. The value of the annual catch of 1.2 million tonnes is also very high (estimated to be between US$2 billion and US$3 billion), as there is a large proportion of valuable fish caught by longlines. Another significant fact is that nearly half the catch comes from artisanal fisheries, whereas in the other oceans most of the catch comes from long-range industrialized operations.

The technical activities that gave rise to IOTC started in 1982 through the Indo-Pacific Tuna Development and Management Programme (IPTP), which was funded by the United Nations Development Programme (UNDP) and executed by FAO. The programme was entrusted with the collection of statistical data on tuna fisheries and provided participating countries with a forum for research and the discussion of stock status. Scientific support was provided throughout the lifetime of IPTP through a project funded by Japan.

stocking (often of exotic species) and other enhancement measures have been adopted. Aquaculture can also be an enhancement measure, but in many rural areas aquaculture production accounts for only a small fraction of inland fisheries production and should not be seen as a substitute for fisheries management. Access to fishing areas is often controlled by powerful individuals within the community. As recreational fisheries become an increasingly valuable source of revenue in developing countries (e.g. through access charges and tourism), local subsistence and commercial fishers are losing access to many water bodies. This poses a problem for the management of individual fisheries, so there is

As of 1986, member parties provided all the funding for the operation of the programme.

The IOTC secretariat has been operational at its headquarters in Seychelles since the beginning of 1998. During this period, staff have been appointed, statistical databases have been constituted, data from tuna fishing countries have been collected and the dissemination of data and information through the Internet and electronic and print media has been organized. The secretariat also provides support in data collection, training and scientific activities to contracting and cooperating parties. The secretariat takes an active role at the international level, cooperating closely with FAO and other regional fishery bodies in such fields as status and trends reporting, the establishment of statistical standards, the exchange of data and information and the international plans of action on seabird by-catch, sharks and fishing capacity. A coordination mechanism has been introduced among tuna management bodies in all the oceans in order to counter the threat posed by illegal, unreported and unregulated (IUU) fishing.

The commission meets every year. Advice on technical and scientific matters is provided through a scientific committee and scientific work is undertaken through working parties. To date, working parties have been constituted for statistics and tagging, as well as for tropical, temperate and neritic tunas and billfish. In the short time since its creation, IOTC has already taken decisions on minimum data reporting standards, the confidentiality of data and measures to regulate IUU fishing. It has also created a new status of Cooperating Party, intended to facilitate the accession of countries that might be hesitant to join or might not have the necessary financial resources. It is anticipated that resource management measures will be taken at the next session.

*Source:* D. Ardill, IOTC Secretary.

***Northeast Atlantic Fisheries Commission***
The foundation of NEAFC can be traced back to the period between the First and Second World Wars. In the 1930s, several conferences were held to address the issue of rational exploitation of fish resources, but attempts to organize an international agreement were interrupted by the Second World War. In 1946, the United Kingdom organized an International Conference on Overfishing, which resulted in the establishment of a Permanent Commission.

This commission, founded in 1953, was the forerunner of NEAFC. Its first meeting was attended by delegations from 12 contracting parties and dealt mainly with minimum fish size and the use of various fishing gears. In 1955, the commission set up an ad hoc scientific committee to look into the issues under discussion and seek advice from the International Council for the Exploration of the Sea (ICES).

During its first years of operation, it was apparent that the measures it could establish were insufficient to protect stocks adequately. Between 1954 and 1958 several informal discussions took place to consider new types of international regulation. In 1959, a conference resulted in the Northeast Atlantic Fisheries Convention, which entered into force in 1963. NEAFC, which was formed under this convention, succeeded the permanent commission. The new commission was given additional powers and was able to establish stricter conservation and management measures.

NEAFC formed the framework for international cooperation in the area of fisheries regulation beyond national fishing limits. Its main purpose was to recommend measures to maintain the rational exploitation of fish stocks in the convention's area, taking scientific advice from ICES. In 1967, NEAFC established a Scheme of Joint Enforcement that contained rules for mutual inspection and control outside national fishery jurisdictions. Although all decisions regarding judicial processes were the responsibility of the flag state, this scheme was considered a

a move to manage watersheds and habitats instead. Protecting the habitat in watersheds and developing access and ownership schemes for inland water bodies are two measures that could help promote responsible inland fisheries, even when there is no accurate information on species catch.

## AQUACULTURE
### Production and value
Most aquaculture has developed in freshwater environments (Figure 9), and mainly in Asia. The development of inland aquaculture is seen as an important source of food security in Asia, particularly in land-locked countries.

Freshwater aquaculture production is

---

significant achievement. In 1969, the commission recommended a complete ban on salmon fisheries outside national limits. It also agreed to enforce a closed season for the North Sea herring fishery from 1971. In 1975 a recommendation to ban directed industrial fishing for North Sea herring was agreed.

During this period, the commission's powers increased, as it was allowed to set limits for total allowable catches (TACs) and effort limitations, including the allocation of quotas. The first quota recommendation was on North Sea herring in 1974 and, the following year, NEAFC recommended TACs and quota allocations for 15 stocks. By the end of 1976, NEAFC was aware that developments taking place after the Third United Nations Conference on the Law of the Sea (UNCLOS III) would result in the extension of fishing limits to 200 miles. In 1977, when the coastal states in the North Atlantic declared 200 miles jurisdiction off their coasts, most of the areas of stocks regulated by NEAFC became national zones. The management of joint stocks became a matter of bilateral or multilateral responsibility, instead of NEAFC's responsibility.

An agreement on membership of the organization was reached between NEAFC's contracting parties and the European Economic Community (EEC) in 1980, enabling the EEC to become a signatory. The 1980 meeting resulted in the Convention on Future Multilateral Co-operation in the Northeast Atlantic Fisheries. A new commission was established in 1982.

The duties and obligations of the new commission were similar to those of the former: it should serve as a forum for consultation and the exchange of information on fish stocks and management and it had the power to make recommendations concerning fisheries in international waters in the convention area. However, since most fisheries activities took place inside coastal state jurisdiction, NEAFC lacked any real responsibility for managing them.

The development of the legal framework for

fisheries management following UNCLOS, in particular the Rio Declaration and the United Nations Agreement on the Conservation and Management of Straddling Fish Stocks and Highly Migratory Fish Stocks, resulted in a new dawn for NEAFC. The commission decided to consider the future of NEAFC in the light of recent developments in the legal framework for fishing in waters outside national jurisdiction.

Recent years have seen increased fishing activity and NEAFC has become responsible for managing several stocks in the convention area. In 1998, the current contracting parties – Denmark (in respect of the Faroe Islands and Greenland), the EC, Iceland, Norway, Poland and the Russian Federation – agreed to strengthen NEAFC by establishing an independent secretariat in London. An agreement was reached on a new Scheme on Control and Enforcement to be applied to waters outside national jurisdiction. This permits the mutual inspection of contracting parties' vessels. Contracting parties are also required to notify the secretariat of vessels authorized to fish in international waters and report the catches taken.

Contracting parties have agreed that, as from 1 January 2000, they require the satellite tracking of vessels fishing outside national jurisdiction in the Northeast Atlantic. The secretariat will supply up-to-date information about ongoing fishing activities to contracting parties with an inspection presence in the area. NEAFC's contracting parties have also agreed measures to be taken when dealing with non-contracting parties fishing in the area; for example, if fishing of NEAFC-regulated stocks takes place contrary to NEAFC recommendations, non-contracting parties may face prohibition of the landing of catches.

*Source:* S. Engesaeter, NEAFC Secretary.

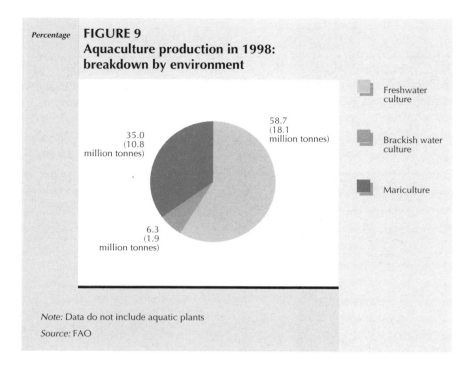

*Percentage* **FIGURE 9**
**Aquaculture production in 1998:
breakdown by environment**

35.0
(10.8
million tonnes)

58.7
(18.1
million tonnes)

6.3
(1.9
million tonnes)

Freshwater
culture

Brackish water
culture

Mariculture

*Note:* Data do not include aquatic plants
*Source:* FAO

dominated by finfish, particularly silver, grass and other carps (Figures 10 and 11). Brackish water aquaculture has most frequently been developed for shrimp production, notably the giant tiger prawn, which accounts for the growth in shrimp export markets. Milkfish production dominated brackish water finfish aquaculture in the 1980s, but has subsequently grown more slowly. In volume terms, mariculture has been dominated by seaweeds, notably Japanese kelp, and molluscs, mainly the Pacific cupped oyster. However, as production figures are given in live weight (including the high water content of seaweeds and the heavy shells of molluscs), the statistics give the impression that these products are greater sources of food and employment than they actually are.

Brackish and saltwater aquaculture has seen a growth in high-value salmon in particular, and in brackish water, shrimp is the major high-value product. Both these types of aquaculture are oriented towards the export market. Shrimp (crustaceans) and salmon (diadromous fishes) make up a lower volume than freshwater fishes such as tilapia and carp but attract a high price, making them a significant component in value terms.

Production is dominated by Asian countries (Figure 12), particularly China which has reported increases in production of 0.7 million tonnes per year until 1992 and 2.6 millions tonnes per year thereafter. For the

rest of the world, combined growth in production has averaged 0.4 million tonnes per year. Within the last decade, LIFDCs, excluding China, have shown an encouraging overall upward trend in production and, in terms of quantity, the increase has kept pace with that reported in non-LIFDCs (Figure 13). China and other Asian countries dominate LIFDC aquaculture production (Figure 14) because they have been much more active in promoting aquaculture, particularly for subsistence. While Asia, the Americas and Europe have seen an expansion in aquaculture production, Africa has been slow to develop its potential. Unlike Asia, Africa has little aquaculture tradition and has been affected by a number of external problems that have prevented proper management and development despite investment. Nevertheless, aquaculture production in Africa has risen from 37 000 tonnes in 1984 to 189 000 in 1998, the majority of which is freshwater carp and tilapia.

## Development and policy
In the Asia region, aquaculture has developed mainly as a rural activity integrated into existing farming systems. Rural aquaculture, including enhancement and culture-based fisheries, has made significant contributions to the alleviation of poverty, directly through small-scale household farming of aquatic organisms for domestic consumption or

*Percentage*

**FIGURE 10**
**Global aquaculture production by species groups in freshwater (A), brackish water (B) and marine (C) environments in 1998**

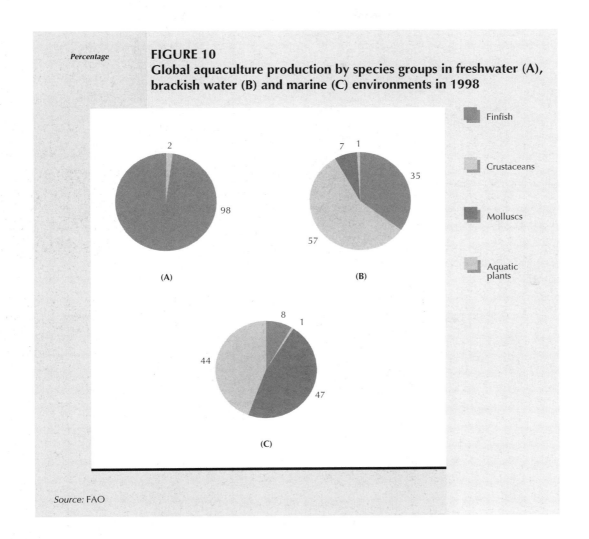

(A)

(B)

(C)

Finfish

Crustaceans

Molluscs

Aquatic plants

*Source:* FAO

**FIGURE 11**
**Global aquaculture production: major species groups in 1998**

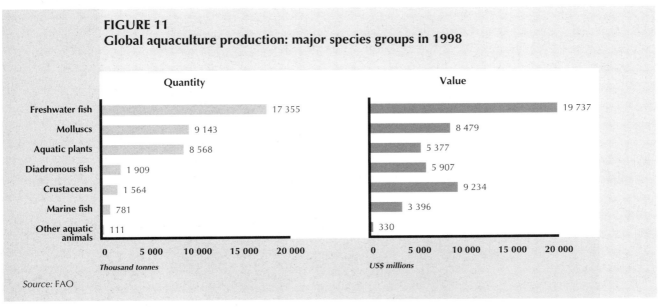

*Source:* FAO

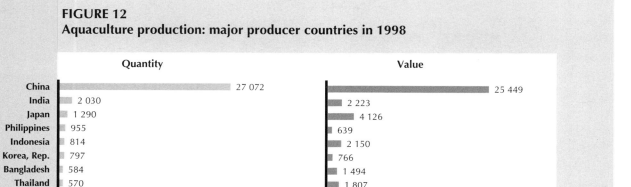

## FIGURE 12
## Aquaculture production: major producer countries in 1998

| | Quantity | | Value |
|---|---|---|---|
| China | 27 072 | | 25 449 |
| India | 2 030 | | 2 223 |
| Japan | 1 290 | | 4 126 |
| Philippines | 955 | | 639 |
| Indonesia | 814 | | 2 150 |
| Korea, Rep. | 797 | | 766 |
| Bangladesh | 584 | | 1 494 |
| Thailand | 570 | | 1 807 |
| Viet Nam | 538 | | 1 357 |
| Other countries | 4 782 | | 12 448 |

Thousand tonnes

US$ millions

*Note:* Data include aquatic plants. Countries listed are those with a production volume of more than 500 000 tonnes

*Source:* FAO

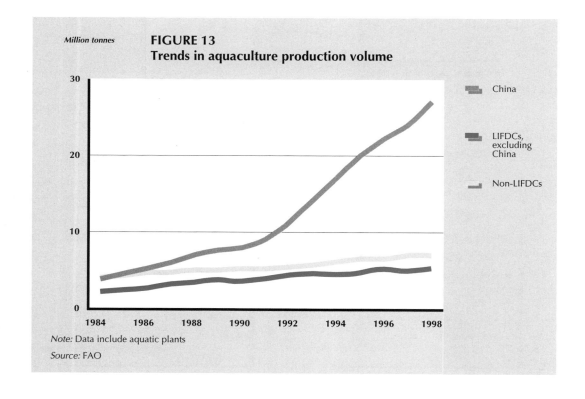

Million tonnes

## FIGURE 13
## Trends in aquaculture production volume

China

LIFDCs, excluding China

Non-LIFDCs

*Note:* Data include aquatic plants

*Source:* FAO

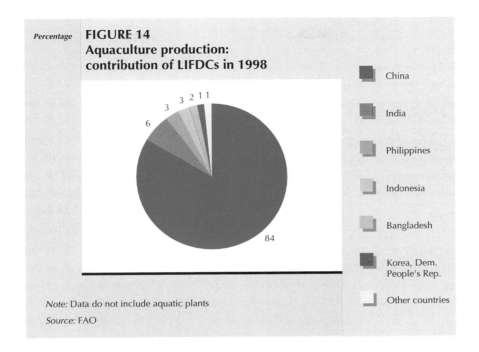

*Percentage* **FIGURE 14**
**Aquaculture production:
contribution of LIFDCs in 1998**

China

India

Philippines

Indonesia

Bangladesh

Korea, Dem.
People's Rep.

Other countries

*Note:* Data do not include aquatic plants
*Source:* FAO

income, and indirectly by providing employment for the poor or low-cost fish for poor rural and urban consumers. Recent experiences in these countries indicate that there are wide opportunities for the poor, who can integrate aquaculture into their existing farming systems.

All countries in the region have a large unfulfilled potential for growth, although rural aquaculture is far better developed in countries such as China and India. In China, significant expansion and intensification of aquaculture are taking place. Intensive systems, based increasingly on formulated feeds, are more common in coastal provinces, where small-scale farms account for 60 percent of production, while in poorer and remoter provinces traditional integrated systems, based mainly on manuring, still predominate. In India, rural aquaculture using extensive to semi-intensive modes of production in ponds and tanks contributes significantly to rural household incomes. In the Philippines, small-scale holders dominate coastal seaweed and mollusc farming. In Bangladesh, where most fish farmers are relatively poor, there is vast potential for the poorest members of society to become new entrant aquaculture farmers. In Nepal, poor fishers are the owner-operators of fish cages, while in the Philippines poor farmers are more likely to be hired to operate such systems and are less likely to be owners. In Indonesia, about 78 percent of farming

households cultivate fish in small ponds of less than 500 m², and aquaculture is the main source of income for 66 percent of the households that cultivate fish in paddies and ponds. Aquaculture is also the main source of income for 65 percent of households with brackish water ponds of an area less than 1 ha. It has been reported that the traditional integrated farming system in Viet Nam may contribute as much to household income as rice cultivation, while occupying a far smaller area.

However, the contribution of rural aquaculture to development is uneven, suggesting that there is still significant unfulfilled potential. Rural aquaculture is increasingly recognized as a way to improve the livelihoods of poor people, and many governments and development agencies attach importance to this sector in the Asia and Pacific region.

Aquaculture still faces a number of problems. Among these are access to technology and financial resources for the poor; environmental impacts; and diseases. The priority areas for further research include:

- the adoption of aquaculture by poor rural households;
- technologies for sustainable stock enhancement, ranching programmes and open ocean aquaculture;
- the use of aquatic plants and animals for nutrient stripping;

- integrated systems to improve environmental performance;
- managing the health of aquatic animals;
- nutrition in aquaculture;
- the quality and safety of aquaculture products;
- emerging technologies, including recirculating systems, offshore cage culture, integrated water use, artificial upwelling and ecosystem food web management, domestication and selective breeding and genetic improvement.

Although many policies are developed specifically for aquaculture, the resulting plans are often integrated with those of the capture fisheries sector. Aquaculture is seen not only as having greater development potential than capture fisheries, but also as an important tool for increasing food security. Many countries have identified a future shortfall in the supply of fishery products and support aquaculture development in order to avoid the importation of scarce fishery products.

Aquaculture is often proposed as a way of providing fish to non-coastal communities, high-value exports, seed stock for replenishing resources and bait for fisheries. As well as the development of new areas, most plans for aquaculture include support for areas that are underutilized as a result of inefficiencies in production, a common problem for many developing countries. Other significant issues addressed by management and development plans include disease control, conflicting land uses and general environmental problems arising from aquaculture development, such as critical habitat loss, species introductions and pollution.

The future development of aquaculture will depend on improvements in new and adaptive research and management. A framework for such cooperation, provided in the Bangkok Declaration and Strategy for Aquaculture Development Beyond 2000,[8] is particularly important to developing countries, which need to share expertise and technology. Regional management of aquaculture is being developed for the Mediterranean region through the application of Article 9 of the Code. This is the first institutional attempt to harmonize the different national principles connected with the Code. The principles

address integrated and improved planning with the participation of all sectors, environmental conservation and economic and trade issues.

## FISH UTILIZATION

Since 1994, there has been a tendency to increase the proportion of fisheries production used for direct human consumption rather than for other purposes (Figure 15). Of the products for human consumption, fresh fish showed significant growth during the 1990s, complemented by a decline in the use of canned fish. This pattern has largely been driven by growth in consumption, which increased the demand for fresh fish and caused a slight decline in other uses (Figure 16).

Fish has a significant capacity for processing. In 1998, only 36 percent of world fisheries production was marketed as fresh fish, while the remaining 64 percent underwent some form of processing. Fish for human consumption had a 79.6 percent share, while the remaining 20.4 percent went to non-food purposes, almost exclusively for reduction to meal and oil. Of the fish destined for direct human consumption, fresh fish was the most important product, with a share of 45.3 percent, followed by frozen fish (28.8 percent), canned fish (13.9 percent) and cured fish (12 percent). Fresh fish increased in volume from 25 million tonnes in 1988 to 42 million tonnes in 1998, live weight equivalent. Processed fish (frozen, cured and canned) increased from 46 million tonnes in 1988 to more than 51 million tonnes, live weight equivalent, in 1998.

### Consumption

The total food fish supply has been growing at a rate of 3.6 percent per annum since 1961, while the world's population has been expanding at 1.8 percent per annum. The proteins derived from fish, crustaceans and molluscs account for between 13.8 and 16.5 percent of the animal protein intake of the human population.

Total food fish supply grew from 27.6 million tonnes in 1961 to more than 93 million tonnes at the end of the twentieth century. Average apparent per capita consumption increased from about 9 kg per annum in the early 1960s to 16 kg in 1997. The per capita availability of fish and fishery products has therefore nearly doubled in 40 years, outpacing population growth, which also nearly doubled in the same period.

In industrialized countries, where diets generally contain a more diversified range of animal proteins, the supply increased from

---

[8] Available at www.fao.org/fi/default.asp.

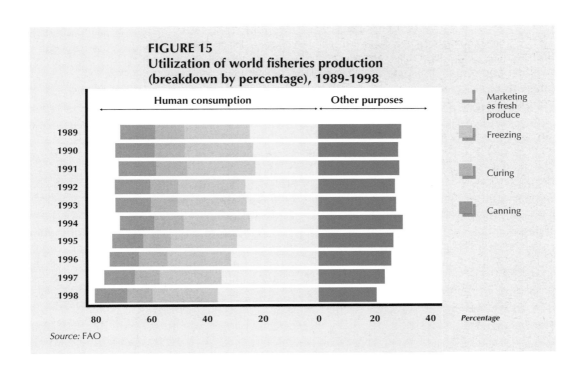

**FIGURE 15**
**Utilization of world fisheries production
(breakdown by percentage), 1989-1998**

*Source:* FAO

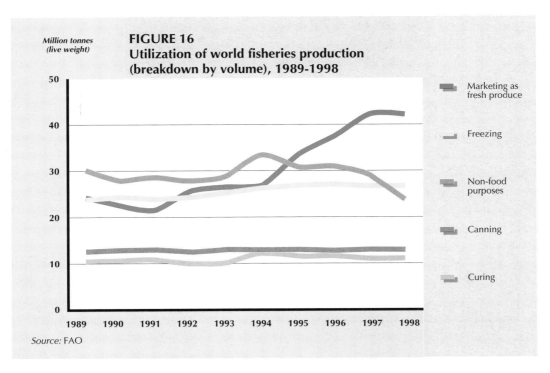

**FIGURE 16**
**Utilization of world fisheries production
(breakdown by volume), 1989-1998**

*Source:* FAO

13.2 million tonnes in 1961 to 26.7 million tonnes in 1997, implying a rise in per capita provision from 19.7 to 27.7 kg. This represents a growth rate close to 1 percent per annum. In this group of countries, fish contributed an increasing share of total protein intake until 1989 (accounting for between 6.5 and 8.5 percent), but its importance has gradually declined since then and, in 1997, its percentage contribution was back to the level prevailing in the mid-1980s.

In the early 1960s, per capita fish supply in LIFDCs was, on average, one-fifth of that of the richest countries. The gap has gradually lessened, however, and in 1997 average LIFDC fish consumption was close to half that of the more affluent economies. If China is excluded, per capita supply in LIFDCs increased from 4.9 to 7.8 kg over the period – an annual growth rate of 1.3 percent.

Despite the relatively low consumption by weight in LIFDCs, the contribution of fish to total animal protein intake is considerable (nearly 20 percent). Over the last four decades, however, the share of fish proteins to animal proteins has exhibited a slight negative trend owing to faster growth in the consumption of other animal products.

As well as income-related variations, the role of fish in nutrition shows marked continental, regional and national differences (Figure 17). For example, of the 93.9 million tonnes available worldwide for consumption in 1997, only 5.2 million tonnes were consumed in Africa (with a per capita supply of 7.1 kg), whereas two-thirds of the total were consumed in Asia – 31.7 million tonnes in Asia excluding China (13.7 kg per capita) and a similar amount in China alone (where the apparent supply amounted to 25.7 kg per capita).

Currently, two-thirds of the total food fish supply are obtained from fishing in marine and inland waters; the remaining one-third is derived from aquaculture. The contribution of inland and marine capture fisheries to per capita food supply has stabilized (at 10 to11 kg per capita in the period 1984-1998). Recent increases in per capita availability have,

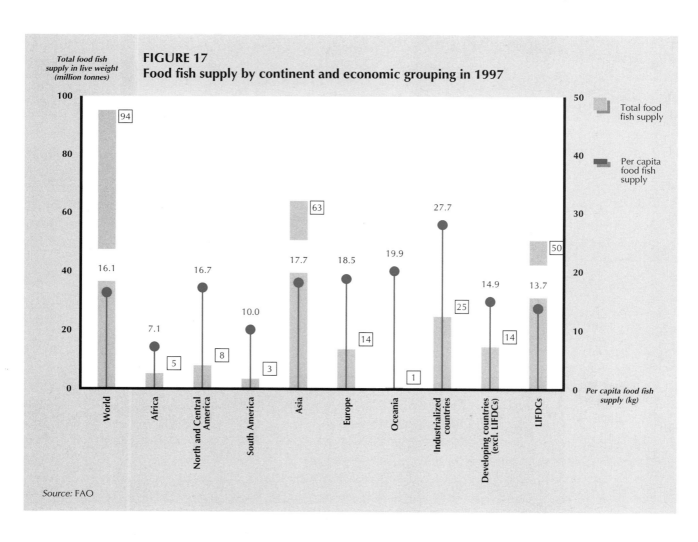

*Total food fish supply in live weight (million tonnes)*

**FIGURE 17**

**Food fish supply by continent and economic grouping in 1997**

*Per capita food fish supply (kg)*

*Source:* FAO

therefore, been obtained from aquaculture production, from both traditional rural aquaculture and intensive commercial aquaculture of high-value species. On average, for all countries in the world except China, aquaculture's contribution to per capita food availability grew from 1.2 kg in 1984 to 2.1 kg in 1998 – at an average rate of 4.1 percent per annum. In China, where fish farming practices have long traditional roots, the per capita supply from aquaculture is reported to have increased from 6 kg to nearly 17 kg in the same period, implying an annual average growth of 15 percent.

The total amount of fish consumed and the species composition of the food supply vary according to region and country, reflecting the different levels of natural availability of aquatic resources in adjacent waters, as well as diverse food traditions, tastes, demand and income levels. Demersal fish are much preferred in northern Europe and North America, and cephalopods are consumed in several Mediterranean and Asian countries,

but to a much lesser extent in other regions. Despite the fast-growing contribution of aquaculture to production, crustaceans are still high-priced commodities and their consumption is mostly concentrated in affluent economies. Of the 16.1 kg of fish per capita available for consumption in 1997, the vast majority (75 percent) was finfish (Figure 18). Shellfish supplied 25 percent – or 4 kg per capita, subdivided into 1.4 kg of crustaceans, 2.2 kg of molluscs and 0.4 kg of cephalopods.

In terms of total supply, 25 million tonnes were made up of freshwater and diadromous species. Marine finfish species provided 45 million tonnes, subdivided into 16 million tonnes of demersal species, 19 million tonnes of pelagics and 10 million tonnes of unidentified and miscellaneous marine fish. The remaining 20 percent of the food supply was shellfish, comprising 8 million tonnes of crustaceans, 2.5 million tonnes of cephalopods and 13 million tonnes of other molluscs. Historically, there have not been dramatic changes in most of the broad groups' shares in

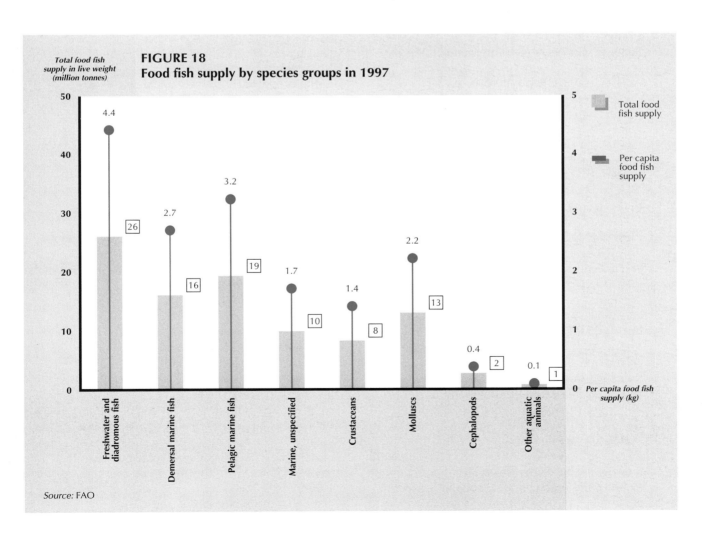

**FIGURE 18**
**Food fish supply by species groups in 1997**

*Total food fish supply in live weight (million tonnes)*

*Per capita food fish supply (kg)*

Total food fish supply

Per capita food fish supply

Freshwater and diadromous fish: 26, 4.4
Demersal marine fish: 16, 2.7
Pelagic marine fish: 19, 3.2
Marine, unspecified: 10, 1.7
Crustaceans: 8, 1.4
Molluscs: 13, 2.2
Cephalopods: 2, 0.4
Other aquatic animals: 1, 0.1

*Source:* FAO

average world consumption: demersal fish species have stabilized at about 2.7 kg per capita and pelagic fish at 3.2 kg. Two groups are exceptions in that they showed considerable increases between 1961 and 1997: the availability of crustaceans per capita more than trebled from 0.4 to 1.4 kg, largely because of the production of shrimps and prawns from aquaculture practices; and molluscs similarly increased from 0.6 to 2.2 kg per capita.

Fish contributes up to 180 calories per capita per day, but reaches such high levels only in a few countries where there is a lack of alternative protein foods grown locally and where a preference for fish has been developed and maintained (examples are Japan, Iceland and some small island states). More typically, fish provides about 20 to 30 calories per day. Fish proteins are essential and critical in the diet of some densely populated countries, where the total protein intake level may be low (e.g. fish contributes more than or close to 50 percent of total proteins in Bangladesh, the Democratic People's Republic of Korea, the Republic of Congo, Ghana, Guinea, Indonesia, Japan and Senegal), and it is very important in the diets of many other countries (e.g. Cambodia, Benin, Angola and the Republic of Korea).

Worldwide, about 1 billion people rely on fish as their main source of animal proteins. Dependence on fish is usually higher in coastal than in inland areas. About 20 percent of the world's population derives at least 20 percent of its animal protein intake from fish (Figure 19), and some small island states depend on fish almost exclusively.

## FISH TRADE

Fish is traded widely – mostly as a frozen food, and increasingly less as a canned or heavily dried food. Its trade has been stimulated by the economic conditions prevailing in most consumer markets and by notions about the health benefits of seafood consumption. In response to higher prices in recent years, production from aquaculture has had a positive influence on supply and consumer prices. However, in 1998 import demand in some important markets was sharply reduced. Although, in some cases, the weak import demand for certain species resulted from increased domestic production, more generally it was a result of the financial crisis affecting some of the more rapidly growing industrial economies. In addition, the global economic

crisis, which began in the summer of 1997 and spread rapidly through East Asia to the Russian Federation and Latin America, dominated the world economy and resulted in reduced trade and lower commodity prices in seafood products. In Japan, the world's largest fish-consuming country and import market, domestic supply remained at more than 8 million tonnes with small fluctuations until 1995, but since then the trend has been to decrease.

Over the last two years, the consumption of fish and fishery products has been strongly influenced by the economic crisis in the Asian countries, in particular Japan. The crisis and the subsequent low value of the yen led to a decline in imports and consumptionin 1998. The main supplying countries had to reduce prices and find alternative outlets for their production. In 1999, the Japanese economy started to recover, but not as quickly as originally forecast because Japanese people were not spending as freely as they had done before the crisis. Food items that consumers consider to be expensive have had difficulty in regaining their pre-crisis market shares. On the other hand, the United States economy has been particularly strong, and consumption of fish continues to increase in that country. The northern European market was strong in the second part of 1999 because of good economic conditions and higher consumption in restaurants. Europe is not the only region to be experiencing a general trend of increased fish consumption in restaurants as people spend more on eating out. Dietary habits are changing, especially in developed countries. Markets have become more flexible and new products and species have found market niches. The trend is for fish to receive greater value added in the catering and retail markets, thus making it easier for consumers to prepare.

Alongside traditional preparations, developments in food science and technology, combined with improved refrigeration and the use of microwave ovens, are making convenience foods, ready meals, coated fish products and other value-added items a fast-growing industry, especially in the EU and in the United States. The reasons for this rapid expansion include changes in social factors such as the increasing role of women in the workforce, the fragmentation of meals in households as well as the general decrease in average family size, and the increase in single-person households. The need for simple meals that are ready to eat and easy

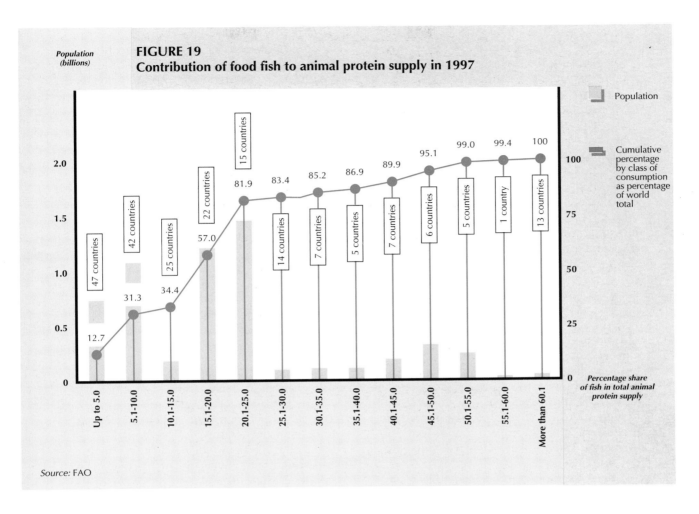

*Population (billions)*

**FIGURE 19**
**Contribution of food fish to animal protein supply in 1997**

Population

Cumulative percentage by class of consumption as percentage of world total

*Percentage share of fish in total animal protein supply*

*Source:* FAO

to cook has thus become more important. Another trend is the increasing importance of fresh fish. Unlike many other food products, fish is still more favourably received on the market when it is fresh rather than processed. However, historically, fresh fish has been of little importance in international trade owing to its perishable nature and very limited shelf-life. Improvements in packaging, reduced air freight prices, and more efficient and reliable transport have created additional sales outlets for fresh fish. Food chains and department stores are also taking an increasing share of the fresh seafood sector, and many have opened fresh seafood counters with an extensive variety of fish and freshly prepared fish dishes or salads next to their frozen food counters. Social changes have greatly influenced the structure of the fish and retail markets. Large food chains and department stores are increasingly common. More and more consumers are limiting their shopping to one day a week and tend to prefer larger food outlets for the sake of convenience.

The United States and EU markets for fishery products are expected to expand in coming years as a result of consumer health consciousness and belief in the positive impact that fish consumption can have on health. Healthy food is a growing concern in developed countries, and calorie counts, dietary and nutritional plans and recipes on packed fish are a useful addition to value-added products.

Outside Japan, the consumption of *sashimi* and *sushi* is increasing in other Asian countries, the United States and Europe. In addition, the consumption of farmed species such as tilapia, catfish and salmon is an alternative to traditional products that are characterized by low supplies and high prices.

The structure of the fish industry in developed countries is also changing. Large, vertically integrated multinational companies are buying smaller producers.

Among the factors that could influence future demand for seafood products are population growth; changes in economic and social conditions (such as lifestyle and family structure); developments in fish production, processing, distribution and marketing strategies; and the prices of fish compared with those of competing foodstuffs. The price of chicken, for example, is making it increasingly attractive on all major markets, resulting in a shift in consumer interest away from fish and towards chicken. Furthermore, globalization and increasing international trade in seafood commodities, as well as international agreements on trade rules, tariffs, quality standards (see Fish quality and safety, Part 2, p. 47) and fisheries management are all having an impact. Long-term global trends in supply and demand, including developments in distribution and consumption, have broad implications for the domestic industry and for domestic consumers. Projections of demand based on population and income growth point to an increasing gap between supply and demand, which could lead to an increase in prices. This, in turn, could lead to a widening of the existing gap in average fish consumption between developed countries and LIFDCs. The consumption trend, as far as species are concerned, points increasingly towards farmed species, whitefish, crustaceans and molluscs in the developed countries and to low-value species, such as small pelagics, in developing countries.

A large share of fish production enters international trade, with about 33 percent exported in 1998 (live weight equivalent).

LIFDCs play an active part in this trade and, at present, account for almost 20 percent of exports. Developing countries as a whole supply nearly 50 percent of total exports in value terms. In 1998, total exports of fish and fishery products were US$51 300 million in value terms, a 3.8 percent decrease compared with 1997.

More than 90 percent of trade in fish and fishery products consists of processed products in one form or another (i.e. excluding live and fresh whole fish). Frozen, fresh and chilled fish make up the majority of exports (Figure 20). Although live, fresh or chilled fish represents only a small share of world fish trade owing to its perishability, trade is growing, reflecting improved logistics and increased demand.

In 1998, total imports of fish and fishery products were US$55 000 million, representing a slight decline of 2.8 percent compared with 1997 and 3.9 percent compared with 1996. Japan was again the largest importer of fishery products, accounting for some 23 percent of total imports, but Japanese imports of fish and fishery products have declined recently as a result of the economic recession (Figure 21). The EC further increased its dependence on imports for its fish supply. The United States, despite being the world's fifth major exporting country, was also its second main importer. More than 77 percent of the total world import value is concentrated in these three areas.

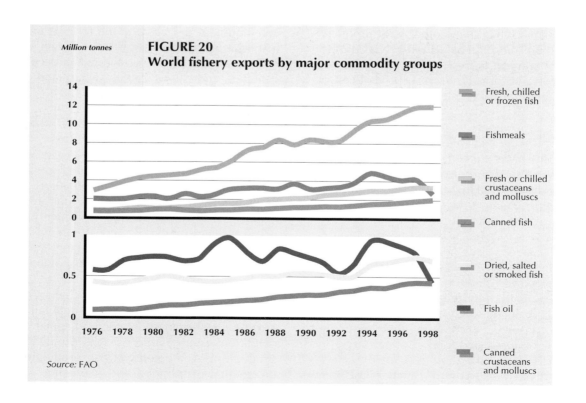

**FIGURE 20**
**World fishery exports by major commodity groups**

*Million tonnes*

Fresh, chilled or frozen fish

Fishmeals

Fresh or chilled crustaceans and molluscs

Canned fish

Dried, salted or smoked fish

Fish oil

Canned crustaceans and molluscs

Source: FAO

*US$ billions*

**FIGURE 21**
**Imports and exports of fishery products for different regions, indicating the net deficit or surplus**

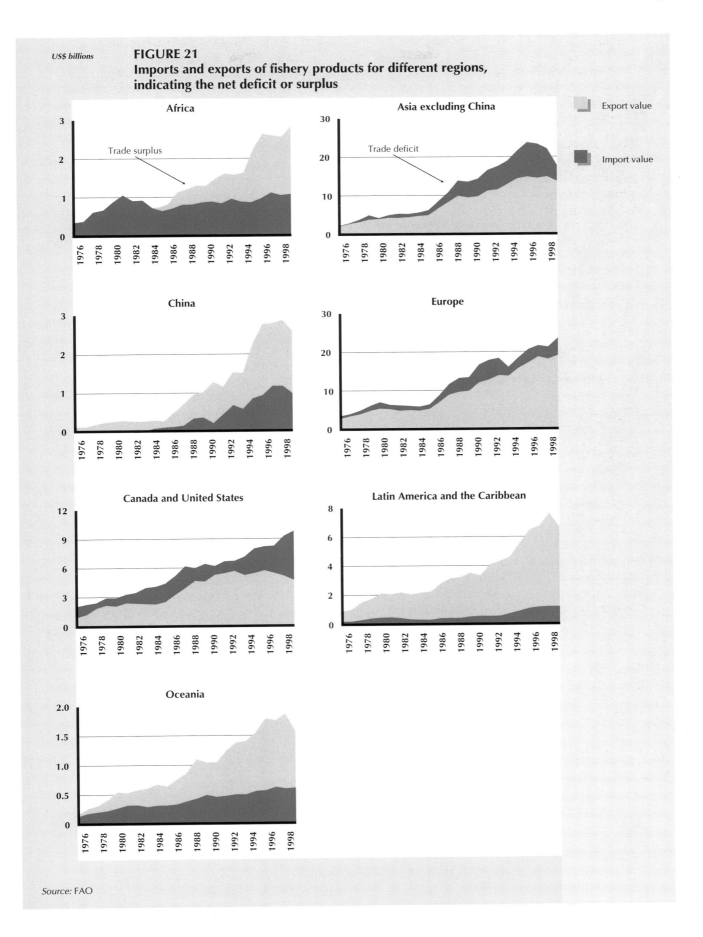

*Source:* FAO

## Shrimp

Shrimp is the main fish trade commodity in value terms, accounting for some 20 percent of the total value of internationally traded fishery products. The international economic crisis in the main producer countries and in their markets, together with disease problems, caused setbacks for shrimp producers, traders and investors in 1998 and 1999. The main producers had to reduce prices and look for alternative outlets in order to sell their production.

In 1998 and 1999, many shrimp-producing countries, particularly in South America, experienced a decline in production mainly owing to disease or weather problems. In Ecuador, Peru, Mexico, Bangladesh and India, shrimp production and exports were disappointing compared with previous years. In contrast, shrimp output in Thailand picked up in 1998 and 1999 after the disease problems of 1996 and 1997. This country continues to be the main shrimp-culturing nation in the world.

After poor trading in 1998, the Japanese shrimp market recovered in 1999, particularly in the second half of the year. The strong yen and high demand were the main reasons for this upturn. The United States market for shrimp was very active in 1999, with record shrimp consumption of 400 000 tonnes, 330 000 tonnes of which were imported.

After a slow start, the European shrimp market was strong in the closing months of 1999. Trade improved in the northern part of the continent as a result of good economic conditions and higher consumption in restaurants. Spain is the main fresh and frozen shrimp importer among the EC countries, followed by France, the United Kingdom and Italy.

## Tuna

Tuna catches in 1999 were well ahead of those of 1998 in practically all major fishing areas. Catches in the Eastern Pacific, in particular (up by 40 percent on 1998), continued the positive trend experienced in 1998. Estimates put the 1999 tuna catch at close to a record of 4 million tonnes. The international tuna market was oversupplied during 1999 and this led to unprecedented low prices, which had already started to decline in mid-1998. In November 1999 skipjack was quoted in Bangkok at a low of US$400 per tonne.

Japanese imports of fresh and frozen tuna were 307 400 tonnes in 1999, a 9.7 percent decrease compared with 1998. Japanese imports of canned tuna expanded slightly in 1999 to reach 21 000 tonnes.

The two main markets for canned tuna are the United States and the EC. While United States imports increased in 1999, the European market was rather weak. United States imports of canned tuna reached 151 700 tonnes in 1999, 32 percent more than the 1998 figure. Canned whitemeat still represents only a small share of United States canned tuna imports, but the product is expanding its presence. The United States accounts for about one-third of the world's canned tuna consumption, but consumption has decreased in recent years. The overall quality of canned tuna in the United States is declining, although the higher-quality segment is growing.

Italian canners' use of tuna loins as raw material is increasing, and loins account for about 60 percent of Italy's total canned tuna production. Spain is now the major tuna processor in Europe, having overtaken Italy.

After the United States, Thailand is the second largest producer of canned tuna in the world, and Thai tuna canning companies are promoting this product on domestic markets by highlighting its low cholesterol content.

## Groundfish

A number of the main groundfish species have experienced reduced stocks and decreased quotas for several consecutive years. In the United States this development has made the market entry of new farmed species such as catfish and tilapia much easier, and in Europe salmon seems to be replacing groundfish. Low supplies of cod have increased the industry's interest in farming cod. However, there are not many alternatives on the market for such traditional products as salted and dried groundfish. Prices in the United States and Europe were relatively depressed in 1999, with an increase towards the end of the year.

Reduced supplies of traditional groundfish species seem to be compensated by increased sales of other products, especially ready-to-eat meals and farmed salmon. In general, world consumption of salmon is rising and farmed Atlantic salmon is becoming more popular, in fresh, smoked and canned forms. Farmed salmon production grew considerably in 1999, reaching nearly 890 000 tonnes compared with 798 000 tonnes in 1998. Chile experienced several problems with its farmed salmon production during 1999, and Norway increased its share in the United States market.

## Cephalopods

Cephalopod fisheries performed well in 1999, especially for *Illex* catches, and supplies on the world market were very strong. The increased supply of squid was initially absorbed without problems, with a strong buying interest reported in Spain and Japan. However, at the end of the year, demand declined suddenly and market prices started to drop.

Squid imports into Japan reached a high of 62 500 tonnes in 1999, almost 30 percent more than in 1998.

In 1999, Japanese cuttlefish imports dropped by 3.1 percent to 43 400 tonnes, with Thailand supplying nearly half of this total. Octopus catches in the Eastern Central Atlantic were good in 1999, leading to higher exports to Japan and lower prices on the world market.

In many of the countries that are not traditional cephalopod eaters, squid consumption is increasing. The best example is the United States, where "calamari" is now well established in fast-food chains. In countries with a low seafood consumption, such as Argentina, squid has found a market niche in the fried fast-food sector.

## Small pelagics

The Russian Federation's financial problems led to a strong price drop in 1998, followed by an upwards trend in mackerel prices during the second half of 1999. Norwegian mackerel exports to the Russian Federation and the Baltic states fell by almost 50 percent between 1998 and 1999. Norway began to focus more on Asia and Eastern European countries such as Poland, Turkey and Ukraine.

In 1999, EC exports of Atlantic mackerel to Eastern Europe dropped compared with 1998, so the EC strongly increased its exports towards African markets (particularly Nigeria).

At the end of 1998, the world herring market collapsed as a result of an oversupply from the 1997/98 season and the economic crisis in the Russian Federation and Japan, the two major markets for herring. The world market price for herring dropped substantially, in some cases by 75 percent. In 1999, imports into Central and Eastern Europe started to pick up and it appears that the Russian Federation will again become the major importer of herring. Prices increased slightly in 1999.

## Fishmeal

Fishmeal production for 1999 is estimated at 6.6 million tonnes, close to the annual average for 1976-1997 of 6.5 million tonnes. This is 29 percent up on the 4.8 million tonnes produced in 1998, which was one of the worst production years ever. Increased production was due to the recovery of fishing in South America after the El Niño phenomenon. Peruvian fishmeal production in 1999 was more than twice the 1998 figure of 815 000 tonnes, representing a return to normal levels. Export earnings from fishmeal increased by 35 percent in 1999 compared with 1998, reaching US$534 million. On the other hand, the situation in Chile did not completely return to normal. Total fishmeal output from this country was 980 000 tonnes in 1999, up from 640 000 tonnes in 1998, but still lower than the 1.2 million tonnes recorded in 1997. Chilean fishmeal exports in 1999 were close to 600 000 tonnes, some 100 000 tonnes more than in 1998.

Increased production led to a strong reduction of prices during 1999. Prices improved somewhat at the end of the year, but competition with soybean meal is still in fishmeal's favour. The present price ratio of 2:1 is one of the lowest in recent history.

Fishmeal exports from the five main exporting countries doubled in 1999, to reach 2.85 million tonnes. China was the main importer, followed by Japan, Taiwan Province of China and Germany.

## Fish oil

World fish oil production reached 1.2 million tonnes in 1999, up from 0.8 million tonnes in 1998. Latin American producers, Peru in particular, reported a strong increase in output, and fish oil production levels went back to pre-El Niño levels. The increase in fish oil availability was coupled with price reductions and, in December 1999, fish oil prices were around US$290 per tonne, compared with US$740 per tonne in mid-1998.

Fish oil use is now dominated by aquaculture, which takes 60 percent of total production. Low production levels in 1998 had a negative impact on the use of edible fish oil, while 1999 saw a recovery in the use of fish oil for direct human consumption.

## Live ornamental fish

Trade in ornamental fish has been increasing since the 1980s. At present, total wholesale trade is estimated at US$900 million and total retail trade at about US$3 billion (live animals for aquariums only). Asia represents more than 50 percent of the world's total ornamental fish supply. Singapore is by far the leading exporter, followed by the United States, Hong Kong Special Administrative Region, Japan, Malaysia, the Czech Republic, Israel, the Philippines and Sri Lanka. Fish farming is a leisure activity that is practised mainly in industrialized countries because it is relatively costly. The main importers are the United States, Japan and Europe, particularly Germany, France and the United Kingdom. ◆

# PART 2
# Selected issues facing fishers and aquaculturists

# Selected issues facing fishers and aquaculturists

## FISHERS' SAFETY

### THE ISSUE

Fishing at sea is the most dangerous occupation in the world. The data gathered from countries that keep accurate records show that occupational fatalities in those countries' fishing industries far exceed the overall national averages. For example, in the United States the fatality rate among fishers is 25 to 30 times the national average;[1] in Italy it is more than 21 times the national average;[2] and in Australia it is 143 per 100 000, compared with the average of 8.1 per 100 000. However, very few countries are able to supply these data. Although the members of the International Maritime Organization (IMO) agreed that the collection and analysis of statistical information on casualties, including fishing vessels and fishers, should be prepared on an annual basis,[3] they acknowledged in 1999 that there had been only a very limited response to their appeal.[4]

It seems plausible that the fatality rate in countries for which information is not available might be higher than it is in those that do keep records. Thus, the International Labour Organization's (ILO) estimate of 24 000 fatalities worldwide, per year, may be considerably lower than the true figure.

Of the 36 million people engaged in fishing and fish farming, FAO estimates that roughly 15 million fishers are employed aboard decked or undecked fishing vessels operating in marine capture fisheries, and that more than 90 percent of these fishers are working on vessels that are less than 24 m in length.

The consequences of loss of life fall heavily on dependants. In developing countries, the consequences can be devastating: widows have a low social standing; there is no welfare state to support bereaved families; and, lacking an alternative sources of income, widows and children may face destitution.

Of particular concern are the reports from fishing administrations and fishers' organizations indicating that fatality rates are increasing in the artisanal sector of developing countries. In most cases, the increase in fatalities can be traced back to changes in the basic nature of fishing operations: overexploitation of coastal resources; advances in vessel and fishing technologies, including motorization and new types of fishing gear; lack of training, experience and skills; commercial pressure; and new fisheries management regimes.

Where inshore resources have been overexploited, fishers are often opting to work farther away from shore, sometimes for extended periods, in fishing craft that are based on designs for inshore fishing, which is limited to daily operations. Such vessels are often built by untrained builders who copy traditional and imported craft, and cost-cutting practices and the builders' lack of experience result in vessels that are unsound. Frequently, they do not comply with national regulations. Furthermore, older generations have no experience of fishing offshore, so there is a lack of traditional knowledge for today's crews about such essential issues as navigation, weather forecasting, communications, living habits during extended periods at sea (several days instead of only one) and the vital culture of safety at sea. The problem is compounded by fishing being a potential source of income for casual workers and the landless or urban unemployed; the fishing industry frequently provides employment for those who have no hope of an alternative source of income.

International voluntary guidelines do not have much effect on artisanal fisheries, largely because standards are directed towards decked vessels of more than 12 m. The Torremolinos Protocol, which is the only international instrument formulated specifically for fishing vessels (decked fishing vessels of at least 24 m in length), is unlikely to come into force because its provisions are seen as being either too stringent or too lenient by the countries whose signatures are required. In the absence of an international instrument, fishers must often rely on national legislation to ensure the safety of their craft, particularly when the vessel owner does not participate as a crewmember. While most countries have regulations concerning the design, construction and equipment of vessels,

[1] United States Bureau of Labor Statistics, 1998.
[2] ILO. 1998. *Yearbook of Labour Statistics, 1998.* Geneva.
[3] IMO. MSC/Circ.539/Add.2 and FSI 6/6/1.
[4] IMO. FSI 7/6/2.

42

BOX 4
**Cyclone in India**

On the night of 6 November 1996, during a severe cyclone, approximately 1 435 fishers perished in the state of Andhra Pradesh on the east coast of India. Of these fishers, 569 were lost while fishing in mechanized boats at sea and 830 were lost while carrying out shrimp seed collection and other shore-based activities in areas remote from the villages. The causes of death differed between the two groups; the former were lost at sea in conditions of high winds and heavy seas, and the latter were lost on land, largely as a result of the storm surge.

The 569 fishers who were reported lost at sea were working on 110 trawlers, which foundered when struck by the cyclone. They had departed from Kakinada port several days before the cyclone struck and were fishing in an area to the southeast of Kakinada, along the coast of the Godavari delta. These trawlers were typically 11 to 15 m long and engaged in fishing trips of 10 to 15 days duration. They were poorly designed and built, yet significant numbers of similar vessels are still being constructed. Few, if any, of the vessels were equipped with safety equipment or even simple transistor radios. Thus, despite the media's transmission of cyclone warnings, the fishers were unaware of the intensity of the approaching cyclone and of its speed of advance.

BOX 5
**Accidents**

Coastal fisheries and coastal sea transport in Guinea (West Africa) depend on open, planked canoes ranging from 6 to 22 m in length. The larger boats are powered by outboard motors of up to 40 HP.

In 1991, Guinea established a National Sea Safety Working Group, which brought together the national Fisheries Department, the Port Authority, the Guinean Navy, national fishers' groups and associated fisheries projects. As its first action, this group established a systematic survey of artisanal canoe accidents along the Guinean marine coast.

In the first three years of the survey, 110 people died in canoe accidents along the coastal stretch of 120 nautical miles – that is nearly one person for each mile of coast. About half of the deaths occurred in fishing canoes, while the other half resulted from transport canoe operations. Comparing deaths at sea with the number of registered small-scale fishers gave an indicative fatality rate of 0.53 percent, or approximately 500 deaths per 100 000 fishers per year. Principal causes associated with the fatalities were given (in order of importance) as capsizing, wind, disorientation (in winter months the sun can become invisible through dust clouds blown off the desert), overloading, waves and motor failure.

A number of other countries along the West African coast, where similar studies have been done, appear to have artisanal canoe fatality rates in the range of 0.3 to 1 percent of fatalities per year.

*Source:* J. Johnson, FAO Fisheries Department.

in developing countries these are sometimes outdated, inappropriate and inadequately enforced. In developed countries, the application of more stringent regulations has not always led to any significant decrease in fatalities; it seems that, as vessels are made safer, operators take greater risks in their ever-increasing search for good catches.

## POSSIBLE SOLUTIONS

There are a number of areas where improvements can be made, including: provision and analysis of data that identify the cause of accidents; training of crews and trainers; and formulation of regulations that are enforced through increased collaboration among fishers, fishers' organizations and the authorities.

It has been argued that the root and causes of accidents in the fishing industry are easy to discern intuitively. While this may often be the case, reliable quantified data would show how the trends vary according to different regions, countries and fisheries, thereby contributing to an understanding of the main causes of fatalities. In order to focus and prioritize the actions to be taken to increase fishers' safety, the most frequent causes of danger and vessel losses must be investigated fully. Vastly improved accident reporting is therefore seen as central to the quest for improved safety in the industry.

Even when accidents are reported, the many diverse approaches to collecting information on their types and causes make it difficult to produce comparable data and statistics and, thus, to identify and address key issues. The nature of the employment arrangements in fishing, which may place many fishers outside traditional occupational accident and disease reporting systems, contributes to this lack of information.[5]

National-level regulations and technical standards must be formulated, reviewed and amended through dialogue among builders, owners, fishers and administrations, to ensure that all parties share a sense of ownership and responsibility in the application of new regulations.

Enforcement of safety regulations is essential and requires collaboration within administrations and, particularly, between fisheries and the marine authorities. However,

very few of the individual inspectors attached to fisheries divisions have a background in boatbuilding, marine engineering or naval architecture, nor have they received any training in how to conduct condition surveys of vessels at the level normally required for classification or insurance purposes. Thus, while part of the solution may lie in regulating the quality standard to which boats are constructed and equipped, attention must also be paid to the necessary skills of the enforcers. Ensuring adequate enforcement implies a significant commitment on the part of the administration, taking into account the cost of establishing, staffing and training a new section.

The training of fishers is clearly one means of channelling the results of lessons learned from the analysis of improved data. Historically, the training of fishers has been limited to skippers, mates and engineers in developed countries. The British Merchant Shipping Act (1894), provided the basis for regulations that covered most of the Commonwealth, including India, Australia and Canada. The IMO Protocol to the Standards of Training, Certification and Watchkeeping for Seafarers (1978) provided standards for countries to follow, but it was never ratified and was superseded by the Convention for the Standards of Training, Certification and Watchkeeping for Fishing Vessel Personnel (1995) (STCW-F). These provisions referred only to vessels over 24 m or powered by more than 750 kW. For smaller vessels, the FAO/ILO/IMO *Document for Guidance on Fishermen's Training and Certification* gave further information on courses and syllabuses. This document has recently been revised in line with STCW-F and retitled *Document for Guidance on the Training and Certification of Fishing Vessel Personnel* (referred to as the *Document for Guidance* in this publication).

---

## RECENT ACTIONS

●

The application of instruments on training, despite the lack of ratification, has been very good in some regions and virtually absent in others. Countries in Europe, the Commonwealth of Independent States (CIS) and South America, along with Canada, Japan and Australasia, have now adopted standards that are in excess of the STCW-F's requirements and in line with the

---

[5] ILO. 1999. *Report on safety and health in the fishing industry.* Geneva.

recommendations laid out in the *Document for Guidance*. The United States has recently started to issue certificates of competency and implement other fishing vessel safety legislation. In Central America, Africa and Asia, many fisheries schools were established in the 1970s and 1980s, and safety training is a major component of their curricula. Unfortunately, the effectiveness of fisheries training schools has been limited by low literacy rates in some countries. In many others, the low status attached to fisheries occupations has resulted in them attracting a high percentage of illiterate workers. Literate individuals with fisheries qualifications have been regarded as potential government employees rather than recruits to the fishing industry. Some training centres have opted to train trainers in order to produce extension agents who can disseminate the training to large numbers of artisanal fishers at the village level. It would appear that the wide disparity in training provision among countries is paralleled by disparities in safety legislation and the compilation of accident statistics. Recent developments have seen a shift in the formal training of fishers from academic to functional training (i.e. assessment is carried out on the basis of what trainees can do rather than what they know). Such training means that lecturers and examiners must have mastered the skills required in order to teach and examine the candidates. Increasingly,

administrations require that entrants into the fishing industry should complete a pre-sea training course in basic safety training, first aid, survival at sea and fire-fighting. Owners and skippers are being encouraged to "think safety" by compiling safety management reports in which they list the main hazards on board their particular vessel and identifying precautions and procedures to minimize the potential effect of such hazards.

A substantial report, entitled *Safety and health in the fishing industries*, was prepared by the International Labour Office as the basis for discussions at the Tripartite Meeting on Safety and Health in the Fishing Industry, held in Geneva in December 1999. It comprehensively examines recent information concerning safety and health in the fishing industry with a view to illustrating these issues and exploring actions that are being taken by international organizations, governments, employers, vessel owners, trade unions, the fishers themselves and other organizations. The meeting concluded that the industry has changed considerably as a result of new management regimes, technology advances and overcapacity, resulting in fishing operations and employment arrangements that create an incentive to work long hours and minimize the number of crewmembers. This, in turn, results in more frequent accidents. The

---

### BOX 6
### Safety and survival training

The first safety courses for fishers were offered in Norway (1981), where they became obligatory in 1989. The other Nordic countries followed this initiative, and all of them established safety education when Finland introduced safety courses for fishers in 1999. Although dispensations are still being granted, the courses will have become obligatory in all Nordic countries within a few years. The length and content of the courses vary considerably. The Nordic Council of Ministers is funding an ongoing project to improve and facilitate safety and survival training by comparing the requirements, courses, instruction materials and practical exercises that each of the Nordic countries has developed and by promoting the sharing of training material, instructors and expertise.

Owing to the different training requirements, Nordic fishers may have difficulty obtaining permits to work as fishers in other Nordic countries. The project aims at facilitating interchange of the workforce by suggesting minimal safety training requirements to be adopted by all the countries, along with guidelines on how to obtain additional training if required.

*Source:* G. Petursdottir, Director, Fisheries Research Institute, University of Iceland.

## BOX 7
## Small boats going offshore

In Samoa, a number of safety problems have been encountered in the development and expansion of the domestic, small-craft (*alia*) tuna longline fishery. In a 15-month period during 1997 and early 1998, at least 14 major accidents occurred, many resulting in the loss of human life. In these 14 accidents, 25 fishers were lost at sea and another 24 were rescued. In addition to the loss of life, nine vessels were not recovered.

In many cases, the specific cause of these accidents is unclear because the vessels and crew disappeared without trace. It is believed, however, that the causes could be attributed to a range of possibilities, including: lack of seaworthiness and stability of the *alia* when loaded in rough weather; poor strength and stability of the *alia* design, which has been modified and "stretched" by builders at the request of owners; an inadequate level of basic skills among many skippers; lack of navigational skills; limited (or non-existent) safety equipment on board; and the rough weather that some skippers and crewmembers were working in.

The national Fisheries Division is working with other government departments to address sea safety issues. The construction of a radio base station in Apia and nine repeater stations around Samoa was completed and put into use in June 1997. The radio is operated around the clock. A vessel registration programme has also been started with a main requirement that every vessel be fitted with a radio. Fishers have to radio in when they are going out to sea, while they are at sea and when they return to port.

As well as the radio requirement for registration, each vessel now undergoes an inspection to check that:

- flotation (foam) is according to the original FAO design;
- the hull is in good condition (with no leaks);
- the main engine is in good running condition;
- the spare engine is in good running condition;
- the boat number is clearly displayed;
- the radio is in good working condition.

Regulations regarding the qualifications of vessel skippers and crewmembers, as well as crew numbers, have been implemented and training in sea safety, vessel surveys, safety equipment requirements and communications has been carried out. A committee to ensure the enforcement of regulations has been set up and includes representatives from the Ministry of Transport, the Police Department and the Fisheries Division.

*Source: SPC Fisheries Newsletter,* 84 (Jan/March 1998), Pacific Community. Updated by P. Watt, Adviser to Samoa Fisheries Division, June 2000.

meeting also concluded that international standards and training related to safety and health in fishing may not be reaching the majority of the world's fishers.

Two sets of guidelines to improve the design, construction and equipment of fishing vessels were formulated in the 1960s and 1970s, not as a substitute for national laws but to serve as a guide to those concerned with framing national laws and regulations. Revision of the two publications *FAO/ILO/IMO Code of Safety for Fishermen* and *FAO/ILO/IMO Voluntary Guidelines for the Design, Construction and Equipment of Fishing Vessels* is being

undertaken by the IMO Subcommittee on Stability, Load Lines and Fishing Vessels, through a correspondence group led by Iceland.

FAO's Fisheries Department has implemented a number of projects aimed at improving sea safety. These have been directed particularly at developing countries and carried out in the field, in cooperation with local people. The issue has been tackled from various perspectives, including improved vessel design and construction, better preparedness for natural disasters, improved collaboration between governments and

---

BOX 8
## Self-help groups

The Icelandic Association for Search and Rescue (IASR) is an NGO that has played a major role in promoting fishers' safety. It was established in 1929. From the very beginning, women – the wives, daughters and mothers of fishers – were very active members of the organization. The first goal was to establish search and rescue groups in all fishing communities around the coast. These were made up of men, but women formed their own affiliates. The groups' main tasks were to raise funds to buy search and rescue equipment, erect shelters in places prone to shipwrecks and build rescue vessels, which were placed in strategic harbours along the coast. IASR has taken an active part in formulating recommendations for safety regulations and in lobbying for their promotion with the authorities.

Another of IASR's major tasks was to organize and carry out safety instruction in fishing communities. At first, this was done by visiting instructors who lectured to voluntary listeners but, with time, the scope broadened considerably and IASR now runs the official obligatory 40-hour safety training courses for fishers on vessels over 12 m. The courses are offered on board a well-equipped teaching vessel, which pays regular visits to the communities around the coast. IASR has grown to be a mass movement in Iceland and is a respected consultant and close cooperator with the authorities. At very short notice, it can call out hundreds of well-trained volunteers, both men and women, for search and rescue missions at sea or on land and using the most up-to date equipment. Volunteers are ready to operate under any circumstances, including wrecked or stranded ships, volcanic eruptions, avalanches and other unforeseen natural catastrophes.

*Source:* G. Petursdottir, Director, Fisheries Research Institute, University of Iceland.

---

fishers' representatives, provision of assistance in the setting up of national sea safety programmes, and institutional support to fisheries training centres.

---

### GLOBAL PERSPECTIVE
IMO, ILO and FAO are the three specialized agencies of the United Nations system that play a role in fishers' safety at sea. IMO is responsible for improving maritime safety and preventing pollution from ships; and the adoption of maritime legislation is still IMO's best-known responsibility. ILO formulates international labour standards in the form of conventions and recommendations, which set minimum standards for basic labour rights. It also promotes the development of independent employers' and workers' organizations, providing training and advisory services to these organizations. However, the working methods and measures of ILO and IMO tend to have little impact on the safety of artisanal and small-scale fishers.

A safe working environment cannot simply be imposed from above. Measures to improve safety can only be truly effective where there is the motivation to apply them. The establishment and maintenance of a culture of safety is a continuous task that demands the participation of fishers and their families, boatowners, legislators and the community at large. There are many examples of individuals interested in safety at sea who have formed fishers' self-help groups or other NGOs and established successful cooperation with the authorities to promote safety in their communities (see Box 8).

In the countries where appropriate regulations, enforcement procedures and training are in place, there has been a measurable (but not always significant) reduction in the annual number of fatalities over the last 15 years. Although these countries account for less than 5 percent of the world's fishers, they demonstrate that results can be achieved. Recognition of safety at sea as a major and continuing problem is the first step towards its mitigation. It is considered that the responsibility for safety at sea should be borne by both administrators and fishers, and similarly that effort and assistance should be shared between those two groups to ensure an effective partnership and hence enable a safer profession.

## FISH QUALITY AND SAFETY

### THE ISSUE
Some 200 different types of illness have been identified as being transmitted by food. In 1999, the Centers for Disease Control and Prevention (CDC) in the United States estimated the following numbers of cases of food-borne disease in the United States:[6]

- 76 million cases of gastrointestinal illnesses;
- 325 000 serious illnesses resulting in hospitalization;
- 5 000 deaths.

These data represent one of the best existing estimates of the impact of food-borne diseases on a developed country. Similar figures (adjusted by the number of inhabitants) could be expected to be found in other developed countries.

Humans have suffered from illnesses transmitted by food throughout the ages. However, in the early 1980s professionals concerned with food safety in developed countries observed what seemed to be a significant increase in the number of disease outbreaks linked to food. This was perplexing, given that an increasing proportion of foods were being – and continue to be – produced under stringent hygienic conditions. Possible reasons for such a "food safety paradox" are:

- increased urbanization;
- improved systems for recording the incidence of illnesses transmitted by food;
- human and industrial pollution;

- non-rational use of antibiotics;
- new emerging pathogens;
- uncontrolled recycling of organic material;
- increased susceptibility to contaminants;
- increased consumption of mass-produced foods;
- the introduction of new technologies for "minimally processed foods";
- prolonged rains, droughts and/or increases in average temperatures, favouring the ecologies of pathogens.

In poorer areas of developing countries, poverty, malnutrition, illiteracy and inadequate public facilities are likely to compound the situation. Although the lack of data makes it impossible to provide quantitative estimates of the situation in developing countries, it seems reasonable to expect that cases of food-borne disease in general are at least as frequent as they are in developed countries and, in most developing countries, probably far more frequent. In poor areas, newborn babies, small children, the elderly, the undernourished and the immune-deficient are the categories most exposed to food-borne diseases. A study conducted in the United Republic of Tanzania from 1992 to 1998[7] indicates that food-borne and water-borne disease is probably one of the four major causes of adult death in the locations studied.

Food-derived illnesses can have several types of cause, including specific toxic substances, pathogenic micro-organisms and parasites that can develop and/or be conveyed by foods. Some toxic substances (biotoxins) may develop naturally in the environment, while others are human-generated contaminants (chemicals). Some pathogenic micro-organisms are part of the normal flora (e.g. of fish) and some are contaminants.

Fish, as is true of any other food, can cause health problems. It can be contaminated at any time from the moment of capture until it is eaten. Contamination may occur because pathogenic micro-organisms form part of the normal flora of the fish. In other cases, toxic substances are introduced through cross-contamination, recontamination or faulty handling and processing.

The extent to which fish products are a source of food-borne diseases is a function of

[6] P.S. Mead, L. Slutsker, V. Dietz, L.F. McCaig, J.S. Bresee, C. Shapiro, P.M. Griffin and R.V. Tauxe. 1999. Food-related illness and death in the United States (review). *Emerging Infectious Diseases*, 5: 607-25. Available at: www.cdc.gov/ncidod/eid/vol5no5/mead.htm.

[7] P.W. Setel and Y. Hemed. 2000. *Cause-specific adult mortality: evidence from community-based surveillance – selected sites, Tanzania, 1992-1998*, p. 416-419. Atlanta, Georgia, USA, CDC.

general food habits, the frequency of fish consumption and the type of products and species consumed. Sometimes, a set of unfavourable circumstances combine to create extremely hazardous health situations. For instance, a recent study conducted by FAO in the village of Xai Udom (Vientiane, the Lao People's Democratic Republic) showed that 67.3 percent of the population was infected by parasites and many villagers were infected by more than one type. The prevailing parasite (affecting 42.1 percent of the population) was liver fluke (*Opistorchis viverrini*), transmitted through the consumption of raw fish, which is the host to an intermediate form of this parasite. Large numbers of people die from a form of liver cancer (cholangiocarcinoma) that it causes.

A study published by the World Health Organization (WHO) in 1995 estimated that about 39 million people worldwide were infested with parasites transmitted by the ingestion of raw or improperly cooked freshwater fish and crustaceans. Almost all of these people – about 38 million – lived in Asia, with the remainder living in Europe and Latin America. In Asia, the problem is concentrated in Southeast Asia and China. Data from Africa were not included in the study, but this type of parasitic infestation is known to occur on that continent in, *inter alia,* Cameroon, Egypt and Nigeria.

Parasitic infestation through the ingestion of fish is only one of the many possible causes of disease, but there is a shortage of reliable information about many of the others. There is a clear need for more information regarding illnesses caused by fish and other foods in developing countries.

## POSSIBLE SOLUTIONS

When the trend of increasing outbreaks of food-related diseases was first identified in the early 1980s, food and fish inspection services in developed countries increased end product sampling. This translated into an increased number of samples of finished foods being analysed and a growing number of inspectors. The effort did not halt the trend of more frequent outbreaks of food-related diseases, however, showing that dependence on end product sampling alone was an inadequate response to the problem.

By the end of the 1980s, it had become clear to public health authorities in developed countries that a new system was necessary. The system had to address all the relevant

hazards in food production and had, therefore, to be incorporated into the harvesting, processing and distribution of fish products. This would require its use on board fishing vessels and by aquaculturists, as well as in fish processing factories, the vehicles used to transport fish and storage and retailing areas. The system that was developed is called the Hazard Analysis and Critical Control Point (HACCP) system. In the HACCP system,[8] each substance, micro-organism or condition of food that can cause disease is called a "hazard". Initially, the system gained credibility through its proven efficiency in controlling the hazard created by *Clostridium botulinum,* a common toxinogenic bacterium, in low-acid canned foods. By applying the HACCP principle, processors were consistently able to ensure adequate timing and temperature control during retorting and improved seaming of cans. This, in turn, virtually eliminated the bacterium from canned foods.

## RECENT ACTIONS

By the beginning of the 1990s, a number of food processing companies, including fish processors, in developed countries were already applying the HACCP system on a voluntary basis. They were soon followed by intermediate and even small food processing companies. Canada was the first country to depart from the traditional approach of fish inspection when it introduced the Quality Management Programme (QMP), a set of regulations that proved to be very similar to those constituting the HACCP system. Eventually, several governments decided to make the HACCP system compulsory.

Regulatory agencies in the European Community (EC) and the United States made fish and fishery products the first category of foods in the food industry to be subject to mandatory application of HACCP systems. The EC issued the first regulation for fish products, "laying down the health conditions for the

[8] FAO. 1997. Hazard Analysis and Critical Control Point (HACCP) System and Guidelines for its Application. Annex to CAC/RCP 1-1969, Rev. 3. Available at: fao.org/codex/standard/fh_basic.pdf.

production and the placing on the market of fishery products", in 1991. In May 1994, the EC adopted an additional regulation which made it mandatory to impose more exact rules for the application of "own health checks".[9] The United States' HACCP-based regulation, Procedures for the Safe and Sanitary Processing and Importing of Fish and Fishery Products – Final Rule, was published on 18 December 1995 and entered into force one year later. Other developed and developing countries soon followed these initiatives.

In 1997, the HACCP system was incorporated into the WHO/FAO Codex Alimentarius in the form of a general guideline.[10] This makes the HACCP system the basic reference for international trade disputes under the World Trade Organization (WTO) Agreement on the Application of Sanitary and Phytosanitary Measures. However, the inclusion of the HACCP system as a general guideline for the Codex Alimentarius does not make all HACCP systems identical. For instance, the United States' HACCP regulations apply to processors, while the EC regulations apply to the whole production chain, from handling fish on board fishing vessels to retailing of fish. In both cases, the HACCP system is therefore very closely linked to the individual food safety and hygiene regulation framework.

Over the last ten years, both the fishing industry and the fish and food inspection services in many developing countries have made a very determined effort to adapt processing and inspection methodologies that satisfy HACCP requirements. Many countries have been successful. Among the countries that were authorized to export fish and fishery products to the EC in mid-1999, 50 operate in full accordance with the EC's HACCP-based regulations.[11] Of these 50 countries, 37 are in Africa, Asia and the Pacific or Latin America and the Caribbean, most received technical assistance from FAO which, during the period 1995 to 1999, organized (mainly through extrabudgetary funding received from

Denmark) 44 workshops and trained more than 1 300 professionals from industry and government in HACCP principles.

However, not all developing countries were able to make the necessary initial investments. Sometimes credit for this purpose was scarce or non-existent and, as a result, some countries suffered a drastic reduction in the number of establishments authorized to export to EC markets. Cape Verde and Guinea-Bissau became extreme examples of this in mid-2000, when the EC banned all imports of fish from these countries.

**GLOBAL PERSPECTIVE**
It is generally agreed that the HACCP system is an improvement on traditional fish inspection and that its use will lead to reduced numbers of food-borne diseases. However, so far little information to prove this point is available. For instance, in a recent report,[12] the CDC stated that "new estimates provide a snapshot of the problem and do not measure trends and do not indicate that the problem is getting better or worse".

The HACCP system is likely to evolve. Developed countries are beginning to introduce a regulatory scheme called risk policy into their food industries. The policy is based on quantitative risk assessment, risk management and risk communication.[13] Risk policy requires additional epidemiological data and studies.

Since there is no possibility of achieving zero risk, the specific relevant hazards to be included in an HACCP system need to be identified. The severity of the hazard therefore needs to be determined. One way of measuring severity is to obtain epidemiology data and establish the ratio between the number of deaths caused by an illness and the total number of diagnosed cases of that illness. Clearly, the first hazards to be controlled through the HACCP system and risk policy should be those that cause illnesses that can lead to death. *Listeria monocytogenes* and *Escherichia coli* O157:H7 are clear examples of this type of hazard. However, control of only these hazards is not enough, and

[9] EC regulations do not use the term "HACCP". Instead they refer to "own health checks".
[10] See op. cit., footnote 8, p. 48.
[11] List No. 1. Commission Decision 97/296/EC.
[12] Op. cit., footnote 6, p. 47.
[13] According to the Codex Alimentarius, risk is "A function of the probability of an adverse health effect and the severity of that effect, consequential to a hazard(s) in food".

## BOX 9
### Risk policy: the case of *ciguatera* control in Cuba

*Ciguatera* is a form of human poisoning caused by the consumption of marine fish that has accumulated naturally occurring toxins. Toxins originate from several algae species (dinoflagellate) that are common to *ciguatera*-endemic regions, particularly in tropical countries. When the HACCP system was introduced in Cuba in the mid-1990s, the available epidemiology data showed that *ciguatera* was one of the main causes of disease from fish products. Between 1993 and 1998, 1 086 outbreaks of *ciguatera* were recorded in Cuba, representing 3 116 individual cases. Mortality attributed to *ciguatera* during this period reached 6 percent of all recorded deaths resulting from food hazards. *Ciguatera* peaked in 1996 with 279 recorded outbreaks. Since 1996, the following measures have been introduced to reduce the impact of this hazard on the population:

- Improved hazard analysis for *ciguatera* was established to determine locations, seasonal variation, species involved, consumers at risk, sources of contaminated fish, etc.

- Detailed analyses of epidemiological records led to dose/response data being defined as functions of the size of fish consumed and allowed limit weights (critical limits) to be set for five of the most important species and potential toxicity to be set for another 15 species (regardless of their weight). This information was included in regulations.
- Fish inspection was made functionally independent of capture and production and included the control of artisanal and recreational fishing. A new regulation was introduced in May 1996.
- A targeted information campaign was conducted in the locations and during the periods of the year in which the problem is more acute.

The industry incorporated this knowledge in their HACCP plans and this led to a drastic reduction in the number of outbreaks caused by industrially processed fish. The total number of *ciguatera* outbreaks has decreased steadily from 1997 and, in 1999, the minimum level so far – 47 cases – was recorded. Most of these outbreaks were caused by unauthorized capture that resulted in the consumption of fish from *ciguatera* endemic areas.

## BOX 10
### The economics of fish safety

The economics of regulatory HACCP systems can be seen from two different point of view, that of the government and consumers and that of the producers. From the viewpoint of government and consumers, the introduction of the HACCP system can be justified in economic terms owing to the possible reduction of illness or death caused by food poisoning, which implies a possible reduction in public and private health costs, insurance costs and lost workdays. In 1993, it was estimated that the total cost of food-borne illnesses caused by the seven major pathogens was between US$5.6 billion and US$9.4 billion per year in the United States alone.

From the point of view of the producers, the application of HACCP systems implies an investment. Some of the initial costs are linked to refitting plants, rearranging processing lines, buying new utensils, purchasing and installing

measurement instruments, training and monitoring of processing activities. The actual figures that are found in practice vary from a few thousand United States dollars, for plants that are already very near to HACCP control requirements, to millions of dollars for large plants that have had to undergo significant refitting. In some cases, it was deemed more convenient to construct a new plant rather than refit an old one, or reduce the level of risk by changing the final product (e.g. from cooked to frozen or fresh product) in order to reduce the level of investments. In even more extreme cases producers decided to cease production.

During the execution of the FAO/Danish International Development Agency (DANIDA) project GCP/INT/609/DEN, a number of plants in developing countries agreed to be monitored to check the effect of HACCP implementation. The plants concerned produced fresh and frozen hake fillets, salted and ripened anchovy, cooked crab meat and cooked lobster tail. They were located in Argentina, Cuba, Ecuador and Uruguay. In all

The case of *ciguatera* control in Cuba is revealing because it shows that application of the HACCP system at the industry level, even if effective, may not be enough to decrease the number of outbreaks associated with a given hazard. It was necessary to enforce policy decisions, including timely communication to places where the population was at risk. It also proved necessary to conduct more in-depth hazard analysis than that ordinarily required for HACCP purposes.

*Source:* Based on data from the Cuban Ministry of Public Health and Ministry of Fishery Industries (FAO/ MIP Workshop on Quantitative Risk Assessment in the Fishery Industry, Havana, March 2000).

cases losses from rejections decreased which, in turn, allowed the plants to recover their investments over periods that ranged from a few months to a few years. In general, the more demanding (risky) the product, the larger the economic gain.

For instance, an Ecuadorian company exporting cooked crab meat managed to reduce internal and external rejections from 4.75 percent of the total production in weight from before the HACCP system was implemented (1997) to 0.81 percent with the system in operation (1998). The company had invested around US$40 000 to implement its HACCP system and, given its level of production (126 tonnes of final product per year), the investment was recuperated within six months.

governments usually rule that relevant hazards also include micro-organisms, chemicals and conditions known to impair human health, temporally or permanently, or cause injury.

Most developing countries do not have useful data about the relevant hazards linked to various food products. Access to better and more refined data would certainly provide a valuable insight into the problem, but the lack of data is not an excuse for failing to take preventive action. In particular, a developing country's lack of information about a possible hazard that is well known in other countries cannot be taken as evidence of that hazard's absence.

Only few developing countries have decided to make the HACCP system obligatory for fish products sold and consumed in internal markets. This may reflect the fact that some people in developing countries see HACCP systems mainly as non-tariff barriers erected by developed countries and submit to them only so that they can export their products to industrial economies. Developing countries that extend the HACCP system to their internal market should expect to reap public health benefits (see Box 9). In fact, HACCP systems could have an enormous impact on fish (and food) safety in developing countries.

The benefits of the HACCP system in developing – and developed – countries are not all linked exclusively to improved public health. Private entrepreneurs would also reap direct benefits because, in order to apply the HACCP, it is first necessary to ensure basic hygiene for all of the activities related to fish production and to improve knowledge of the overall process. FAO's experience in this field has shown that the introduction of the HACCP system has helped entrepreneurs to improve their profits (see Box 10). The investments made to introduce the system are recovered through declining rejection rates and fine-tuning of the production process.

The HACCP system contributes to better quality, because safety is an indispensable requirement for quality. For conceptual and regulatory reasons, the fishing industry separates safety and quality, but in-plant safety and quality go together. Implementation of the HACCP system requires an improved understanding of all aspects of the processes that lead to the final product, and this knowledge can be used immediately to reduce costs and improve overall product quality. The introduction of HACCP principles is shaping the fishing industry of tomorrow.

## PROPERTY RIGHTS AND FISHERIES MANAGEMENT

### THE ISSUE

Since the 1950s, economists concerned with the management of capture fisheries have been aware that the rules for access to resources create incentives and participatory responses, and that these rules and incentives can have a fundamental effect on the long-term status of fisheries. In most fisheries, ineffective strategies for regulating access can lead to situations where the level of fishing effort wastes society's resources and overexploits species.

There is a growing realization that part of the remedy to this management problem lies in designing appropriate access rights to wild stocks, and fishery administrators are now increasingly considering how to provide explicit rights of various sorts to fisheries participants. This process is sometimes referred to as "applying rights-based fisheries management", but the precise meaning of this term and of the concept of assigning "property rights" is often unclear.

The basic concept of property and the rights associated with property is a simple one. So-called "property rights" are bundles of entitlements that confer both privileges and responsibilities. The establishment of property rights in fisheries management therefore involves the definition and specification of the entitlements, privileges and responsibilities created by all the various types of fisheries management. However, it is not uncommon to hear about a lack of clearly defined property rights in fisheries management, and it is quite accurate to note that "property rights, like the dorsal fins on different fishes, come in many different shapes and sizes".[14]

To complicate the matter further, references to rights-based management systems can be references to just about anything along the very broad spectrum of different types of fisheries management systems. Rights-based fisheries management systems may be based

on the use of input controls or on the use of output controls. Some property rights are created by licensing and other forms of access limitation systems. Some are created by fisheries management systems and specify the use of fisheries resources for particular communities (community development quotas [CDQs]), in particular areas or territories (territorial use rights in fisheries [TURFS]) and of particular stocks (stock use rights in fisheries [SURFS]). Other property rights are created by individual quota (IQ), individual fishing quota (IFQ), individual transferable share quota (ITSQ) and individual transferable quota (ITQ) systems.

Ultimately, the basic issues of property rights systems in fisheries management are related to an understanding of:

- how the rights are defined – namely, who has the right to use the resources of a fishery, which portion of the fishery may be used, and how and when it may be used;
- how the rights are conferred and upheld;
- precisely how the respective rights create incentives for those involved – by virtue of the fact that they, to lesser or greater degrees, allocate potential benefits, which may or may not reinforce management objectives.

### POSSIBLE SOLUTIONS

In very general terms, there are three basic ways in which the difficulties of understanding, discussing and applying property rights in fisheries management can be mitigated, if not overcome.

First, one of the major sources of confusion when discussing the matter of property rights and fisheries management is miscommunication. Difficulties frequently arise simply because the term "property rights" means different things to different people and can refer to vastly diverse bundles of entitlements, privileges and responsibilities, each of which will produce very different incentives and, hence, management outcomes. It is important to have a very clear definition of exactly what the property rights in question are, even though this information is not typically part of discussions on the use of property rights in fisheries management.

Before any possible solutions can be developed, the property rights (and their associated issues) that are part of fisheries management need to be defined, and this depends on describing the following attributes

---

[14] D.E. Lane. 1999. Applications of rights-based fisheries: experiences and consequences. In A. Hatcher and K. Robinson, eds. *The definition and allocation of use rights in European fisheries.* Proceedings of the second Concerted Action Workshop on Economics and the Common Fisheries Policy, Brest, France, 5-7 May 1999. University of Portsmouth: Centre for the Economics and Management of Aquatic Resources (CEMARE) Miscellaneous Publications No. 46, p. 19. Portsmouth, UK.

---

*BOX 11*
**Factors affecting the concept of property rights in fisheries management**

Rights-based fisheries management systems and the property rights conferred by them are a function of the legislative, legal, economic, social, cultural, biological and political institutions that shape the environment in which they occur. For example, the legal system of a country will have a direct effect on what entitlements can be conferred under property rights in fisheries. In many instances, fisheries rights do not convey actual ownership of the resources themselves to individuals. For example, in the United States and Australia, natural resources such as fisheries are, respectively, the public's and the Crown's resources, and property rights in fisheries are defined in terms of an individual's right to try to harvest or otherwise use fisheries resources. In

other countries, such as in Japan and Taiwan Province of China, there are instances where the property rights for fisheries resources belong to local communities.

---

of the property rights granted or assigned by a fisheries management strategy or plan:[15]

- the *exclusivity* of participation in the fishery;
- the *durability* (duration) of the rights conferred;
- the *security* or quality of the title conferred by the rights;
- the *transferability* of the rights;
- the *divisibility* of the rights assigned;
- the *flexibility* associated with the use of the rights.

Second, there needs to be recognition and acceptance of the fact that, just as for any other management situation, there is no single fisheries management strategy that will solve all fisheries problems. When working to find solutions, fisheries management requires the most appropriate combination of the available management tools and the rights associated with them. This is another simple point that is often overlooked.

Third, as part of the design process of a management strategy, and before work starts on the design of a particular regulatory solution to the rights-related issues of a fishery, managers and participants need to give explicit descriptions of:[16]

- the fishery management unit;[17]
- the total amount that can be caught;[18]
- to what extent the different participants can assume a successful harvest.[19]

Possible regulatory solutions can then be constructed on the basis of the nature of the property rights that can be conferred (i.e. their

---

[15] Anthony Scott described his characterization of the elements of property rights in a keynote address, entitled Moving through the narrows: from open access to ITQs and self-government, at the Fremantle conference FishRights99, Use of Property Rights in Fisheries Management. Available at: www.fishrights99.conf.au.

[16] L.G. Anderson. 1992. *Consideration of the potential use of individual transferable quotas in US fisheries overview document.* The National ITQ Study Report Volume 1. Washington, DC, National Oceanic and Atmospheric Administration (NOAA).
[17] Preferably, the management unit is the fish stock throughout its range, but this may not always be possible. When the management unit is not the stock throughout its range, it becomes critical that other uses of the stock are accounted for.
[18] If total allowable catches (TACs) cannot be quantitatively determined and/or set, it is still important to try to set them qualitatively in order to help guide regulatory decision-making and compare the incentives created by different TACs.
[19] Focusing attention on individual allocations, regardless of whether they are explicit or implicit, helps to identify possible regulatory options and their impact on participants' behaviour.

---

BOX 12
## Property rights and conflict minimization

Most conflicts over fisheries resources arise when the resource is (or is perceived to be) so scarce that sharing it becomes difficult. When rights, particularly those relating to participants' activities regarding their own portions of a stock, are well defined, understood and observed, allocation conflicts tend to be minimized. However, when rights to the use of a stock are not well defined, understood or upheld, divergent assumptions about what the rights may convey often result in conflicts over scarce fisheries resources.

Fisheries resources are becoming increasingly scarce, so conflicts over the allocation and sharing of these resources are likely to become more frequent, unless there are mechanisms that allocate resources explicitly. Conflicts can be minimized by clarifying the property rights conferred by the management of a fishery, following risk-based decision strategies and using conflict mitigation processes.

---

exclusivity, durability, security, transferability, divisibility and flexibility). The management solutions that are created in this way are likely to reflect either:

- bundles of rights where some of the six elements of the entitlements held by participants are relatively weak and unspecified (such as those conveyed by management programmes based firmly on spatial or temporal limitations to access, the use of other input controls such as gear restrictions or total quota systems); or
- bundles of rights where the elements of entitlements are relatively well specified (such as those conveyed by the use of IQs or community development quotas, SURFS, individual transferable effort [ITE] or individual vessel quota [IVQ] systems, or such systems as ITQs, ITSQs and IFQs).

This approach to the issue of property rights in fisheries leads to the following basic questions:

***When is it useful to take property rights systems into consideration?*** What sorts of sociological, biological and economic conditions will shape property rights? What institutions, administrative conditions and legal needs (instruments, legislative practices, etc.) are useful?

***Who holds and who should hold property rights?*** What are the requisite legal bases for property rights? If property rights are changed, who should receive the new rights? Are there advantages in defining communal property rights? How are different scales of fishing activities accommodated? How do different property rights systems of management accommodate indigenous or other user groups?

***How can property rights systems improve the incentives for economic efficiency, stewardship, conservation and profitability?*** Where and how do the incentives created by different types of property rights become apparent? What sorts of distributional implications are there? What sorts of operational requirements do different types of property rights management strategies require in terms of research, enforcement, administration and actual fishing operations?

The solution to the issue of property rights in fisheries management requires a return to the fundamental elements on which all fisheries management systems are based, allowing for the comparative assessment of the management options offered by different types of property rights. Although there is little need for new fisheries management tools, current use of the available tools must be improved so that they can impart incentives more vigorously.

## RECENT ACTIONS

●

Over the last decade, there has been considerable international interest in the issues of property rights in fisheries management. The property rights associated with fisheries that extend beyond or occur outside national jurisdictions are being clarified by a rapidly growing set of international memoranda and agreements. In addition, international organizations are increasingly interested in how different types of rights-based fisheries management systems can affect the conservation and sustainable use of fisheries.

The ongoing maturation of the concepts embodied in the 1982 United Nations Convention on the Law of the Sea, coupled with conflicts over the issue of who has the rights to catch fish in situations where stocks cross national jurisdictions and/or national and international areas,[20] has led to the development of the following agreements, which clarify and define more precisely various aspects of property rights in fisheries:

●

In 1993, the FAO Compliance Agreement[21] was adopted to strengthen the exclusivity of the property rights of those fishing on the high seas. The Agreement focused on which vessels had the authority to fish on the high seas, and it also underlined the responsibilities of fisheries management authorities in controlling such activity.

●

Two years later, the adoption of the UN Fish Stocks Agreement[22] extended the definition of property rights relating to the fishing of straddling and highly migratory fish stocks by strengthening both the flag state's responsibilities associated with the right of

exploiting such stocks and the enforceability and security of the privileges conferred by those rights with provisions on compliance and enforcement.

●

Currently, the development of an international plan of action to deal with illegal, unreported and unregulated (IUU) fishing will serve to define more clearly and enforce the property rights to harvest fish on the high seas. Various types of property rights systems continue to be discussed in more general terms at such meetings as:

- the Expert Group on Economic Aspects of Biodiversity, held by the Organisation for Economic Development and Co-operation (OECD) in 1998 to consider the pros and cons of using ITQs in a property rights-based fisheries management system that would create positive incentives for the conservation and sustainable use of marine biodiversity;
- the 1999 Fremantle Conference, FishRights99, on the use of property rights in fisheries management, where participants from 49 countries examined the use of rights-based management systems from the perspectives of governments and administrators, the commercial fishing industry and various types of communities.

●

While such institutions as the United Nations and the World Bank are addressing issues arising from the conservation of marine biodiversity, there is increasing interest in examining fisheries management tools and their property rights characteristics to see if these are of use in effecting ecologically sustainable development.

At the regional level, discussions regarding the use of property rights in fisheries management have been benefiting from both the growing recognition that the use of ITQs is only one of a range of relevant types of rights-based fisheries management and the realization that adjustment programmes need to be coupled with new management strategies if their results are to be consolidated. One example of this was the 1999 Concerted Action on Economics and the Common Fisheries Policy workshop on the Definition and Allocation of Use Rights in European Fisheries, funded by the EC and its Agriculture and

---

[20] For example, Canada's enforcement actions against Spanish vessels fishing for Greenland halibut in 1995.

[21] The Agreement to Promote Compliance with International Conservation and Management Measures by Fishing Vessels on the High Seas was adopted by the FAO Conference in November 1993 but has not yet entered into force.

[22] The Agreement on the Implementation of the Provisions of the United Nations Convention on the Law of the Sea of 10 December 1982 Relating to the Conservation and Management of Straddling Fish Stocks and Highly Migratory Fish Stocks was adopted and opened for signature in 1995.

Fisheries Programme (FAIR).[23] This workshop was followed by another, held in Bergen, Norway in October 2000, focusing on specific rights-based solutions to EC fisheries management problems.

At the national level, interest in the use of property rights is continuing to develop, albeit cautiously. Politicians are aware that there are potentially significant political ramifications when property rights are made increasingly specific and when allocation issues have to be addressed explicitly. For example, in Iceland, allocation issues have inspired first political and then legal battles to challenge the implementation of ITQ programmes. In Australia, recent efforts to discuss and implement fisheries management systems based on clearly specified property rights such as ITQs have been stalled in the political arenas of several states, while fishers are making increasing demands on fisheries management agencies for clarification of their commercial fishing rights and mechanisms that allocate fisheries resources in ways that are defensible and predictable.

Since 1998, governments and the industry in some Latin American countries have been debating the merits of introducing more clearly defined rights for those involved in industrial pelagic fisheries (in Chile and Peru) and groundfish fisheries (in Uruguay and Argentina). So far, however, it is not clear that agreements on how to proceed will emerge.

In contrast, the characteristics of the rights held by artisanal fishers in Latin America are gradually becoming more clearly and exclusively defined.[24] Although generally applied to situations where there are stocks of fish dwelling on the bottom or in other localized and non-migratory areas (including relatively small bodies of freshwater), these arrangements have given rights-holders the legal wherewithal to exclude those who do not have rights in such fisheries. For example, in 1998 Peru began to provide artisanal fishers' organizations with exclusive rights in some inshore marine resources, and in Ecuador fishers have received exclusive rights to enhance and exploit fisheries in some inland waters. In Brazil, moves to allocate exclusive fishing rights – and management obligations – to local communities are currently under way. In Chile, Mexico and Cuba, similar programmes have been under way for some time and are now relatively well established.

Although there has not yet been any systematic assessment of all the economic and other impacts of such issues as the assignment of rights to fishers and the state of stocks, some potentially positive outcomes have already been recorded. Initial regional assessments indicate that, for many communities, the assignment of rights has meant that wild resources have recovered, the prices received by fishers have improved (sometimes because fishers have become involved in processing and marketing) and fishers' organizations have been able to grow stronger through the accumulation of capital.

## GLOBAL PERSPECTIVE

It is clear that open access utilization of such natural resources as fisheries is not sustainable. It is also clear that current approaches to controlling and regulating the use of fisheries resources do not necessarily lead to sustainable use, and in addition often create incentives that work against management objectives.

Around the world, in artisanal and industrial fisheries, both large- and small-scale, the increasing scarcity of resources is driving stakeholders to demand greater clarification of their property rights in fisheries. As increasing numbers of people exploit fisheries resources (often using better technology than was available in the past) there is an ever-growing need to examine the advantages and limitations of the existing role of property rights in fisheries management and to consider strategies that are based on more clearly defined rights.

At all levels, political and administrative interest regarding property rights and fisheries management, and the opportunities created by the spectrum of rights that may be conferred, will continue to grow, particularly as fisheries resources come under even greater pressure and the linkages between well-specified property rights and fisheries management become more widely understood. This interest

[23] The Concerted Action Workshops Series is being organized by CEMARE. Held in Brest, France, from 5 to 7 May 1999, the meeting focused explicitly on The Definition and Allocation of Use Rights in European Fisheries.

[24] Workshop on the Management and Allocation of Fishery Resources to Artisanal Fishers in Latin America, Valparaiso, Chile, 25-28 April 2000.

is likely to be coupled with a growing use of capacity adjustment programmes as mechanisms for shifting fisheries management systems towards the use of more clearly defined and specified property rights.

In the future, all those involved with fisheries and their management will give greater consideration to the property rights – entitlements, privileges, responsibilities and incentives – that are conferred by different types of fisheries management strategies.

## ILLEGAL, UNREPORTED AND UNREGULATED FISHING

### THE ISSUE
Illegal, unreported and unregulated (IUU) fishing is found in all capture fisheries, irrespective of the location, species targeted, fishing gears employed or level and intensity of exploitation (see Box 13). IUU fishing occurs in small-scale and industrial fisheries, inland and marine fisheries, and fisheries in zones of national jurisdiction as well as those on the high seas. IUU fishing is not confined to high seas fisheries, to particular groups of fishers or to specific fisheries. Regional fisheries management organizations see cases of IUU fishing by both contracting and non-contracting parties and by vessels from countries with open registers.

IUU fishing is not a new phenomenon. It has been a source of concern for resource custodians ever since fishing communities first started to implement measures to conserve fish stocks. In societies where indigenous resource-use practices continue (e.g. Melanesian communities in the South Pacific Islands), infringements of these practices by fishers carrying out IUU fishing often carry substantial social and economic sanctions.

Efforts are under way to assess how serious and widespread IUU fishing is, but no complete and comprehensive picture of the situation has yet emerged. FAO has been informed that, in some important fisheries, IUU fishing accounts for up to 30 percent of total catches, and in one instance it has been indicated that IUU catches could be as high as three times the permitted catch level. Many of the world's regional fisheries management organizations have taken steps to address the problem. Where IUU fishing is common, it has major consequences for national and regional scientific assessments and, in turn, for the determination of catch levels and other

management measures adopted and implemented by national administrations and regional fisheries management organizations.

The international community has identified IUU fishing as a major fisheries management issue because of its far-reaching consequences for the long-term sustainable management of fisheries resources; when IUU fishing is unchecked, the system on which fisheries management decisions are based becomes fundamentally flawed. This situation leads to a failure to achieve fisheries management goals and the loss of both short- and long-term social and economic opportunities (see Box 13). In extreme cases, IUU fishing can lead to the collapse of a fishery or seriously affect efforts to rebuild fish stocks that have been depleted.

IUU fishing has many facets and motivations, although the most obvious underlying incentives are economic in nature. Other factors that may encourage IUU fishing include the existence of excess fleet capacity, the provision of government subsidies (where they maintain or increase capacity), strong market demand for particular products, weak national fishery administration (including inadequate reporting systems), poor regional fisheries management and ineffective MCS, including a lack of VMS.

### POSSIBLE SOLUTIONS
To combat IUU fishing, concerted international cooperation is required, and this depends on the collaboration of all states, irrespective of whether their primary roles are as coastal states, flag states, port states or fish-importing countries. A clear focus on the issues that contribute to IUU fishing and a common international resolve to address them in a timely and realistic manner should enable progress to be made towards greatly reducing or eliminating IUU fishing.

In zones of national jurisdiction where IUU fishing is practised by both authorized and unauthorized fishers, national administrations need to strengthen, *inter alia*, licensing procedures; conservation and management measures; data reporting, collection and analysis; and MCS. An international plan of action to combat IUU fishing will be helpful. Such a plan, if comprehensively developed and effectively implemented, should reduce, if not eliminate, the incidence of IUU fishing. Based on recent international discussions of this issue, it seems likely that an international plan of action to address this type of fishing

## BOX 13
## IUU fishing in
## the CCAMLR region

The term "IUU fishing" is new to the fisheries literature. It first emerged during recent sessions of CCAMLR, where it evolved from discussions concerning fishing activities that are illegal and/or not compliant with CCAMLR on the part of Parties (illegal and unreported) and non-Parties (illegal and unregulated) in the Convention[1] area. The first formal mention of IUU fishing on a CCAMLR meeting agenda occurred in 1997.

The IUU fishing problem in CCAMLR waters has not been confined to the vessels of non-contracting parties. In some instances, vessels flagged to CCAMLR member countries have been involved in IUU fishing. To date, the measures adopted by CCAMLR in seeking to address the IUU problem have not included elements related to the control of nationals, or the control of flag vessels, by members of the Commission.

The scale of IUU fishing that has taken place in CCAMLR toothfish fisheries is unlikely to be repeated in many other fisheries. In 1997/98, CCAMLR estimated that the toothfish catches from IUU operations were in the order of 33 583 tonnes or more. This figure was estimated to represent in excess of 50 percent of the total global catch of the species. Estimates for 1998/99 suggest that the IUU catch has decreased but is still at least 10 773 tonnes and, when compared with the 17 435 tonnes reported for this species in CCAMLR waters, it still represents a significant proportion of the toothfish product on the market.

A number of factors have influenced the high levels of IUU fishing in the CCAMLR toothfish fisheries. Two of the more significant points are:

• The product is highly sought after in the international market, thus offering the potential for significant monetary gain to participants in the IUU fishery.
• The isolated location of the fisheries is such that the deployment of surveillance and enforcement resources is extremely expensive, making it unlikely that an offending vessel will be caught while fishing illegally.

One of the impacts of the combination of these two factors has been to limit the effectiveness of more traditional MCS tools in addressing the IUU problem in CCAMLR toothfish fisheries. As a result, CCAMLR has introduced a series of measures in its attempt to address the IUU problem. The most recent mechanism adopted by the Commission has been the introduction of the Catch Document Scheme for *Dissostichus* species. The purposes of the scheme are to monitor international trade in toothfish products, identify the origin of toothfish products entering the markets of contracting parties, determine whether such products were caught in CCAMLR waters and, if so, whether they were taken in a manner consistent with CCAMLR conservation measures. Since 7 May 2000, CCAMLR contracting parties have been required to ensure that any toothfish product landed in their ports, transshipped to their vessels or imported into their markets is accompanied by a valid catch document.

---

[1] The Convention on the Conservation of Antarctic Marine Living Resources was signed in May 1980 and entered into force in April 1981.

*Source:* G. Bryden, Chairman of the Standing Committee on Observation and Inspection, CCAMLR.

would promote, *inter alia,* the following short- and long-term measures:

- strengthening of national conservation and management arrangements, including national fisheries administrations;
- conformity of national legislation with regional and international obligations, including the ratification of the 1995 UN Fish Stocks Agreement, and the 1993 Compliance Agreement; [25]
- the promotion of flag state responsibility by ensuring that the state authorizes all vessels flying its flag to fish, irrespective of whether such authorization is for operations in zones of national jurisdictions, in the exclusive economic zones (EEZs) of other countries or on the high seas;
- complete, accurate and timely catch and other reporting;
- encouragement of port states to take action that will hinder the landing, transshipment or sale of fish as a result of IUU fishing;
- encouragement, consistent with WTO-related measures, of the closure of markets for IUU-harvested fish;
- certification of product origin;
- support of regional fisheries management organizations in taking steps to strengthen measures that will permit them to assess more effectively the extent and impact of IUU fishing on their work and to adopt and implement measures to curb such fishing in their respective areas of competence;
- empowerment of MCS systems for the monitoring of both in-zone and high seas fisheries, and the facilitation of close collaboration among all states, irrespective of whether they are coastal, flag, port or market states.

---

## RECENT ACTIONS

●

During 1999 and 2000, IUU fishing has been addressed in several important international fora.[26] FAO was given a clear mandate at the 23rd Session of its Committee on Fisheries (COFI) and the 1999 FAO Ministerial Meeting on the Implementation of the Code of Conduct for Responsible Fisheries to develop a voluntary international plan of action to

combat IUU fishing within the framework of the Code.[27]

Development of the plan of action has followed a two-step approach:

- An Expert Consultation on IUU Fishing was hosted by the Government of Australia in cooperation with FAO. The meeting, which was attended by some 60 experts from a wide geographical distribution and range of professional backgrounds, was held in Sydney, Australia, from 15 to 19 May 2000. The experts who attended prepared a preliminary draft international plan of action.
- An FAO Technical Consultation on IUU Fishing was held at FAO headquarters from 2 to 6 October 2000.

---

## GLOBAL PERSPECTIVE

Regional fisheries management organizations are taking steps to combat IUU fishing. Action has already been taken by the:

- Commission for the Conservation of Antarctic Marine Living Resources (CCAMLR) (see Box 13);
- Commission for the Conservation of Southern Bluefin Tuna (CCSBT);
- Indian Ocean Tuna Commission (IOTC);
- International Commission for the

---

[25] See footnotes 22 and 21, p. 55.

[26] The 23rd Session of COFI in February 1999; the FAO Ministerial Meeting on Fisheries in March 1999; the 7th Session of the Commission on Sustainable Development in April 1999; the 116th Session of the FAO Council in June 1999; the Asia-Pacific Economic Cooperation Fisheries Working Group in July 1999; the 54th Session of the United Nations General Assembly in November 1999; the 8th Session of the IMO Sub-Committee on Flag State Implementation in January 2000; the Chilean International Conference on Monitoring, Control and Surveillance in January 2000; the 44th Session of the IMO Marine Environment Protection Committee in March 2000; the 72nd Session of the Maritime Safety Committee in May 2000; and the United Nations Open-ended Informal Consultative Process on Oceans and the Law of the Sea in May 2000.

[27] In February 2000, FAO reported to the 24th Session of COFI on progress achieved in fulfilling the mandate provided concerning IUU fishing, and in particular the request to develop an international plan of action to combat IUU fishing. Given the urgency of the IUU fishing problem and the strong international focus on the issue, FAO anticipates that it will be possible to provide COFI with a draft plan of action for consideration and possible adoption in 2001.

Conservation of Atlantic Tunas (ICCAT);
- Northwest Atlantic Fisheries Organization (NAFO);
- Northeast Atlantic Fisheries Commission (NEAFC).

Other regional fisheries management organizations are in the process of assessing and addressing IUU fishing.

Members of regional fisheries management organizations will have to decide how to enhance flag state control and how to improve cooperation with port states. Non-parties to regional fisheries management organizations will be urged to take steps to control their vessels so that they do not engage in activities that undermine the work of regional fisheries management organizations. As a result, it will become of primary importance that these organizations try to accommodate new entrants. The establishment of a joint FAO/IMO ad hoc working group is expected to lay the groundwork for cooperative action on IUU fishing between the two organizations, in response to calls that they should collaborate to find solutions to the problem.

FAO will to continue its cooperation with regional fisheries management organizations and to facilitate cooperation among these organizations. A manifestation of this collaboration is FAO's annual consolidated reporting to the United Nations General Assembly on the activities of regional fisheries management organizations and the biennial meeting it holds with other interested parties to address matters of mutual concern.

## INDICATORS OF SUSTAINABLE DEVELOPMENT AND THE PRECAUTIONARY APPROACH IN MARINE CAPTURE FISHERIES

### THE ISSUE
Widespread concern about the sustainability of present uses of natural renewable resources led to the United Nations Conference on Environment and Development (UNCED), held in Rio de Janeiro, Brazil in 1992, and to the adoption of its Agenda 21. The event reflected a global consensus for more ecosystem-based sustainable development across all sectors of human activity, as a means of improving the human welfare of present generations without sacrificing that of the future. It called for a substantial shift in governance, improved scientific support to decision-making and a

substantial increase in strategic information.

Simultaneously, UNCED recognized the cost and scarcity of such information and, therefore, the high degree of uncertainty about the functions and state of productive ecosystems as well as the resulting risk for the resources and the people dependent on them for a living.

The combination of these requirements presents a formidable challenge for modern fisheries governance. The capacity of fishery managers and industry to comply with the requirements will condition the views of an increasingly aware society on the future role of fisheries in global sustainable development and food security.

### POSSIBLE SOLUTIONS
In order to assist fisheries policy-makers and managers, allow monitoring and performance assessment and facilitate people's participation, Chapter 40 of Agenda 21, Information for decision-making, calls for
"a harmonized development of sustainable development indicators at the national, regional and global levels, and for incorporation of a suitable set of these indicators in common, regularly updated, and widely accessible reports and databases, for use at the international level, subject to national sovereignty considerations" (Paragraph 40.7). In 1995, the United Nations Commission on Sustainable Development (CSD) followed up and approved a work programme aimed at making such indicators available to decision-makers at the national level by the year 2000.

In addition, Principle 15 of UNCED's Rio Declaration states that "In order to protect the environment, the precautionary approach shall be widely applied by States according to their capabilities. Where there are threats of serious or irreversible damage, lack of full scientific certainty shall be not used as a reason for postponing cost-effective measures to prevent environmental degradation." The General Principles and Article 6.5 of the Code followed this up by prescribing a precautionary approach to all fisheries in all aquatic systems, regardless of their jurisdictional nature.

### RECENT ACTIONS

During the last few years, considerable effort has been devoted to elaborating frameworks for the development of sustainability indicators and procedures for their integration with the precautionary approach. The following is a review of the progress made.

●

***Indicators of sustainable development.*** Since 1995, CSD has promoted, *inter alia,* the exchange of information among interested actors; identification, testing and evaluation of relevant indicators; training and capacity building; and the development of frameworks for sustainability indicators. Taking the lead in the development of sectoral indicators in fisheries, FAO, in collaboration with the Government of Australia, reviewed the issue and drew up technical guidelines for the development and use of indicators for the sustainable development of marine capture fisheries.[28] It is recognized that the adoption and reporting of sustainable development indicators are practicable and cost-effective means of tracking progress towards sustainable development (e.g. in the implementation of the Code); detecting potential problems in good time; learning by comparing performances among different fisheries; and, as a consequence, optimizing policies and fisheries management.

Several complementary frameworks have been proposed for the design, organization and reporting of sustainable development indicators, such as the pressure-state-response (PSR) framework. In the case of fisheries, the Code provides an alternative framework. When indicators have been established for similar frameworks, they can be shared at the relevant national, regional and global levels. To that effect, similar concepts, definitions and processes need to be agreed and implemented when comparable systems of indicators that follow minimum standard requirements are being developed.

In general, indicators should reflect the state of the system and its outcomes in relation to societal goals and objectives, the long-term sustainability of the fishery, the ecosystem

---

*TABLE 4*

**Indicators for the main dimensions of sustainable development**

| Dimension | Indicator |
| --- | --- |
| **Economic** | Harvest and harvest value |
| | Fisheries contribution to GDP |
| | Income |
| | Value of fisheries exports (compared with value of total exports) |
| | Investment in fishing fleets and processing facilities |
| **Social** | Employment/participation |
| | Demography |
| | Literacy/education |
| | Fishing traditions/culture |
| | Gender distribution in decision-making |
| **Ecological** | Catch structure |
| | Relative abundance of target species |
| | Exploitation rate |
| | Direct effects of fishing gear on non-target species |
| | Indirect effects of fishing: trophic structure |
| | Direct effects of gear on habitats |
| | Change in area and quality of important or critical habitats |
| **Governance** | Compliance regime |
| | Property rights |
| | Transparency and participation |

supporting it and the generation of net benefits to fishers and society.

Indicators of sustainability should reflect the well-being of (or the problems related to) the resource and human components of the system, as well as the progress (or lack of it) towards the objective of sustainable development (Figure 22). Indicator-based systems are becoming a useful complement to conventional management support systems, as well as a promising way of monitoring and managing fisheries subsectors, or the sector as a whole, offering an alternative to the fishery-by-fishery approach.

The selection of appropriate geographic units for the reporting of indicators is critical and, while recognizing national and subnational jurisdictions, should reflect the geographic

---

[28] FAO. 1996. *The precautionary approach to fisheries and its implications for fishery research, technology and management: an updated review,* by S.M. Garcia. FAO Fisheries Technical Paper No. 350/2, p. 1-75. Rome; FAO. 1999. *Indicators for sustainable development of marine capture fisheries.* FAO Technical Guidelines for Responsible Fisheries No. 8, Rome; S.M Garcia and D. Staples. 2000. Sustainability reference systems and indicators for responsible marine capture fisheries: a review of concepts and elements for a set of guidelines. *Marine and Freshwater Research.*

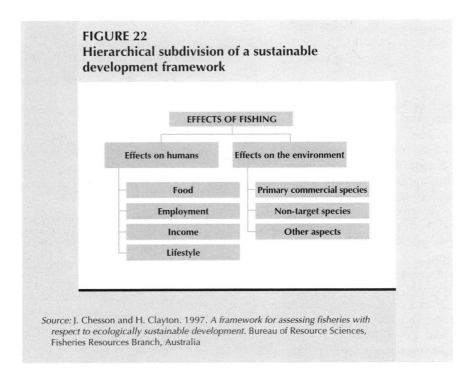

**FIGURE 22**
**Hierarchical subdivision of a sustainable development framework**

EFFECTS OF FISHING

Effects on humans — Food, Employment, Income, Lifestyle

Effects on the environment — Primary commercial species, Non-target species, Other aspects

*Source:* J. Chesson and H. Clayton. 1997. *A framework for assessing fisheries with respect to ecologically sustainable development.* Bureau of Resource Sciences, Fisheries Resources Branch, Australia

location of the ecological processes that define aquatic ecosystem boundaries. While commitments have been made for national reporting, it might sometimes be appropriate to aggregate reports at a subnational level (e.g. by fisheries or by small districts within the same nation) or multinational level (e.g. for transboundary stocks).

There are many ways of representing the interdependent components of a fishery or of a fishery sector in a sustainable development reference system. The minimum critical components are the ecosystem, the economy, society and governance. The ecosystem comprises the fishery resources that support the fishery as well as other aspects of the ecosystem  that control the productivity of the resource, including dependent and associated species. The economy reflects the results – expressed in terms of benefits and costs – that are derived from the use of the ecosystem. The benefits and costs are experienced by consumers, producers and society at large. Short- and long-term equity is included. The society component of the system consists of non-monetary costs and benefits, which are important elements of human welfare. Governance includes the institutions as well as the rules governing the system. Indicators should reflect the performance of the system in each of these components.

Ideally, indicators for each component should be developed by identifying objectives that are relative to that component, by specifying a conceptual or numerical "model" of the available scientific understanding; and determining indicators of performance that relate to the objectives for which information is available or can easily be collected. Indicators can be very numerous and need careful selection (Table 4). They must be scientifically validated as really reflecting the changes that they imply; based on the "best scientific information available", as required by UNCLOS; easy to develop and cost-effective; and easily understood by the target audience.

The value of indicators must be interpreted in relation to target, limit or threshold reference values (or reference points) derived in various ways, even when there is a shortage of data. The target reference values define desirable states of the system and good performance. Limits indicate undesirable states of the system and bad performance. Thresholds identify situations in which action, possibly pre-agreed, should be taken. Together, these reference points give an indication of societal value judgements regarding the indicators. For example, an indicator of biomass below the limit level may be considered as illustrating a "bad" situation. An indicator of biomass at the maximum sustainable yield level may be considered as "good".

Collaborating nations that share a resource should strive to establish some common indicators for each component of a system

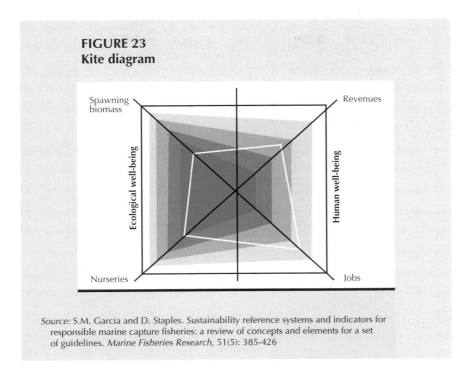

**FIGURE 23**
**Kite diagram**

*Source:* S.M. Garcia and D. Staples. Sustainability reference systems and indicators for responsible marine capture fisheries: a review of concepts and elements for a set of guidelines. *Marine Fisheries Research,* 51(5): 385-426

and, possibly, common evaluation criteria. This will make it easier to assess the status of fishery resources within the ecosystem and to establish costs and income for which there are generally agreed objectives and methodologies. It may, however, be less practical for social components, for which it is difficult to make generalizations.

Simple representations of a fishery system in relation to the dimensions of sustainable development are proposed in the relevant FAO guidelines and by Garcia and Staples.[29] The kite diagram is one such representation in which each dimension (e.g. spawning biomass and revenues) is represented by one of the axes. Each axis is appropriately scaled and there are established societal evaluation criteria to qualify the various levels on each scale (e.g. bad, mediocre, acceptable, good). In Figure 23, the position of the fishery is shown by a white polygon. The degree of shading represents value judgements, from bad (black) to good (clear). Thus, the fishery illustrated in Figure 23 is satisfactory in so far as it creates a high number of jobs and adequate revenues, although its spawning biomass is inadequate in size and its nursery areas are threatened. A complete system of sustainable development indicators should include mechanisms for effective communication among fisheries stakeholders,

those responsible for governance and the general public. A number of visual reporting methods would greatly enhance communication in this regard. The system of indicators should be reviewed regularly in order to provide the necessary incentives to maintain and improve it.

Although the indicators should be easy to understand, they can still be misinterpreted or misused (as can any statistical data). Authoritative interpretation and reporting by an expert group, collaborating with industry and stakeholders, will guard against this, and nations and international organizations should convene such groups of experts to evaluate and interpret indicators every few years. Policy-makers will then be able to act in response to whatever the indicators show.

●

***The precautionary approach.*** Before integrating the precautionary approach into the Code and promoting its application in the UN Fish Stocks Agreement,[30] FAO reviewed its implications for fisheries.[31] In collaboration with Sweden, the Organization also developed technical guidelines for the precautionary approach to

---

[29] Garcia and Staples, op. cit., footnote 28, p. 61.

[30] See footnote 22, p. 55.

[31] S.M. Garcia. 1994. The precautionary principle: its implications in capture fisheries management. *Ocean and Coastal Management,* 22: 99-125.

capture fisheries and species introductions, in support of implementation of the Code.[32]

There is considerable uncertainty about the data, parameters and processes involved in fisheries. The situation is aggravated by natural variability, climate change and the need to consider fisheries within their respective ecosystems. Fisheries management has always had a number of "precautionary" elements that make it possible to take action in response to risk to the resources before enough scientific data are available to guide decision-making. Unfortunately, over the last half-century, these elements have been either scarcely used or poorly enforced. The precautionary approach recognizes that: all fishing activities have significant impacts; the impacts of fisheries should not be considered negligible unless proved to be so; the complex and changing fisheries system will never be perfectly understood, which means that scientific advice to management is always affected by uncertainty; management decision processes and the sector's compliance have their own uncertainties, so fisheries' impacts on the system are difficult to predict accurately; and the consequences of management errors may take a long time to put right.

As a consequence of these factors, and of the fact that the nature of fisheries is such that management decisions have to be made on the basis of incomplete knowledge, the approach requires, *inter alia,* that: a level of precaution commensurate to the risk be applied at all times to all fisheries and that it be applied systematically, i.e. across all research, management and fishing operations; potentially irreversible changes be avoided (to maintain options for future generations); undesirable outcomes be anticipated, and measures taken to reduce their likelihood; corrective measures be applied immediately and become effective within an acceptable time frame; priority be given to conserving the productive capacity of the resource; precautionary limits be put on fishing capacity when resource productivity is highly uncertain; all fishing activities be subjected to prior authorization and periodic review; the burden of proof be appropriately (realistically) placed; standards of proof that are commensurate with the potential risk to the resource be established; and a comprehensive legal and institutional management framework be used.

The precautionary approach has now been widely adopted by a number of fishery bodies, including CCAMLR, the International Pacific Halibut Commission (IPHC), the International Whaling Commission (IWC), NAFO, the North Atlantic Salmon Conservation Organization (NASCO), ICCAT, the Multilateral High-Level Conference on the Conservation and Management of Highly Migratory Fish Stocks in the Western and Central Pacific and the Southeast Atlantic Fisheries Organization (SEAFO). The implementation of the approach is actively discussed in others, including the Asia-Pacific Fishery Commission (APFIC), the Western Central Atlantic Fishery Commission (WECAFC) and the General Fisheries Commission for the Mediterranean (GFCM), and is advancing rapidly in ICES. The approach has also been indirectly applied by the International Tribunal for the Law of the Sea (ITLOS) in relation to the southern bluefin tuna cases. It is also advancing rapidly in a number of countries, including the United States, Canada, Australia and South Africa.

●

***Merging both concepts.*** The precautionary approach is based on a range of key indicators of the state of the critical components of the fishery system (e.g. spawning stock size, fishing pressure, critical habitats) that are similar to those recommended as sustainability indicators. It also requires determination of the related target, limit and threshold reference points (taking into account the uncertainty inherent in their estimations). As a consequence, recent developments in fisheries have led to a merging of the concepts related to indicators of sustainable development with those related to the precautionary approach. This represents a valuable and original advance in the field of natural resources management.

Thus, mixed frameworks (although not explicitly identified as such) are now being considered by ICES (which is leading the movement), NAFO and ICCAT. The approach consists in formally reporting the indicators of fishing mortality and reproductive biomass on a graph that represents the limit, threshold and target reference points as well as including areas corresponding to overfishing, target and buffer or precautionary situations. On such a graph, the agreed harvest control rules can also be reported, indicating what action is to be taken (in terms of fishing mortality) for observed levels of spawning biomass (Figure 24).

---

[32] FAO. 1996. *Precautionary approach to capture fisheries and species introductions.* FAO Technical Guidelines for Responsible Fisheries No. 2. 54 pp.

**FIGURE 24**
**Type of precautionary plot used to monitor fisheries in ICES or NAFO**

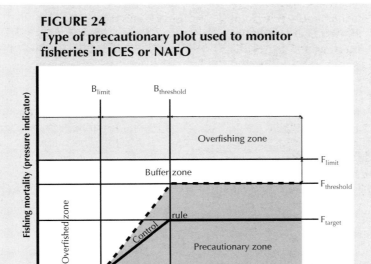

*Source:* Modified from ICES CM 1997/Assess: 7, p. 41; and F.M. Serchuk *et al.,* 1988. *In* V.R. Restrepo, ed. *Proc. 5th National NMFS Stock Assessment Workshop,* Florida, USA

**FIGURE 25**
**Precautionary plot position of several North Atlantic stocks in 1970**

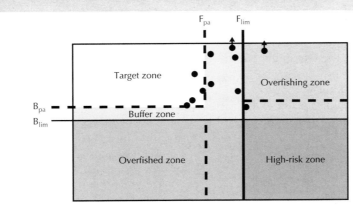

*Source:* S.M. Garcia and I. De Leiva Moreno. 2000. Proposal for a synoptic presentation of state of stock and management advice in a precautionary indicators framework. *Report of the CWP Intersessional Working Group on Precautionary Terminology,* 14-16 February 2000, Copenhagen, Denmark

As illustrated in Figure 24, the precautionary approach, as it is currently applied, is essentially based on biological considerations. Despite this shortcoming, the approach can be very useful for comparative purposes, as it allows many stocks to be represented on a single graph. Figure 25 illustrates this point, showing the position of a number of North Atlantic stocks in 1970. The mapping of this information on similar graphs over a period of several years provides a useful way of following trends in the resources of a region.

## GLOBAL PERSPECTIVE

While the development of sustainability indicators in fisheries has only just started and the application of the precautionary approach has largely been confined to biological elements, a combination of the two concepts and their active implementation by regional fishery bodies represents a major advance in the global fisheries management landscape, with potentially significant implications for the resources and the sector. The outcomes of ongoing efforts have been as follows: determination of limit reference points that represent biological constraints and minimum requirements for sustainability; determination of thresholds (or buffers) to ensure that the limits are not accidentally violated; improved methodology for assessing uncertainty and the risk attached to it; elaboration and evaluation of precautionary harvest control rules and assessment of their effectiveness; and elaboration of strategies, plans and special control rules for the rebuilding of overfished stocks.

In addition, these efforts have led to the incorporation of uncertainty about the state of stocks into management scenarios; improved communication between scientists and managers regarding explicit uncertainty considerations and their impacts; more explicit statements of objectives on the part of policy-makers as a basis for establishing target reference points; development, adoption and implementation of precautionary fisheries management plans; and implementation of recovery plans for depleted resources.

Increased effort is needed to build on the progress already made. As the matter is of the utmost importance, it seems likely that additional resources will be assigned and used for the identification, analysis, systematic organization and formal adoption of a limited number of reference points covering the ecosystem, economic, institutional and other social aspects; further identification of sources of uncertainty and their impact in terms of risk to the fishery system, including its human component; explicit linking of reference points to the objectives of fisheries management and development policies, as well as to the constraints imposed by ecosystems and the need for human well-being; appropriate representation of reference points as a means of conveying the issues, trade-offs, alternatives, etc. to managers, industry and the public; and systematic analysis of the ability of management strategies and processes to operate with uncertainty.

## MONITORING THE IMPACT OF FISHING ON MARINE ECOSYSTEMS

### THE ISSUE

In addition to the concern expressed about individual stocks, there is increasing interest in ecosystems and the impact that fishing may be having on their structure and function. There is little information at either the regional or global level on the relationship between the state of marine ecosystems and fishing. However, broad indicators of change are available from reported capture fisheries landings in the major fishing areas. These can indicate changes, although it is usually difficult to separate changes in exploitation patterns from changes in the underlying ecosystem.

*Trophic index.* One concern is that fishing may cause large (and valuable) predatory fish to be replaced by other species lower down the food web.[33] This may not only affect the value of fisheries, but may cause significant problems in the structure and function of marine ecosystems. For example, some species may cease to be controlled by predators after those predators have been reduced by fishing. The potential effect of such ecosystem disruption can be seen when new species are introduced into environments where there are none of the predators that usually control them. A spectacular example occurred in the Black Sea, where the ctenophore (jellyfish) *Mnemiopsis leidyi*, which was first found there

---

[33] D. Pauly, V. Christensen, J. Dalsgaard, R. Froese and F. Torres Jr. 1998. Fishing down marine food webs. *Science,* 279: 860-863.

in 1982, had increased to average abundance levels of 1 to 5 kg/m² wet weight by 1991/92. It has subsequently decreased in numbers but remains common, and it has permanently changed the structure of the Black Sea marine ecosystem. Although ecosystems are generally robust, there is a fear that this sort of secondary effect could also be triggered by overfishing.

One way to detect changes is to study the ratio of landings of predatory fish (piscivores) to landings of fish that feed on plankton (planktivores). As predatory fish are removed from the population, the proportion of plankton feeders in catches may grow, suggesting increased relative abundance and, perhaps, some underlying change in the ecology.

There are no clear overall trends in the piscivore-planktivore ratio for most regions. Landing statistics vary significantly because of changing vessel activities and fishing patterns, and other environmental factors may well play a role. For example, although the Mediterranean and Black Seas are heavily exploited, there has been significant nutrient pollution, which may have influenced the relative abundance levels of piscivores and zooplankton feeders.[34] An area where there is

particular cause for concern is the Northeast Atlantic (Figure 26), which has been heavily exploited over a long period and has some of the most reliable statistics available. These indicate a long-term trend towards a greater ratio of plankton-feeding fish in landings which may represent a structural shift in the underlying ecosystem, caused by chronic heavy fishing.

***Landings composition index.*** In statistics regarding landings as a whole, the species yielding the most abundant catches tend to dominate. This is not necessarily a clear reflection of the underlying impact of changes on the ecosystem, as some rarer species may have critical ecological roles. Furthermore, it is difficult to interpret the meaning of an array of landings data by species, and more useful to use indices that summarize landings composition.

Landings composition can be summarized by two indices, the landings volume averaged over categories and a measure of the variation in landings among categories – the variance. The variance is the average of the squared difference between the overall average landing and the actual landings in each case. These calculations are carried out on the logarithm of landings, because the landings composition follows the log-normal frequency distribution.

The log-normal frequency has been found to describe a wide variety of distributions, such as income distribution in some countries,

[34] For a discussion of this and other aspects of trophic changes, see J.F. Caddy and L. Garibaldi. Apparent changes in the trophic composition of world marine harvests: the perspective from the FAO capture database. *Ocean and Coastal Management*, 43 (8-9):615-655.

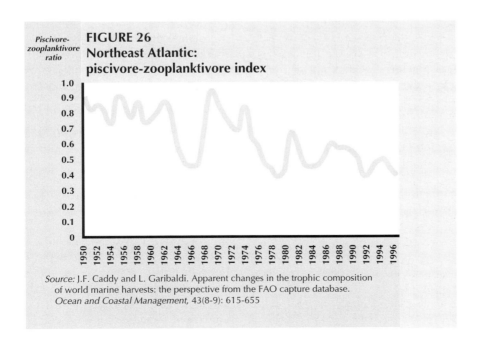

**FIGURE 26**
**Northeast Atlantic: piscivore-zooplanktivore index**

*Source:* J.F. Caddy and L. Garibaldi. Apparent changes in the trophic composition of world marine harvests: the perspective from the FAO capture database. *Ocean and Coastal Management*, 43(8-9): 615-655

distribution of sizes of rocks when they are crushed and, most important, species abundance in ecological communities.[35] In landings statistics, the log-normal distribution captures the fact that only a few species are very abundant in the statistics and the large majority of categories have far smaller annual landings. A log-normal distribution fitted to landings statistics can be defined by two values, the mean and the standard deviation, which can be used as indices of the changing exploitation pattern. The distribution has the additional advantage that it can account for some of the landings that were not reported, particularly in the early years.[36] However, interpretation requires care as the values are given on the log scale. For example, an increase in the variation would increase the perceived arithmetic average even when the log average remains constant.

The indices are related to the way in which exploitation of the ecosystem can develop. The level of landings across all categories can change among individual categories equally or differentially. An equal increase implies a proportional increase in the total harvest of all species and would produce an increase in the mean landings. The landings variance can change for a number of reasons. Developing fisheries for only a few of many species would change the variation in landings, but would have less effect on the mean. As a fishery develops, both the mean and the variance in landings can be expected to increase as all the fisheries in a region, particularly the more valuable ones, are exploited more heavily. Overfishing may then cause the landings of some stocks to decline, thereby decreasing the average landings. However, declines in landings of categories that are below the average will increase the variance, whereas declines in landings for categories that are above the average will decrease it. It can be seen that the indices do not directly represent simple causes.

Most regions, notably the Northern, Central and Southeast Atlantic and the Northern Pacific, show a negative trend in average landings; that is, the average reported landings are broadly in decline across categories. Most other areas show no significant change, with

the exception of the Western Central and Southeast Pacific and the Eastern Indian Oceans, where average landings are increasing (Figure 27). This occurs when fishing pressure increases across all exploited groups, and reflects the proportional change that can be attributed to all categories.

In terms of variation of landings among species, all areas show some increase over time (Figure 28). This represents changes in landings quantities, which are not the same across categories. In particular, increasing variation among species suggests relatively greater landings of the most abundant species and increasing numbers of smaller landings. However, changes in landings may also be due to improved reporting as well as to underlying changes in the ecosystem and fishing activities.

In the case of the North and South Atlantic and the Western Central and Southern Pacific Oceans, the increase in variation is not significant. In these cases, the range of exploitation appears to be stabilizing, perhaps because these regions are approaching full ecosystem exploitation. However, reporting will play a part, at least in the case of the Western Central Pacific which classifies the majority of its very diverse catch as "marine fish".

Nevertheless, the broader pattern of increasing variation probably reflects an increasing concentration on the largest stocks, as well as an increased variety of resources being exploited. Two major driving forces are the expansion of markets for larger quantities of a wider range of fishery products and the increase in prices of previously neglected species. These phenomena are mainly the result of the emergence of new markets for fish, including previously discarded species, the separation of species that were previously lumped together and the development of new stocks.

### The state of ecosystem exploitation by region.
As exploitation of an ecosystem develops, it can be expected that new species will be added to the landings and that the levels of landings will increase across all categories, with catches of some of the more abundant and valuable species increasing relatively more rapidly. This would be shown on the indices as a positive relationship over time between the average landings and the variance in landings per category as the fisheries of the region expand to utilize more and more categories within the ecosystem.

[35] For a discussion of models, see A.E. Magurran. 1988. *Ecological diversity and its measurement*. Princeton, New Jersey, USA, Princeton University Press. 179 pp.

[36] This is achieved by fitting the truncated log-normal, which allows for the absence of reports on the smallest landings.

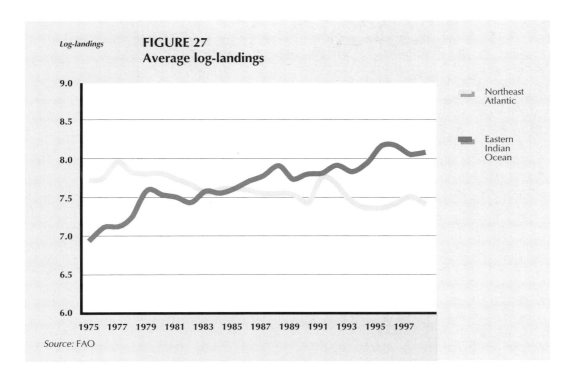

**Log-landings**

**FIGURE 27**
**Average log-landings**

Northeast Atlantic

Eastern Indian Ocean

*Source:* FAO

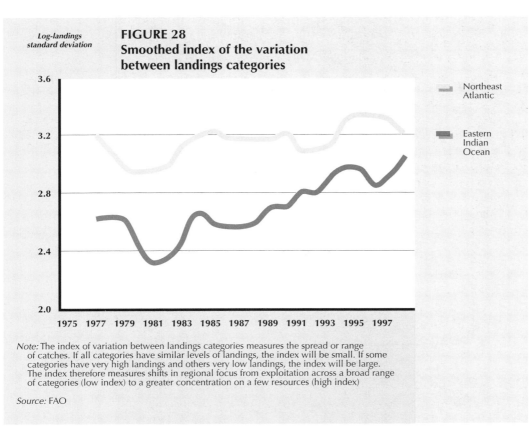

**Log-landings standard deviation**

**FIGURE 28**
**Smoothed index of the variation between landings categories**

Northeast Atlantic

Eastern Indian Ocean

*Note:* The index of variation between landings categories measures the spread or range of catches. If all categories have similar levels of landings, the index will be small. If some categories have very high landings and others very low landings, the index will be large. The index therefore measures shifts in regional focus from exploitation across a broad range of categories (low index) to a greater concentration on a few resources (high index)

*Source:* FAO

As more species are included in the landings, the variation in landings among categories will increasingly tend to match the underlying variation in species abundance and the potential for further diversification will decline. This will tend to produce a negative relationship between average landings and landings variation, as fisheries are unable to increase the two simultaneously. For example, directing capacity away from a fully or overexploited very abundant species to a number of less abundant species may make landings among categories more similar (decreasing variation) while raising the average individual category landings.

For most areas there is a negative relation between variation and mean landings, suggesting that the potential for expanding landings in these regions is limited. The Northeast and Eastern Central Atlantic, where much of the Northeast Atlantic's excess capacity is being diverted, show this pattern (Figure 29). An exception to the general rule is the Eastern Indian Ocean, where both the variation and the amount of the harvest appear to be increasing. The Eastern Indian and the Western Central Pacific Oceans represent the most biologically diverse regions. Trends between the mean and the variance do not necessarily represent time trends, although trends over time will have an effect (Figures 27 and 28).

## POSSIBLE SOLUTIONS
Given the diversity of ecosystems within each region, is not possible to describe the state of ecosystems at the regional level with any certainty. The statistics show that marine ecosystems have come under increasing pressure, the full consequences of which are unknown. Improved monitoring through fishery-independent indices and research on the impacts of fisheries on fish communities would both go some way towards identifying, preventing and solving the problems.

Marine reserves represent an important tool to be used in conjunction with other appropriate management measures, not just for protecting many ecosystems and leaving proportions of them intact, but also for providing a baseline state for monitoring. To be effective, reserves have to cover a relatively large proportion of the ecosystem at the regional level. At present, marine reserves are frequently proposed to protect particular stocks or periods of their life cycle, rather than to offer general protection for the ecosystem. A more general approach coordinated at the

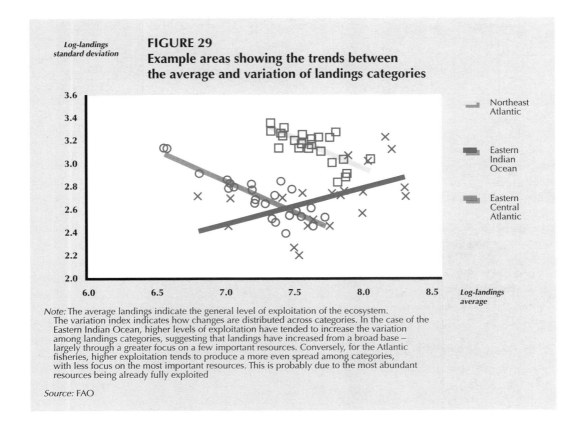

FIGURE 29

**Example areas showing the trends between the average and variation of landings categories**

Log-landings standard deviation

Northeast Atlantic

Eastern Indian Ocean

Eastern Central Atlantic

Log-landings average

*Note:* The average landings indicate the general level of exploitation of the ecosystem. The variation index indicates how changes are distributed across categories. In the case of the Eastern Indian Ocean, higher levels of exploitation have tended to increase the variation among landings categories, suggesting that landings have increased from a broad base – largely through a greater focus on a few important resources. Conversely, for the Atlantic fisheries, higher exploitation tends to produce a more even spread among categories, with less focus on the most important resources. This is probably due to the most abundant resources being already fully exploited

*Source:* FAO

regional level would probably be required if wider benefits are to be acquired, particularly for pelagic ecosystems.

In protecting the ecosystem, the most important course of action is to protect the various parts that make it up – the individual stocks. When the abundance of individual species is maintained, the ecosystem derives protection. However, because individual stock assessments do not take account of interactions among species, recommendations on exploitation levels may have to become more cautious as increasing numbers of species become fully exploited.

## GLOBAL PERSPECTIVE

With the possible exception of the Eastern Indian Ocean and the Western Central Pacific, the indicators show fully exploited ecosystems with little room for manoeuvre in all areas. However, if one area were to be singled out for particular concern, based on the available indices it would be the Northeast Atlantic (Figures 27, 28 and 29). Several indices suggest that this ecosystem has been shifted away from its unexploited state, giving cause for concern that continued heavy fishing may lead to more widespread problems.

## GENETICALLY MODIFIED ORGANISMS AND FISHERIES

### THE ISSUE

*"We have no problem with genetically modified organisms (GMOs) as long as they are proved to be safe to human beings and have no negative impact on the environment. That is a very clear position."*

**Jacques Diouf, FAO Director-General**
**7 March 2000**

Genetic modification of aquatic species has the potential to increase, greatly, both the quantity and the quality of products from aquaculture. Traditional animal breeding, chromosome-set manipulation and hybridization have already made significant contributions to aquaculture production, and their contributions are expected to increase as aquatic species become more domesticated and as breeding and genetic technology continue to improve.

Although such techniques all involve genetic modification, GMOs are defined by

international agreements and much national legislation in a very narrow sense as being essentially transgenic organisms, i.e. organisms that have had foreign genes inserted into their cells (Box 14).

Several useful genes that can be transferred into different aquatic species have been identified (Table 5). Among the genes identified are those that produce:

- growth hormones for increased growth and efficiency (among other important traits);
- anti-freeze protein for increased cold tolerance and growth;
- lysosyme for increased disease resistance;
- prolactin hormones that influence hatching, osmoregulation, behaviour and general metabolism.

Some genes can create a "loss of function". For example, they can block the release of gonadotropin, thereby delaying or reducing reproduction. Other genes that are useful in basic research and genetic marking have been identified and transferred into the fish that are used in laboratory studies, such as the medaka and platyfish.

Experimental and pilot projects on transgenic organisms have demonstrated that growth rates can be improved dramatically; and other commercially important traits, such as disease resistance and increased environmental tolerance, can also be improved. Although no transgenic aquatic species are yet available to the consumer, transgenic fish may well be on the market within the next few years. There is concern in aquaculture, as in other food-producing sectors, that transgenic technology poses new risks and must therefore be carefully monitored and regulated to ensure that the environment and human health are not endangered. A contrasting opinion is that GMOs are not substantially different from other genetically improved or domesticated species, that they will not survive well in the wild should they escape and, therefore, that they need no additional testing or oversight.

Issues regarding environmental and human health safety must be addressed if this technology is to fulfil its potential. Other areas that need to be considered include intellectual property protection, trade and ethics. Key questions are: To what degree are GMOs different from organisms that have not been genetically modified? What, if any, additional regulations, safeguards, testing or monitoring need to be put in place?

---

*BOX 14*
## Nomenclature

The development of a common nomenclature is crucial in establishing legislation and policy for the responsible use of GMOs. However, this is proving to be a formidable task. The tendency in international legal bodies and industry is to restrict use of the term GMO to transgenic species, whereas some voluntary instruments adopt a wider definition that includes other genetic modifications such as hybridization, chromosome manipulations, sex reversal and selective breeding. The following are some of the definitions of GMOs that are currently in use.

***ICES.***[1] "An organism in which the genetic material has been altered anthropogenically by means of gene or cell technologies. Such technologies include isolation, characterization and modification of genes and their introduction into living cells or viruses of DNA, as well as techniques for the production involving cells with new combinations of genetic material by the fusion of two or more cells."

***USDA.*** The United States Department of Agriculture states that its Performance Standards (which are voluntary) on conducting research on GMOs apply to the following organisms:
1. "Deliberate Gene Changes – including changes in genes, transposable elements, non-coding DNA (including regulatory sequences), synthetic DNA sequences and mitochondrial DNA;
2. Deliberate Chromosome Manipulations – including manipulation of chromosome numbers and chromosome fragments; and
3. Deliberate Interspecific Hybridization (except for non-applicable species discussed below) – referring to human-induced hybridization between taxonomically distinct species."

To clarify further, USDA states that non-applicable organisms are intraspecific, selectively bred species and widespread and well-known interspecific hybrids that do not cause adverse ecological effects.

***Convention on Biological Diversity.*** In the language of the Convention on Biological Diversity, GMOs have become living modified organisms (LMOs). "Living modified organism" means any living organism that possesses a novel combination of genetic material obtained through the use of modern biotechnology. "Living organism" means any biological entity capable of transferring or replicating genetic material, including sterile organisms, viruses and viroids. "Modern biotechnology" means the application of: i) *in vitro* nucleic acid techniques, including recombinant DNA and direct injection of nucleic acid into cells or organelles; ii) fusion of cells beyond the taxonomic family that overcome natural physiological reproductive or recombination barriers and that are not techniques used in traditional breeding and selection.

***EC.***[2] "An organism in which the genetic material has been altered in a way that does not occur naturally by mating and/or natural recombination. ... Genetically modified micro-organisms are organisms in which genetic material has been purposely altered through genetic engineering in a way that does not occur naturally."

*TABLE 5*

## Some aquatic GMOs (transgenic species) being tested for use in aquaculture

| Species | Foreign gene | Desired effect and comments | Country |
|---|---|---|---|
| Atlantic salmon | AFP | Cold tolerance | United States, Canada |
| | AFP salmon GH | Increased growth and feed efficiency | United States, Canada |
| Coho salmon | Chinook salmon GH + AFP | After 1 year, 10- to 30-fold growth increase | Canada |
| Chinook salmon | AFP salmon GH | Increased growth and feed efficiency | New Zealand |
| Rainbow trout | AFP salmon GH | Increased growth and feed efficiency | United States, Canada |
| Cutthroat trout | Chinook salmon GH + AFP | Increased growth | Canada |
| Tilapia | AFP salmon GH | Increased growth and feed efficiency; stable inheritance | Canada, United Kingdom |
| Tilapia | Tilapia GH | Increased growth and stable inheritance | Cuba |
| Tilapia | Modified tilapia insulin-producing gene | Production of human insulin for diabetics | Canada |
| Salmon | Rainbow trout lysosome gene and flounder pleurocidin gene | Disease resistance, still in development | United States, Canada |
| Striped bass | Insect genes | Disease resistance, still in early stages of research | United States |
| Mud loach | Mud loach GH + mud loach and mouse promoter genes | Increased growth and feed efficiency; 2- to 30-fold increase in growth; inheritable transgene | China, Korea, Rep. |
| Channel catfish | GH | 33% growth improvement in culture conditions | United States |
| Common carp | Salmon and human GH | 150% growth improvement in culture conditions; improved disease resistance; tolerance of low oxygen level | China, United States |
| Indian Major carps | Human GH | Increased growth | India |
| Goldfish | GH AFP | Increased growth | China |
| Abalone | Coho salmon GH + various promoters | Increased growth | United States |
| Oysters | Coho salmon GH + various promoters | Increased growth | United States |
| **Fish to other life forms** | | | |
| Rabbit | Salmon calcitonin-producing gene | Calcitonin production to control calcium loss from bones | United Kingdom |
| Strawberry and potatoes | AFP | Increased cold tolerance | United Kingdom, Canada |

*Note:* The development of transgenic organisms requires the insertion of the gene of interest and a promoter, which is the switch that controls expression of the gene.

AFP = anti-freeze protein gene (Arctic flatfish).

GH = growth hormone gene.

***Environmental issues.*** Environmental issues centre on the import and release into the environment of GMOs. GMOs may either be introduced into the environment on purpose, as in stock enhancement programmes, or accidentally through escape from aquaculture. Even in contained aquaculture facilities there is a high probability that organisms will escape. In Norway, escaped farmed salmon make up about 30 percent of the salmon in rivers and outnumber the resident salmon in many inland streams.[37] There is currently concern that GMOs will either have an adverse impact on local biodiversity through increased predatory or competitive ability, or that they will breed with related species and disrupt the local genetic diversity. The proponents of GMOs maintain that these organisms will be very domesticated, will have very low fitness in the wild and, therefore, will not compete successfully with wild fish.

However, the low fitness of GMOs in the wild is a genetic concern if they breed with local stocks. Local stocks have adapted to the local environment, whereas GMOs have adapted to the farm environment, so breeding between GMOs and resident organisms would mix the different sets of genes, thus changing the local diversity. Work that concerned mainly salmonids (non-transgenic salmons) suggested that the mixing of farmed and wild genes usually has an adverse effect on wild stocks, but real examples of damage are few and it is difficult to attribute adverse impacts on wild stocks to genetic causes alone when habitat degradation, overfishing, etc. are also influencing them.

The issue is whether GMOs can interbreed with local stocks, how fit their offspring will be in the wild and, hence, what their real impact on local genetic diversity will be. Evidence indicates that many aquaculture species escape and are capable of establishing reproducing populations even when they are genetically improved and have moved into new areas, as in the case of farmed Atlantic salmon escaping and reproducing in British Colombia.

***Human health issues.*** Although most fishery resource managers agree that environmental

issues are of primary importance, the human health concerns associated with GMOs probably receive the most attention worldwide, probably as a result of news about crops. Crops have been genetically modified to contain pesticides, herbicides and general antibiotics, and there are fears that these toxins could affect people.

There have also been instances in crops where the foreign gene has caused allergic reactions; for example, a gene from a Brazil nut was placed in soybean and people who were allergic to Brazil nuts reacted to the soybean. In the fisheries sector, the most common gene construct involves a growth hormone gene (Table 5) and not the herbicides or pesticides used in plants. Many of the GMOs being tested for use in aquaculture only produce more of their own growth hormone.

Thus, from the human health perspective the risks with the present use of the technology are clearly circumscribed and minor. One area of potential concern is the future development of disease resistance. A theoretical possibility is that, if a GMO is more disease-resistant, it may become a host for new pathogens, some of which may be transmissible or pathogenic to humans.

***Trade.*** The WTO agreements contain components that apply to GMOs (e.g. the removal of trade barriers, the requirements for intellectual property protection and labelling requirements).

Although no aquatic GMOs are traded, genetically modified soybean is an ingredient of shrimp and other animal feeds that are traded globally. The EC and Japan have labelling requirements for this feed, and the feed industry is studying the worldwide reaction to the labelling and may look for soybean replacements for feeds.

***Intellectual property protection.*** The research, development and production of reliable GMOs and the environmental and human health monitoring infrastructure that should be installed have financial implications for biotechnology companies promoting the use of GMOs. One mechanism to help recover these costs is through intellectual property rights, for example patents that protect the inventors and developers of a product. Article 27(3)(b) of the Agreement on Trade-Related Aspects of Intellectual Property Rights (TRIPS) allows for the patenting of life forms. The United States Patent Office has granted patents on

---

[37] D. Gausen and V. Moen. 1991. Large-scale escapes of Atlantic salmon (*Salmo salar*) into Norwegian rivers threaten natural populations. *Canadian Journal of Fisheries and Aquatic Science*, 48:426-428.

transgenic salmon and abalone. However, worldwide patenting laws are extremely complex and sometimes even contradictory; WTO and some countries allow the patenting of living organisms, but the EC does not. Many groups have moral objections to the patenting of life (see the paragraph on Ethics) and innovations that are contrary to public morality cannot be patented.

**Labelling.** Europe and the United States are in conflict over the labelling of genetically modified crops. Some countries maintain that labelling is impractical and would, in any case, be ambiguous while others think that it is necessary for informed consumer choice and to prevent a public relations disaster. A major issue in labelling is that of "substantially equivalent" which means that, if the GMO or product is equivalent to the non-GMO counterpart, no extra labelling is needed. How to assess equivalence, how much information should go on to a label and how the authenticity of labels can be established will be difficult matters to resolve.

**Ethics.** The field of ethics is extremely broad and ethics issues are often discussed under different terminology. For example, some aspects of "responsible fisheries" could also be referred to as "ethical fisheries". Ethical questions with regard to aquatic GMOs usually focus on whether humans have the right to modify natural creations. The Prince of Wales (UK) stated that "[genetic modification] takes mankind into realms that belong to God, and to God alone". Yet humans have been modifying plants, animals and the habitats they live in for millennia. The development of agriculture has been proposed as one of the most significant aspects of civilization in that it provided the time and resources that allowed humans to feed more people and left them free to develop fine arts and science. Other ethical dimensions include autonomy and the right to information. Again, from the crop sector it appears that a main cause of concern are multinational agribusinesses, which are seen as taking control away from farmers and withholding information from consumers. These issues are less important in fisheries at present, mainly because no fisheries GMOs are available to consumers.

**Public perceptions.** Although no genetically modified fish, shellfish or seaweed are available to consumers, the issue permeates the popular media and is a topic of discussion in nearly every general meeting on aquaculture development. This is because the public perceives that there is a problem, and policy-makers and NGOs strive to address the issues their publics find important. Because this is such an emotive issue, much of the news and research reports are presented by special interest groups in ways that suit their particular agendas; industry claims that the technology has been carefully tested and is safe, while opponents forecast environmental and health disasters.

The use of GMOs needs to be evaluated objectively and rationally. Recently, scientific papers that deal with GMOs have been capturing headlines in major newspapers throughout the world. Unfortunately the journalists and interest groups concerned have not managed to report the science completely or accurately. This has been the case in respect of genetically modified salmon. Although there are theoretical causes for concern, there are no real data to support the recent claim that genetically modified salmon are extremely dangerous to the environment. On the other hand, although fish that have not been genetically modified and that have escaped from culture facilities or been introduced into environments outside their native range have already caused environmental damage and are a clear and present danger, they have not received nearly so much press coverage.

**POSSIBLE SOLUTIONS**
International legislation, guidelines and codes of conduct for the sustainable use and conservation of aquatic genetic diversity have been, and continue to be, established. These represent a valuable first step in the responsible use of GMOs. Performance standards for conducting safe research on GMOs have been established by the United States Department of Agriculture.[38] It has been recognized that GMOs share many of the same traits as alien species and alien genotypes.

Management and risk management should therefore follow the methodology, established by such groups as ICES[39] and the European

---

[38] Available at: www.nbiap.vt.edu/perfstands/psmain.html.
[39] ICES. 1995. *ICES Code of Practice on the Introductions and Transfers of Marine Organisms – 1994.* ICES Cooperative Research Report No. 204.

Inland Fishery Advisory Committee, for the transfer of marine organisms from one aquatic environment to another.

Concerning human health, the EC and the FAO/WHO Codex Alimentarius Commission (CAC) play leading roles in the enhancement of food safety. Codex standards, guidelines and other recommendations on food safety considerations, descriptions of essential food hygiene and quality characteristics, labelling, methods of analysis and sampling and systems for inspection and certification are not binding on Member Nations, but are a point of reference.

There are also technical solutions to the problem of environmental impact. The production of sterile GMOs would reduce their impact on native genetic diversity by making breeding impossible should they escape into the wild. Commercial developers of GMOs have stated that, once approved for grow-out, only sterile fish will be used in production. Sterility has been achieved easily by chromosome-set manipulation in many species, although the technique is not always successful. Genetic engineering itself may provide sterility by inserting loss of function genes.

The adoption of closed systems and the location of farms in areas that are not environmentally sensitive would be other ways of lessening the impact of GMOs. Commercial promoters of GMOs believe that, through increased production efficiency, farms that have closed systems and are located away from certain areas (e.g. the coast) would be profitable.

Solutions to the problem of using GMOs will only come from addressing all sides of this complex issue. Technically, there must be good scientific backup with adequate testing and monitoring to reduce the uncertainties of environmental impact. The non-technical issues will be equally important and include being aware of the perceptions of consumers and civil society, acknowledging that these groups know and understand very little about how their food is produced, and taking steps to educate the general public. A group of aquaculture geneticists established a key component in the Network of Aquaculture Centres in Asia-Pacific (NACA)/FAO Bangkok Strategy for Aquaculture Development in the Third Millennium, which gave high priority to "encouraging public awareness and providing information to consumers on the application of genetics".

## RECENT ACTIONS

It seems likely that aquatic GMOs will soon be available for sale to consumers. A private company, operating in the United States and Canada, is leading the drive to commercialize genetically modified salmon and has requested approval for distribution from the United States Food and Drug Administration (USFDA) and the Canadian Department of Fisheries and Oceans. The commercial distribution of genetically modified salmon has provoked expressions of concern about the potential lack of adequate regulatory mechanisms, but these have been countered by claims that groups such as USFDA do have adequate testing and regulatory procedures in place.

Regarding food safety, at its 23rd Session (July 1999), CAC established an Ad Hoc Intergovernmental Codex Task Force on Foods Derived from Biotechnology. Its objective is to develop standards, guidelines or recommendations for foods derived from biotechnology or traits introduced into food by biotechnology, on the basis of scientific evidence, risk analysis and other factors that are relevant to the health of consumers and the promotion of fair trade practices.

The most significant international action regarding GMOs is the establishment of the Cartagena Protocol on Biosafety, a legally binding agreement under the Convention on Biological Diversity to protect the environment against risks posed by the transboundary transport of LMOs, which are similar to GMOs. Under this agreement, governments can decide whether or not to accept genetically modified commodities, and commodities that may contain GMOs must be clearly labelled. When genetically modified organisms such as live fish are released into the environment, advanced informed agreement procedures must be followed, requiring that exporters provide detailed information to each importing country in advance of the first shipment and that importers authorize shipments. Pharmaceuticals produced by genetic engineering are not covered by the protocols, however. The relationship between protocols that can restrict trade and existing WTO agreements that aim for liberalized trade need to be refined.

●

Recently, a framework for addressing ethical issues was proposed by the FAO Committee on Ethics in Food and Agriculture. It includes basic elements on:

- *beneficence* – including hunger alleviation, increased standards of living and environmental protection;
- *safety* – including the precautionary approach, human and animal rights and human and environmental health;
- *autonomy* – including participation, the right to knowledge and access to resources;
- *justice* – including equity, food security, intergenerational equity and sustainability.

The ethical dimension of GMOs in food and agricultural development is being addressed by the relevant subcommittee through the preparation of documents and other media.[40]

## GLOBAL PERSPECTIVE

Globally, more than a dozen transgenic fish are being developed for aquaculture – and more are in the early stages of development or being used in basic research into gene action, physiology and development. Development of aquatic GMOs is carried out primarily in developed countries (Table 5, p. 73). However, developing countries have also produced transgenic fish such as carp, mud loach and tilapia. In spite of this activity, there are no confirmed reports of transgenic fish being released into commercial culture conditions or into the environment. No transgenic fish are available to the consumer.

The use of gene-transfer technology in molluscs and crustaceans lags behind its use in fishes. Molluscs such as oysters have been genetically improved through the use of chromosome manipulation and conventional selective breeding. Genetic improvement of crustaceans is still hampered by difficulties in closing the life cycle of many important species, such as the tiger prawn.

## ECOLABELLING IN FISHERIES MANAGEMENT

### THE ISSUE
The idea that ecolabelling would lead to improved management of marine capture fisheries is of recent origin. It was first publicly promoted by Unilever PLC/NV and the World Wide Fund for Nature (WWF) at their Marine Stewardship Council (MSC) initiative in early 1996.

The usefulness of ecolabelling in creating a market-based incentive for environment-friendly production was recognized about two decades ago when the first ecolabelled products were put on sale in Germany in the late 1970s. Since then, and especially during the 1990s, ecolabelling schemes have been developed in most industrialized countries for a wide range of products and sectors. In recent years, they have been gaining importance in a number of developing countries, including Brazil, India, Indonesia and Thailand. The concept was globally endorsed in 1992 at UNCED, where governments agreed to "encourage expansion of environmental labelling and other environmentally related product information programmes designed to assist consumers to make informed choices".[41]

Despite the international community's general acceptance of product ecolabelling, the approach has caused controversy in several international fora, including the WTO Sub-Committee on Trade and Environment and FAO's COFI. General concerns about ecolabelling are its potential to act as a barrier to trade and its coherence, or lack of it, with international trade rules. More specific concerns arise when applying ecolabelling to products from marine capture fisheries because these have special characteristics.

***Definitions.*** OECD has defined environmental labelling as the "voluntary granting of labels by a private or public body in order to inform consumers and thereby promote consumer products which are determined to be environmentally more friendly than other functionally and competitively similar products".[42] A distinction is usually made between labels assigned on the basis of product life cycle criteria and so-called

[40] FAO. *GMOs, the consumer, food safety and the environment.* Rome (in preparation).

[41] UNCED. Agenda 21, Paragraph 4.21.

[42] OECD. 1991. *Environmental labelling in OECD countries,* by J. Salzman. OECD Report No. 1. Paris.

"single issue labels", and the latter are often excluded from ecolabelling programmes. This is in accordance with the general principles adopted by the International Organization for Standardization (ISO)[43] which prescribe, *inter alia*, that "the development of environmental labels and declarations shall take into consideration all relevant aspects of the life cycle of the product".[44] The product life cycle approach is followed by many ecolabelling programmes, including the EC Flower, the Nordic Green Swan and United States Green Seal ecolabel award schemes.

While no explicit definition has been adopted by either WTO or FAO, an implicitly wide definition of ecolabelling has been used in past debates at sessions of WTO's Committee on Trade and the Environment (WTO/CTE) and COFI. This broader definition encompasses product labelling that conveys any type of environmental information. However, as the central concerns of primary resource-based industries include sustainable use of the exploited natural resources and the conservation of habitats and related ecosystems, future ecolabelling in fisheries is likely to focus on these aspects and not encompass all of the other environmental impacts (e.g. energy use) that are assessed for most of the industrial products for which a life cycle approach is used.

## HOW ECOLABELLING WORKS

Ecolabelling is a market-based economic instrument that seeks to direct consumers' purchasing behaviour so that they take account of product attributes other than price. Such attributes can relate to economic and social objectives (fair trade;[45] support to small-scale fishers; discouragement of child labour) in addition to environmental and ecological ones. Consumers' preferences are expected to result in price and/or market share differentials between products with ecolabels and those that either do not qualify for them or whose

producers have not sought to obtain them. Potential price and/or market share differentials provide the economic incentive for firms to seek certification of their product(s).

The label helps consumers to distinguish a product according to desirable attributes without requiring them to have the detailed technical knowledge and overview of production processes and methods that underlie the certification criteria and certification itself. The label is a cost-effective way of supplying consumers with relevant product information that may influence their purchasing and consumption decisions.[46]

Consumers' product choices and their willingness to pay a higher price for an ecolabelled product will depend on their general capacity to address, and willingness to respond to, environmental concerns through purchasing behaviour, and on their level of awareness and understanding of the specific objectives pursued through the labelling scheme.[47] While there is considerable evidence that consumers' responsiveness to environmental product attributes varies among countries as well as within them (among

---

[43] ISO, established as an NGO in 1947, is a federation of national standards bodies from about 100 countries. Its mission is to promote the development of worldwide standardization and related activities with a view to facilitating the international exchange of goods and services and to developing cooperation in the spheres of intellectual, scientific, technological and economic activity. Additional information is available at: www.iso.ch.

[44] ISO. 1998. *Environmental labels and declarations: general principles.* Principle 5. ISO 14020. Geneva.

[45] The German company Fair Trade e.V. launched a fair-traded fish initiative at the Bremen 2000 Seafood Fair. It aims at improving the living and working conditions of artisanal fisheries workers in developing countries and is based on partnership between associations of marine fisheries workers and Fair Trade. Criteria for participation include practising fisheries activities that adhere to ILO's core labour standards, are small-scale labour-intensive and environmentally friendly and have no negative impacts on local fish supplies and traditional marketing and processing practices. For details, see S. Mathew. 2000. Sustainable development and social well-being: which approach for fish trade? In *Bridges*, April 2000, p. 11-12. International Centre for Trade and Sustainable Development (ICTSD), Geneva.

[46] The theoretical aspects of product labelling are based on the economics of information. For a discussion of this, see C. R. Wessells. *Ecolabelling of products from marine capture fisheries: technical and institutional aspects and trade implications.* FAO Fisheries Technical Paper (in preparation).

[47] The findings of a recent sample survey among United States consumers suggest that current awareness and understanding of the sustainability issues in fisheries are still limited and that preferences for ecolabelled seafood are likely to differ by species, geographic region, consumer group and, perhaps, certifying agency. See C.R. Wessells, R.J. Johnston and H. Donath. 1999. Assessing consumer preferences for ecolabelled seafood: the influence of species, certifier and household attributes. *American Journal of Agricultural Economics,* 81(5): 1084-1089.

different strata of the population), there is still a scarcity of reliable data on the gains in market shares and prices of ecolabelled products compared with non-labelled products. Northern European and North American consumers with good incomes and a high level of education have a moderate, and sometimes, strong, tendency to choose an ecolabelled product over a non-labelled one, even when the former costs slightly – but not much – more. There is evidence that ecolabels covering product attributes that relate not only to lower environmental impacts, but also to assumed higher product quality in terms of nutritional and/or health benefits, can realize significant price premiums and show strong growth in market shares, although such products are still operating from a small base. This applies to organic food products, for example.

Consumer confidence and trust are essential for a successful ecolabelling programme. If the purchase of ecolabelled products is to be sustained, consumers need to be confident that the scheme's objectives are being reached. If consumers feel misled or become confused by a large variety of competing ecolabelling schemes within the same product group, they are likely to return to cheaper non-labelled products. Certification criteria that are clear and precise and a certification procedure that is independent and verifiable ensure that the label conveys accurate and sufficient information. Third-party certification through private or public certifying agents whose qualification and independence have been established would ensure the reliability and accountability of the programme and consumers' confidence in it. The international harmonization of criteria and standards can prevent the consumer confusion that could arise with multiple, competing ecolabelling schemes based on different, and perhaps deceptive, criteria and standards.[48]

All ecolabelling schemes require a stringent chain of custody, so that the product can be traced throughout the full production, distribution and marketing chain down to the

retail level. This presents particular difficulties in marine fisheries, where fleets are often away from port for considerable periods, may fish several different species in one trip and may transship and/or transform products for different markets at sea. Although these difficulties can be overcome, the costs associated with performing fisheries tasks within a system that includes proper inspection and control procedures can be a problem.

The feasibility of achieving fisheries management objectives through ecolabelling schemes depends on certain requirements being met. The economic incentive created by the labelling scheme needs to be sufficiently high to encourage the fishery management authority and participants in the fishery to seek certification and cover the related fisheries management and labelling costs. However, the fact that many of the fisheries that are currently biologically and/or economically overexploited could produce high economic returns if they were managed on sound economic and biological principles, suggests that economic incentives may not be the most important constraint to realizing effective fisheries management. Instead, political and social considerations are likely to be important reasons why many marine fisheries will remain poorly managed. Nevertheless, the public relations, awareness creation and educational activities that may accompany an ecolabelling programme could eventually also make a difference in the political arena, and contribute to the kind of political will that is needed if society and politicians are to shoulder the short-term costs of fisheries management for the longer-term good.

There is no guarantee that the widespread adoption of ecolabelling programmes for marine fisheries would result in the better management of global fisheries *in toto*. At present, only a small fraction of global fish consumers (most of them living in Europe and North America) are likely to be responsive to ecolabels. Most of the future growth in global fish demand, however, will be in Asia, Latin America and Africa. The private sector is likely to react by directing to ecosensitive markets only those products that can be certified at a low cost, while other products will be directed to markets that are not ecosensitive. It cannot be guaranteed therefore, that when a particular fishery fulfils the certification criteria, excess fishing capacity will not be redirected to other uncertified fisheries. This could increase the

---

[48] The problems arising from multiple labelling schemes and how to resolve them in the case of banana production and trade have recently been the subject of useful discussions in FAO. For details, see FAO. 2000. *Report of the Ad Hoc Expert Meeting on Socially and Environmentally Responsible Banana Production and Trade*. Rome, 22-24 March 2000. Available at: www.fao.org/es/esc/ESCR/BANANAS/ExMConcl.pdf.

pressure on some fish stocks in favour of those for which certification is profitably applied. Such negative spillover effects are not unique to ecolabelling schemes and can arise from any fisheries management approach that does not encompass specific measures to avoid the undesirable transfer of excess fishing capacity.

Although some of the best managed marine fisheries are currently found in developing countries, in general these countries face greater difficulties in achieving effective fisheries management and, therefore, in participating in ecolabelling programmes than industrialized countries do. The reasons for this are manifold and include the preponderance of small-scale and artisanal fisheries, where management is more complex because of the large number of participants and their lack of alternative remunerative employment opportunities; the multispecies characteristics of tropical fisheries; a lack of the financial resources needed to retire significant amounts of excess fishing capacity; and the limited technical and managerial capacities of government agencies, many of which face reductions in their budgetary allocations. Consequently, technical and financial support would be needed to facilitate the participation of developing countries, as well as of several countries in transition, in ecolabelling programmes.

***Ecolabelling and international fish trade.*** Fish and fishery products are among the most widely traded natural resource-based goods. About 37 percent of global fisheries production enters international trade. For many developing countries, foreign exchange revenues from fish exports make a major contribution to the balance of payments and are thus of strategic macroeconomic importance. In the three major global fish importers (Japan, the EC and the United States), the processing, wholesaling and retailing of imported fish are of considerable economic significance, and they satisfy the consumer demand that is not met by domestic production.

The large and increasing trade of global fisheries production and the fact that much of the trade flow is from developing to industrialized countries indicate the potential of ecolabelling as both an incentive to improved fisheries management and a barrier to trade. Currently, much of the ecologically aware consumer demand is concentrated in the main fish-importing countries, with the

exception of China which has become a major fish importer only in recent years.

There is no unanimous view on how international trade rules, including the WTO Agreements, can be interpreted by and applied to ecolabelling schemes. One area of divergent opinions is the extent to which WTO rules encompass production processes and methods that are not product-related. Another area of concern, which is not exclusively or specifically addressed by ecolabelling, is the establishment procedures and characteristics of international standards.[49]

## RECENT ACTIONS

•

In October 1998, FAO convened a Technical Consultation on the Feasibility of Developing Non-discriminatory Technical Guidelines for Ecolabelling of Products from Marine Capture Fisheries. Although this consultation did not reach an agreement on how practical and feasible it would be for FAO to draft technical guidelines for the ecolabelling of marine fisheries products, it did identify a number of principles that should be observed by ecolabelling schemes. They should:

- be consistent with the Code of Conduct for Responsible Fisheries;
- be voluntary and market-driven;
- be transparent;
- be non-discriminatory, by not creating obstacles to trade and allowing for fair competition;
- establish clear accountability for the promoters of schemes and for the certifying bodies, in conformity with international standards;
- include a reliable auditing and verification process;
- recognize the sovereign rights of states and comply with all relevant laws and regulations;
- ensure equivalence of standards among countries;
- be based on the best scientific evidence;

---

[49] For details on ecolabelling and international trade rules see, for example, C. Deere. 1999. *Ecolabelling and sustainable fisheries.* Washington, DC-Rome, IUCN/FAO; and A.E. Appleton. 1997. *Environmental labelling programmes: trade law implications.* The Hague, Netherlands, Kluwer Law International.

- be practical, viable and verifiable;
- ensure that labels communicate truthful information;
- provide for clarity.

There are no a priori criteria that can be considered essential or that can be applied automatically to products derived from fisheries. Within any labelling scheme, the criteria will reflect a compromise between the demands of the consumers and the capabilities and willingness of the producers and intermediates to meet those demands. Hence, in principle, labelling schemes in fisheries could aim to encompass all or any subset of the environmental, biological, social, political or economic issues that characterize a fisheries venture.

The set of criteria applied in any ecolabelling scheme should be developed jointly by representatives of the different interested parties, including the producers, processors, retailers and consumers. In fisheries, criteria related to the sustainable use of the exploited natural resources are of central concern, but social and economic criteria might also be considered. Criteria should be developed in a participatory and transparent process, and those selected should be "practical, viable and verifiable".[50] Practicality and verifiability are very important requirements in assessing fisheries, where high levels of uncertainty, arising from poor understanding of important ecosystem principles in aquatic systems and difficulties of measuring what is happening in the sea, commonly prevent the totally objective interpretation of the status of stocks and ecosystems. This may prove to be a substantial obstacle to the widespread application of ecolabelling schemes in marine capture fisheries.[51]

●

The Marine Stewardship Council (MSC) is an independent, international non-profit body,

created by WWF and the large fish retailer Unilever to promote sustainable and responsible fisheries and fishing practices worldwide. In collaboration with a selected group of parties that have interests and experience in fisheries issues, MSC has established a broad set of Principles and Criteria for Sustainable Fisheries.[52] Fisheries meeting these standards will be eligible for certification by independent certifying bodies accredited by MSC. On a voluntary basis, fishing companies and organizations are expected to contact certifiers in order to have a certification procedure carried out. Currently, two fisheries – the Thames Herring Fishery (total annual production of about 150 tonnes) and the Western Australia Rock Lobster Fishery (with an annual production of about 10 000 tonnes this is Australia's most valuable single fishery, contributing approximately 20 percent to the total value of national fisheries) – have been certified and awarded the Fish Forever MSC ecolabel. The United States Alaska salmon fishery is likely to be certified soon, and initial assessments are under way for some crustacean fisheries in Southeast Asia and Central America and a tuna fishery in the Pacific.

●

The Marine Aquarium Council (MAC) is an international non-profit organization that brings together representatives of the aquarium industry, hobbyists, conservation organizations, government agencies and public aquariums. MAC aims to conserve coral reefs by creating standards and educating and certifying those engaged in the collection and care of ornamental marine life, from the reef to the aquarium. It is working to establish standards for best practices in the supply of marine aquarium organisms; an independent system to certify compliance with these

[50] FAO. 1998. Report of the technical consultation on the feasibility of developing non-discriminatory technical guidelines for ecolabelling of products from marine capture fisheries, 21-23 October 1998. Rome. FAO Fisheries Report No. 594. 29 pp.

[51] Certification criteria for ecolabelled marine fishery products are discussed more fully in K. Cochrane and R. Willmann. Ecolabelling in fisheries management. In Proceedings of the 2000 Conference on Current Fisheries Issues, 16-17 March 2000, Rome. FAO and the Centre of Ocean Law and Policy, University of Virginia, United States (in preparation).

[52] According to MSC "A sustainable fishery is defined, for the purposes of MSC certification, as one that is conducted in such a way that: it can be continued indefinitely at a reasonable level; it maintains and seeks to maximize ecological health and abundance; it maintains the diversity, structure and function of the ecosystems on which it depends as well as the quality of its habitat, minimizing the adverse effects that it causes; it is managed and operated in a responsible manner, in conformity with local, national and international laws and regulations; it maintains present and future economic and social options and benefits; and it is conducted in a socially and economically fair and responsible manner". See www.msc.org.

standards; and increased consumer demand and confidence for certified organisms, practices and industry participants.[53]

●

The Responsible Fisheries Society (RFS) of the United States and the Global Aquaculture Alliance (GAA), which also has its headquarters in the United States, have announced a joint ecolabelling scheme to recognize industry's commitment and participation in responsible fisheries and aquaculture. The new ecolabel will be offered to industry members who endorse the Principles for Responsible Fisheries of RFS or the Principles for Responsible Aquaculture of GAA and incorporate these principles into their business. The RFS and GAA programmes are open to all segments of the industry (e.g. producer, importer, distributor, retailer or restaurant operator) and require the preparation of reports or plans that document implementation of the RFS/GAA principles. The RFS programme targets all types of United States domestic seafood products while GAA focuses principally on farm-raised shrimp and operates on a worldwide basis. GAA evaluates shrimp farms on the basis of a system of self-assessment questionnaires. RFS is considering developing a third-party certification system.[54]

●

Following an initiative by the Nordic Council of Ministers (NCM) in August 1996, a Nordic project group was established to review criteria for sustainable production of fish and fish products. The work of this group led to a number of related initiatives by NCM and, in 1999, its Senior Officials for Fishery Affairs created a Nordic Technical Working Group on Ecolabelling Criteria. The participants in this group are drawn from Denmark, Iceland, Norway and Sweden and include observers from the European Commission.

The Technical Working Group concluded that, in the marine capture fisheries of the Northeast Atlantic, state authorities ought to establish ecolabelling criteria, which can then be used by private bodies and NGOs to ecolabel fish products. Ecolabelling is seen as voluntary and consumer-driven. The Technical

---

[53] For more information, see www.aquariumcouncil.org/.
[54] For more information, see www.nfi.org/ and www.gaalliance.org/GAA-RFSecolabel.html.

*BOX 15*
**Labelling for origin and species**

Working Group emphasized that the process should be transparent, be based on scientific findings and use verifiable criteria. The essential elements are a fisheries management plan, the availability of regular scientific advice, the establishment of pre-agreed management actions to adopt when precautionary reference points are approached, efficient monitoring and control systems, the absence of destructive fishing practices, a minimum of discards, and consideration of ecosystem issues. The procedure should assure the consumer that ecolabelled products derive from stocks that are harvested in a sustainable way and that the

The labelling of fisheries products by country of origin and species is not a counterproposal to ecolabelling or an alternative to it. Rather, it is an independent way of providing minimal information where none currently exists. The importance of identifying the origin of fishery products was highlighted in the Code. Article 11.1.11. states that "States should ensure that international and domestic trade in fish and fishery products accords with sound conservation and management practices through improving the identification of the origin of fish and fishery products treated". From January 2002, labelling for origin and species will become mandatory in the EC for fish and fishery products offered for retail sale to final consumers.[1]

Identification of the origin of fisheries products can provide a way of weeding out those products that are deemed to be caught illegally or caught in a fashion that undermines national or international management efforts. For example, in recognition of the problem of trade in unreported, illegally harvested Patagonian toothfish, the Parties to the 1980 Convention on the Conservation of Antarctic Marine Living Resources have drafted a catch certification scheme for toothfish. The idea is that international trade in illegally caught Patagonian toothfish would be restricted by requiring that imports be accompanied by a valid certificate of origin.[2]

Similarly, ICCAT introduced a Bluefin Tuna Statistical Document Programme for frozen bluefin (1992) and fresh bluefin (1993). The aim of the programme was to increase the accuracy of bluefin statistics and track unreported fish caught by non-members and fleets flying flags of convenience. The programme obliged all contracting parties to require that all imported bluefin tuna be accompanied by an ICCAT Bluefin Statistical document that details the name of the exporter and importer, the area of harvest, etc.[3]

[1] According to Article 4 of Council Regulation (EC) No. 104/2000, labelling is required to indicate: (a) the commercial designation of the species, (b) the production method (caught at sea or in inland waters or farmed), and (c) the catch area.
[2] *CCAMLR Newsletter*, December 1998. Hobart, Tasmania, Australia.
[3] WTO. 1998. Communication from the Secretariat of the International Commission for the Conservation of Atlantic Tunas. Committee on Trade and Environment, WT/CTE/W/87. Geneva.

*Source:* Based on C. Deere. 1999. *Ecolabelling and sustainable fisheries.* Washington, DC-Rome, IUCN/FAO.

fish processing methods used do not have serious ecosystem effects.

## GLOBAL PERSPECTIVE

Ecolabelling is a new concept in capture fisheries and there is no empirical evidence as yet about its future ability to make a significant contribution to improving the management of the world's aquatic resources. As has been observed in the forestry sector, it is likely that ecolabelling will first be applied to those fisheries that are already fairly well managed or that could achieve good management at a comparatively low cost. Such fisheries are currently primarily found in industrialized countries, but not in great numbers, and there are important exceptions in developing countries. For example, Namibia's fisheries and national economy could eventually benefit greatly if higher sale prices were realized from ecolabelled fish and fishery products. Once the success of pilot ecolabelling schemes has been established, these could provoke significant interest among governments and industry and could create the kind of political will that is needed to attain effective fisheries management, often in the face of economically and socially difficult adjustment.

The financial and technical resources needed for these adjustments may be beyond the means of several developing countries, and the international community may be called on to provide assistance and fulfil the commitments made in various international instruments, including the Code, the WTO Agreements and Agenda 21. However, such assistance would be needed irrespective of whether or not ecolabelling were considered as part of improved fisheries management.

There is increasing acceptance on the part of those who are familiar with ecolabelling that such labels should not be used to discriminate against those who cannot, in the short term, afford to develop and implement the management practices needed for sustainable fisheries management. It is also realized, not least among the promoters of ecolabelling, that it would be to the detriment of all schemes if a large number of competing ecolabelling schemes were to develop. This would undermine one of the principle objectives of ecolabelling, namely to give consumers more information that is relevant for their product choice. Success hinges on respecting this principle. It therefore seems plausible that governments, industry and consumers should promote international collaboration in order to agree on basic principles for the introduction and use of ecolabels in fisheries and aquaculture. ◆

# PART 3
# Highlights of special FAO studies

# Highlights of special FAO studies

## BACKGROUND

In 1995, a conference on the Sustainable Contribution of Fisheries to Food Security was convened by the Government of Japan, in collaboration with FAO, in Kyoto, Japan. One of the conclusions of the conference was that an understanding of the culture of fishing communities is fundamental for equitable governance and management of capture fisheries and aquaculture and for sustaining food security in fisheries-dependent regions.

As part of the follow-up to the conference, FAO commissioned a study on the culture of fishing communities. It was decided that the study should be based on a review of the literature, supplemented by a set of specially commissioned case studies. The study has been completed and will be published as an FAO Fisheries Technical Paper.[1] It provides guidance to fisheries officials with the aim of increasing their understanding of the cultures of small-scale fisher communities and, ultimately, helping them to improve living standards within such communities. It is based on the generally accepted notion that ensuring decent living conditions for fishing people is just as important an aim as sustaining healthy fish stocks or obtaining the maximum economic yield from fisheries resources, and that achieving this aim will require a greater understanding of and respect for fishers' cultures and social arrangements.

A few highlights of the case studies are given in the following section, which is followed by a summary of conclusions. Most of these are drawn from a review of the literature and some are illustrated by the case studies.

---

[1] FAO. *Understanding the cultures of fishing communities: a key to fisheries management and food security,* by J.R. McGoodwin with T. Akimichi, M. Ben-Yami, M.M.R. Freeman, J. Kurien, R.W. Stoffle and D. Thomson. FAO Fisheries Technical Paper No. 401 (in press). Rome.

## HIGHLIGHTS FROM CASE STUDIES

The six case studies of contemporary fishing communities from distinct cultural regions throughout the world illustrate how fisheries management practices and policies may strengthen or weaken small-scale fishing cultures.

### Community-based, species-oriented fisheries management

The case study by T. Akimichi, on species-oriented resource management on reef fish conservation in the small-scale fisheries of the Yaeyama Islands, describes the complex and highly participatory steps that must be taken in order to promote cooperative community-based fisheries comanagement.

Around the Yaeyama Islands in southwestern Japan, recent degradation of coral-reef marine ecosystems and heightened fishing effort by both commercial and recreational fishers have prompted concerns about introducing new and more comprehensive methods of fisheries management. Responding to these concerns, the prefectoral government launched a project to promote the community-based management of a single species of emperor fish (*Lethrinus mahsena*), which has long been one of the most important food fishes in the region. The commercial fishers who target this species do not comprise a homogeneous or unified group, but instead take different approaches to fishing and use different methods. However, they are all members of the region's fisheries cooperative association (FCA), which coordinates fishing effort within the territories ascribed to it and has prerogatives regarding certain management measures, although it does not have jurisdiction over recreational fishers. Recreational fishing interests in the region are also somewhat diverse, consisting mainly of party-boat operators, fishing guides and the owners of fishing tackle shops.

Prefectoral and local governments coordinate among the FCAs within their jurisdiction and exercise some other management prerogatives. They also play an especially important role as mediators in disputes among the various FCAs under their jurisdiction, as well as in disputes between these and the FCAs in bordering jurisdictions or with non-FCA sectors, such as recreational fishing. Japan's national Fisheries Agency in Tokyo oversees the administration of the prefects and local governments.

During 1996 and 1997, the prefectoral government prompted a series of meetings at Yaeyama's FCA, at which management proposals were presented to the various commercial fishers of emperor fish. FCA members, prefect and other government officials as well as individuals from the recreational sector took part in these meetings. It proved difficult to obtain a consensus among FCA members about the proposed management measures, mainly because of their diverse approaches to fishing, as well as some members' scepticism about the need for a new management programme and doubts that all members would abide by it. On the other hand, FCA members were virtually unified in their concern about the impact of recreational fishers on emperor fish stocks.

Eventually, after reworking the proposed management programme, a tentative consensus was reached among FCA members regarding their willingness to abide by it, while members of the recreational sector voluntarily agreed to promote its acceptance within their sector.

The FCA members' knowledge of the ecology helped the government authorities to develop the programme, while dialogue among all the parties with interests in emperor fish stocks helped to ensure that it was comprehensive and effective. The current programme is not complete and is expected to evolve as greater experience is gained among the various interest groups, which have started to collaborate with one another more fully than before.

### Using traditional credit systems for small-scale fisheries development in Nigeria

M. Ben-Yami's case study, on the integration of traditional institutions and people's participation in an artisanal fisheries development project in southeastern Nigeria, illustrates how limited access to credit can constrain the productivity of small-scale fishers. It reports on a successful credit development scheme aimed at helping small-scale fishing communities in southeastern Nigeria. The success of this project depended on a high degree of community participation in all of its phases, from initial planning to final project implementation.

Ben-Yami observes that the overall fishing effort in the small-scale sector was not limited by fish stocks, which had long remained stable and underutilized, but rather by difficulties in gaining access to reasonably priced credit, which was needed for sustaining fishing operations. The local communities already had traditional credit institutions, but these were not able to provide the higher levels of reasonably priced credit that would facilitate significant increases in fishing production. By connecting traditional community-based credit institutions with a modern lending bank, the development effort was able to capitalize on an important, pre-existing component of local community culture.

Overall, the project enhanced the well-being of many of the people living in small-scale fishing communities, although its success was eroded by individuals (usually from outside the communities) who tried to exploit the project for their own benefit, and by inflationary trends in the national economy. A few years later, other development projects were launched in the same region. However, project organizers did not consult the local people first, which resulted in considerable expenditures being made on technological innovations that turned out to be inappropriate and did little to improve the well-being of the people living in the fishing communities.

### Cultural identity and small-scale whaling in North America

M.M.R. Freeman's case study on small-scale whaling in North America focuses on the aboriginal Inuit people of northern Alaska and Canada, and illustrates how the Inuits' traditional whaling practices have helped them to maintain their cultural identity while also promoting effective conservation of whale stocks. Thus, although whaling plays a significant role in the contemporary Inuit subsistence economy, its symbolic importance within their cultural identity is perhaps even more important.

In particular, the community-wide distribution of foods derived from whale is an important means of maintaining social cohesion and a cultural identity in which it is the distribution process itself, rather than the actual quantities distributed, that is most valued. Thus, over the past two decades, while the Inuit population has doubled, the average number of whales taken annually has remained nearly constant, and there is little interest in increasing the commercialization of these resources.

Freeman argues that conventional fisheries management approaches, which treat whales as merely another wild stock to be conserved and allocated as a human food resource, would threaten the sustainability of the Inuits' unique cultural identity, as well as the whale stocks themselves. The key to sustaining both the Inuit culture and the whales lies in understanding the multidimensional significance that whale hunting and the distribution of whale products hold in the Inuit culture.

## Socio-cultural considerations in small-scale fisheries development in India

J. Kurien's case study on the socio-cultural aspects of fisheries and their implications for food and livelihood security reports on a project in Kerala State, India, and illustrates the inappropriateness of developments in small-scale fishing communities that ignore traditional cultural adaptations. He describes the small-scale fishing communities in Kerala, where the population's level of well-being declined as a result of development initiatives that ignored their long-established traditional approaches to managing their fisheries.

Before the developments, access to fisheries and the allocation of fisheries resources were regulated by communal traditions and institutions that emphasized the sharing of seafood and the incomes derived from it, as well as promoting community-based participation in fisheries management. Traditional practices had also provided effective means of conflict resolution and ensured that an abundant supply of seafood was sustained throughout the region. However, since about four decades ago, development policies that favour the expansion of a modern shrimp-exporting industry have refocused fisheries policies on the needs of that sector, although it provides comparatively little employment for the people living in small-scale fishing communities.

Important marine ecosystems started to become degraded, while regional seafood supplies decreased and the employment of women in the region's seafood markets declined. Within the small-scale communities themselves, other development efforts were compelling small-scale fishers to turn away from traditional approaches to fishing and promoting a new ethos of competitive individualism that was oriented towards markets rather than the communities themselves. This subverted the cultural traditions that had long guided social and economic life in the region, prompting new

social and political divisions both within and among the communities.

Kurien maintains that future fisheries policies should make the promotion of well-being within small-scale fishing communities their first priority. He also recommends that the traditional communal ethos and community-based fisheries management be revitalized, that traditional approaches to fishing be given greater consideration, and that women's return to regional seafood markets be promoted as a way of reviving those markets.

## External effects on traditional resource management in a Dominican Republic fishing community

R.W. Stoffle's case study, entitled When fish is water: food security and fish in a coastal community in the Dominican Republic, illustrates the range of interconnections that a small-scale fishing community has with people and cultural systems outside its own area. He describes a small, rural-coastal village in the Dominican Republic, which seems to be isolated but which, in fact, has a web of interconnections at the local, national and even global level. This case study outlines the ramified implications of a fishing community's linkages with the outside world and illustrates how these can influence the well-being of the various people involved.

The village's full-time fishers – who are referred to locally as fishing specialists – produce fish to supply their families with food and to sell in regional and national marketplaces, where it generates income. Much of the lower-quality fish that they catch is sold in the nation's coastal cities, where it provides an important source of animal protein for the urban poor. However, in order to understand the local, national and global roles that the village's fishers play, their interconnections with village farming people must also be taken into account. When local farmers experience declines in their subsistence food production and incomes, brought on by localized drought or by national or international economic policy changes that depress the prices of cash crops, many turn to fishing as a temporary measure to augment their household food and income deficits. Such increases in the overall fishing effort lead to corresponding reductions in local fish stocks.

During these periods of decline in farming, the village fishers sell relatively more of their lower-quality catch to their agricultural neighbours instead of to urban markets. This, in turn, diminishes the fish supplies of the urban poor, many of whom cannot afford alternative sources of animal protein. At the same time, the village fishers have increasingly had to resist the encroachment of better-capitalized fishers from outside the community, as well as the expansion of national and international tourism which is having a negative impact on fish stocks and other important fisheries resources.

Furthermore, because the village's potable water is often in short supply – a common problem for fishing communities, especially in developing countries – local fishers are sometimes compelled to sell their families' subsistence fish supply in order to buy potable water for drinking and for cooking inexpensive, high-calorie staple foods.

## The effect of fisheries policies on small-scale fishers in Scotland

D. Thomson's case study on the social and cultural importance of coastal fishing communities and their contribution to food security illustrates how small-scale fishing communities in the Hebrides and on the west coast of Scotland are being culturally and economically impoverished by fisheries policies that favour larger-scale, more industrialized approaches to fishing.

Thomson notes that western Scotland is one of the most remote, rural and economically peripheral regions of the EC where, despite long-term declines, capture fisheries and their ancillary activities still provide about 20 percent of total employment. Until the early 1980s, the natural marine resources of this region had been abundant, supporting a robust and localized small-scale fishing sector, as well as a large number of fishing enterprises that came from outside the region. Since the early 1980s, however, the region's fisheries have steadily and continuously declined as a result of years of overharvesting and the encroachment of marine pollution.

The impact of this decline has been devastating for small-scale fishing communities, not only in the production sector, but also in the fish processing and distribution sectors, which formerly employed many women. Recently, large-scale fishing enterprises from other parts of Scotland have been competing for and buying fishing licences (only a limited number of which are issued) from economically marginal, smaller-scale localized fishers, who can no longer sustain fishing activities. This has led to

increased prices of licences and has further decreased the small-scale fishing communities' participation in the very fisheries they had long depended on.

In addition to this, the region's small-scale fishing communities are now likely to be impoverished further when the EC's Common Fisheries Policy (CFP) is fully implemented, permitting access for all member countries' fleets. This will almost certainly lead to an escalation in the trade of licences and quotas, putting them well beyond the reach of most of western Scotland's small-scale operators and transferring more and more of the economic benefits of the region's fisheries to foreign interests. Thus, while regional development is one of the objectives of the CFP, Thomson argues that its current structure favours larger-scale approaches to fishing so much that it may lead to the demise of small-scale fishing communities and cultures.

He recommends that the EC make the well-being of the region's small-scale fishing communities the first priority in its fisheries policies. The widespread benefits of doing so would be increased food security and employment in the coastal communities of western Scotland; more efficient harvesting of the region's fish stocks, with a correspondingly less deleterious impact on its marine ecosystems than is the case when larger-scale fishing is adopted; and a general reversal of the long-term loss of population and economic decline that has been affecting this region.

## HIGHLIGHTS OF MAIN FINDINGS

The principal conclusions of the FAO Fisheries Technical Paper underline the importance of focusing on small-scale fishing communities in the future development of fisheries management practices and policies, as well as the need for a more thorough understanding of the cultures and social arrangements within fishing communities. The paper emphasizes the importance of community participation in the establishment of fisheries management practices and policies and recommends that communities buy guaranteed rights of access to and exploitation of fisheries resources.

These conclusions and recommendations are based on the accumulated knowledge and expertise of a large number of individuals. The experiences of those who have tried to achieve sustainable and equitable fisheries in small-scale fishing communities, and have encountered a set of cultural characteristics that are common to many other small-scale fishing communities, are of particular relevance and importance to fisheries officials. In most cases, the cultural characteristics of a small-scale fishing community are developed by its members in order to sustain fishing livelihoods and meet other human needs. In many instances, fisheries management can be more successful when it capitalizes on certain characteristics, or at least helps to minimize those that are problematic. The following are some of the most important and common of the cultural characteristics of fishing communities:

- Such communities undertake small-scale capital commitments and levels of production and have limited political power. This makes them vulnerable to external threats, especially the large-scale fishing sector.
- Such communities are dispersed along coastlines and, because they depend mainly on marine ecosystems that are close to home, they are particularly vulnerable to resource depletions.
- Community members, especially those who are primary producers, derive much of their personal identity from the fishing occupation and are often particularly tenacious in their adherence to it.
- The nature of the ecosystems and the particular species that are exploited are important determinants of many cultural characteristics, including the social and economic organization and the fishing gear and technologies that are utilized.
- The various fishing occupations that community members pursue will be interwoven through the whole fabric of a community's culture.
- Small-scale fishers develop intimate, detailed and function-oriented knowledge about the marine ecosystems and species that they exploit.
- There is a systematic division of labour according to both gender and age, with corresponding role expectations regarding men, women, children, adults and the elderly.
- In most (although not all) communities, the primary producers are men, while women are expected to play a dual role: as mainstays of their household and children, and as mainstays of fish processing, marketing and distribution systems.
- Fishing crews and other fisheries-related workers are often recruited on the basis of important social ties in the community,

rather than on the basis of skill, experience or labour costs.
- Primary producers are often dissociated from everyday community life, which may cause serious problems for them, their families and other community members.
- Small-scale fishing cultures develop ways of adapting to the risks and uncertainties that are associated with fishing activities. These include taking a conservative approach to fishing, maintaining occupational pluralism, establishing share-payment compensation systems, and developing beliefs, ritualized behaviours and taboos that provide psychological support.
- Access to credit and insurance is problematic in most small-scale fishing communities and constrains fishing effort and production.
- Nearly all small-scale fishing communities develop systems of community-based management, which can be distinguished from management that is instituted by government authority.
- Most community-based management practices entail the assertion of rights to fishing spaces and aim at excluding non-community members from fishing in them.
- Contemporary small-scale fishing communities are increasingly stressed by external problems, including expanding globalization, marine pollution and, in some regions, the growth of a coastal tourism industry.

## THE ECONOMIC VIABILITY OF MARINE CAPTURE FISHERIES

### BACKGROUND
In the first half of the 1990s, FAO's Fisheries Department studied the viability of the world's fishing fleets. For these studies, countries provided FAO with information about the size of their fishing fleets and recorded landings. Drawing on its accumulated knowledge of the various fleets' operations, FAO developed broad estimates of the costs and incomes of fishing operations for different size categories of fishing vessels. The results showed that, for the world's fishing fleets as a whole, costs exceeded incomes by substantial amounts.

This result seemed to be contradicted by the fact that most individual fisheries appeared to be economically successful. The Fisheries Department then decided to monitor the incomes and costs of the world's major fisheries. This task was begun in 1995, in close cooperation with fisheries research institutions and national fisheries in selected countries in Asia, Africa, Latin America and Europe.[2] A first comparative analysis of the findings of the national-level studies completed in 1997 were published as an FAO Fisheries Technical Paper.[3] The highlights of the findings are summarized in this section. The data presented are based on the studies, which were carried out between 1995 and 1997, with the exception of a traditional Indian fishing craft (*kattumaram*), for which information collected in 1999 is used.

## FINDINGS
### Overview and comparison by continent
In spite of heavily and sometimes overexploited fisheries resources, marine capture fisheries are still an economically and financially viable undertaking. In most cases, they generate sufficient revenue to cover the cost of depreciation and the opportunity cost of capital, thus generating funds for reinvestment. Marine capture fisheries are an important source of income and generate employment and foreign exchange earnings, particularly in developing countries. When comparing the findings of the studies by continent, the following picture emerges.

---

[2] By 1997, national sample surveys and case studies had been completed in 13 countries in Asia, Africa, Latin America and Europe. In 1995, these countries accounted for 49 percent of the marine capture fisheries production of their regions and 41 percent of global marine production. The parameters studied include the techno-economic, operational and economic characteristics of fishing fleets and individual fishing units; the availability of such financial services as institutional credit programmes for the fisheries sector; levels of exploitation of fisheries resources; and national plans for fleet restructuring and adjustment. At present, the studies are being updated and expanded to include the role and impact of catch utilization. Information on the impact of subsidies on profitability and the sustainability of fishing operations will also be sought. Among the additional countries being included are some in the South Pacific, the Caribbean and northern Europe. The methodology for studying and analysing data on costs and earnings of fishing units follows the one used in: Agricultural Economics Research Institute. 1993. *Costs and earnings of fishing fleets in four EC countries*. The Hague, Netherlands, Agricultural Economics Research Institute, Department of Fisheries.

[3] FAO. 1999. *Economic viability of marine capture fisheries. Findings of a global study and an interregional workshop*. FAO Fisheries Technical Paper No. 377. Rome.

*Africa.* The following practices in Ghana and Senegal were studied: small-scale hook and line fisheries, driftnetting, bottom set gillnetting, beach seining, purse seining, small-scale multipurpose fishing operations, medium- and large-scale fish and shrimp trawling, and pole and line fishing. Only small-scale gillnetters in Senegal generated a negative cash flow. All the others generated a positive net surplus.

*Latin America.* All of the various types of trawlers and purse seiners studied in Peru and Argentina generated a positive net surplus.

*Asia.* All of the fishing fleet units studied in the Republic of Korea, Taiwan Province of China and Malaysia generated a positive net surplus, as did five of the seven typical medium- and large-scale fishing units in Indonesia. The fishing units that generated positive net returns include purse seiners, bottom and mid-water trawlers and pair trawlers, jiggers, stow netters, set netters, seiners, tuna and other longliners, and pole and line vessels. Negative net results were recorded for small-scale gillnetters in Indonesia and smaller bottom pair trawlers and stow netters in China. In India, three types of medium- and large-scale fishing units – tuna longliners, purse seiners and trawlers – generated a positive net surplus, while two of the three small-scale fishing units studied – seiners and handliners – scarcely broke even or had a negative cash flow.

*Europe.* Of the 27 types of small-, medium- and large-scale fishing vessels studied in France, Spain and Germany, only two types of deep-sea trawlers operating in France had negative net results. The other 25 types – including handliners, gillnetters, seiners, pole and line vessels, longliners, and inshore and offshore trawlers – all generated positive net surpluses.

These results are similar to those found by a study of the economic performance of marine capture fisheries in European countries, which was carried out on behalf of the EC.[4]

It is interesting to note that those few categories of fishing units that incurred operational losses at the time of the study are located at the extreme ends of the scale of fishing operations (i.e. the very small-scale and the very large-scale) and include both artisanal gillnetters and large industrial

---

[4] Agriculture Economics Research Institute, op. cit. footnote 2.

deep-sea trawlers. In the former case, overexploitation of inshore fisheries resources and competition from more efficient capture technologies, such as purse seiners and coastal trawlers, seem to be responsible for the negative financial performance. In the latter case, excess capture capacity and related excessive operational and investment costs for limited fishing grounds and fisheries resources seem to be the important factors.

## Cost structure of trawlers and small-scale fishing vessels

The cost structure of trawl fisheries differs significantly between developing and developed countries. The differences seem to be related mainly to variations in the remuneration of labour, which depends on the overall level of economic development.

As could be expected, and is illustrated in Figure 30, labour is the most important cost component in the developed countries studied (i.e. France, Germany and Spain). The second most important cost component is running costs, closely followed by vessel costs.[5]

---

[5] Labour costs include wages and other labour charges such as insurance and employers' contributions to pensions funds. Running costs include fuel, lubricants, the cost of selling fish, harbour dues, the cost of ice, and food and supplies for the crew. Vessel costs include vessel and gear repair and maintenance expenses, and vessel insurance.

In the developing countries studied (i.e. Peru, Senegal, India, Malaysia and China), labour costs only account for between 17 and 40 percent of the total operation costs for trawlers, while running and vessel costs account for the major share. As countries develop and their levels of remuneration increase, these differences in the cost structure can be expected to disappear. The Republic of Korea, where the cost of labour has become at least as important as it is in the European countries studied, exemplifies this trend.

When looking at the cost structure of trawl fisheries in absolute terms and in relation to gross earnings, it is interesting to note that the cost of production per unit of gross earnings is significantly higher for trawler fleets in OECD countries (i.e. Argentina, France, Germany, the Republic of Korea and Spain) than for trawler fleets in developing countries (i.e. China, India, Malaysia and Peru). An exception is Senegal, where a French company operates trawlers under a joint venture arrangement. (This also explains the relatively high vessel costs shown in Figure 30.)

As can be seen from Figure 31, the cost of producing US$1 of gross earnings varies between US$0.91 and US$0.78 in the OECD countries studied, while the corresponding range for developing countries lies between US$0.74 and $0.68.

The cost structure of small-scale fishing vessels (Figure 32) compared with that of

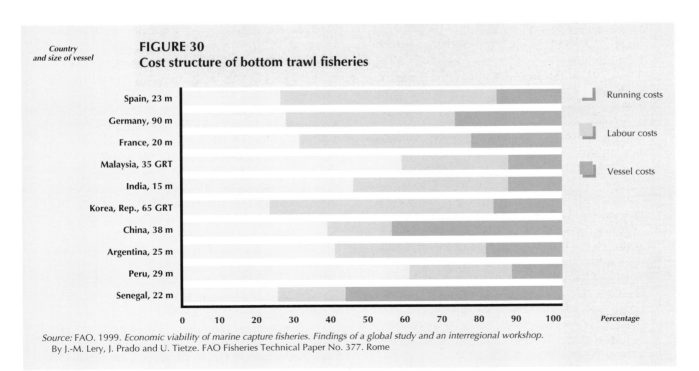

FIGURE 30
**Cost structure of bottom trawl fisheries**

Country and size of vessel

Running costs
Labour costs
Vessel costs

Spain, 23 m
Germany, 90 m
France, 20 m
Malaysia, 35 GRT
India, 15 m
Korea, Rep., 65 GRT
China, 38 m
Argentina, 25 m
Peru, 29 m
Senegal, 22 m

0  10  20  30  40  50  60  70  80  90  100   *Percentage*

*Source:* FAO. 1999. *Economic viability of marine capture fisheries. Findings of a global study and an interregional workshop.* By J.-M. Lery, J. Prado and U. Tietze. FAO Fisheries Technical Paper No. 377. Rome

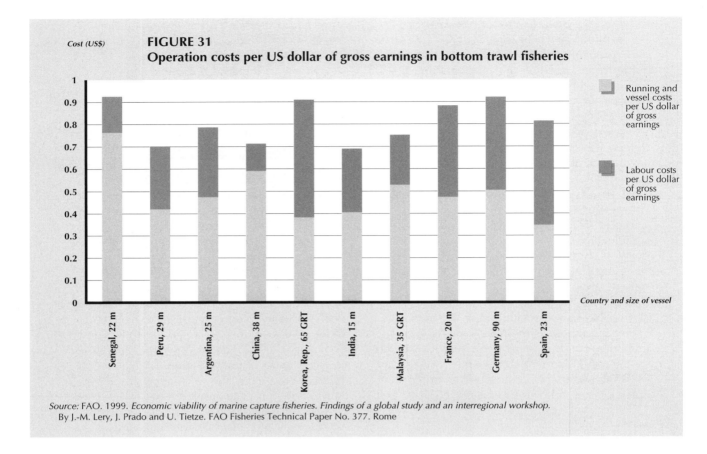

Cost (US$)

**FIGURE 31**
**Operation costs per US dollar of gross earnings in bottom trawl fisheries**

Running and vessel costs per US dollar of gross earnings

Labour costs per US dollar of gross earnings

Country and size of vessel

Senegal, 22 m
Peru, 29 m
Argentina, 25 m
China, 38 m
Korea, Rep., 65 GRT
India, 15 m
Malaysia, 35 GRT
France, 20 m
Germany, 90 m
Spain, 23 m

Source: FAO. 1999. *Economic viability of marine capture fisheries. Findings of a global study and an interregional workshop.* By J.-M. Lery, J. Prado and U. Tietze. FAO Fisheries Technical Paper No. 377. Rome

industrial trawl fisheries (Figure 30) shows some interesting differences. In France, as a developed country, the labour costs of small-scale fishing vessels remain the most important cost component, as is the case for industrial trawl fisheries. Running costs, however, are the least important while vessel costs emerge as the second most important cost component.

In three of the four developing countries included in Figure 32 (i.e. India, Senegal and Ghana), labour costs emerge as the most important cost component of some of the small-scale fishing units studied. This is related to a system of remuneration in which the proceeds from fish sales are shared among the crewmembers. In cases where crewmembers are paid on a fixed wage basis, running costs remain the most important cost factor.

The production costs of the small-scale fishing vessels studied in relation to their gross earnings show some distinct differences from the production costs of trawlers. First of all, they are lower. As shown in Figure 33, for most of the small-scale fishing vessels, the cost of producing US$1 of gross earnings ranges between US$0.56 (for Ghanaian gillnetters) and $0.78 (for French gillnetters).

At the extreme ends of the cost range are the traditional sail-powered Indian trammel netter, which spends only US$0.19 to produce US$1 of gross earnings, and the large Senegalese handliner, which spends as much as US$0.91. The data suggest that, unlike industrial trawl fisheries, small-scale fishing vessels do not show any typical differences between developing and OECD countries as far as the costs of production in relation to gross earnings are concerned.

**Productivity and financial performance**
Regarding the productivity and financial performance of trawl fisheries, noticeable differences can be observed between OECD and developing countries. While productivity, measured as the value of production per crewmember was found to be generally higher in developed countries, the rate of return on investment was found to be generally higher in developing countries (Figure 34).

Productivity was highest in France, followed by Argentina, Peru, Germany, Spain and the Republic of Korea. The highest rate of return on investment, on the other hand, was found in the Republic of Korea (37 percent), followed by Peru (34 percent), India (24 percent), Ghana

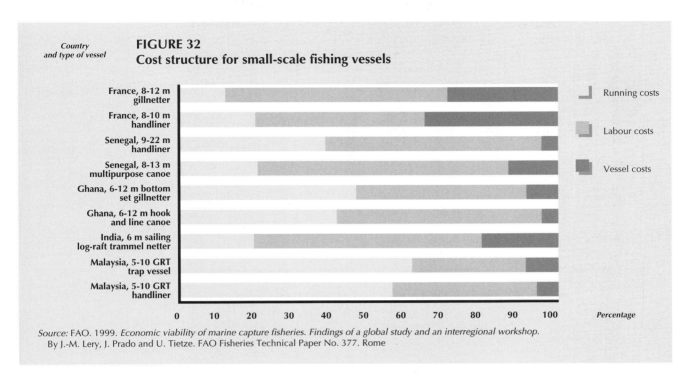

**FIGURE 32**
**Cost structure for small-scale fishing vessels**

*Source:* FAO. 1999. *Economic viability of marine capture fisheries. Findings of a global study and an interregional workshop.* By J.-M. Lery, J. Prado and U. Tietze. FAO Fisheries Technical Paper No. 377. Rome

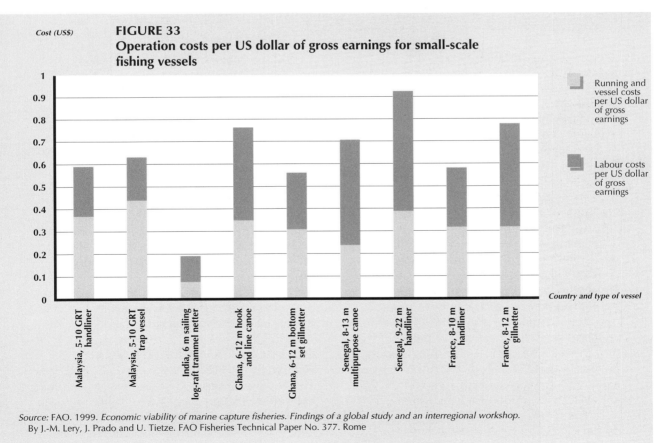

**FIGURE 33**
**Operation costs per US dollar of gross earnings for small-scale fishing vessels**

*Source:* FAO. 1999. *Economic viability of marine capture fisheries. Findings of a global study and an interregional workshop.* By J.-M. Lery, J. Prado and U. Tietze. FAO Fisheries Technical Paper No. 377. Rome

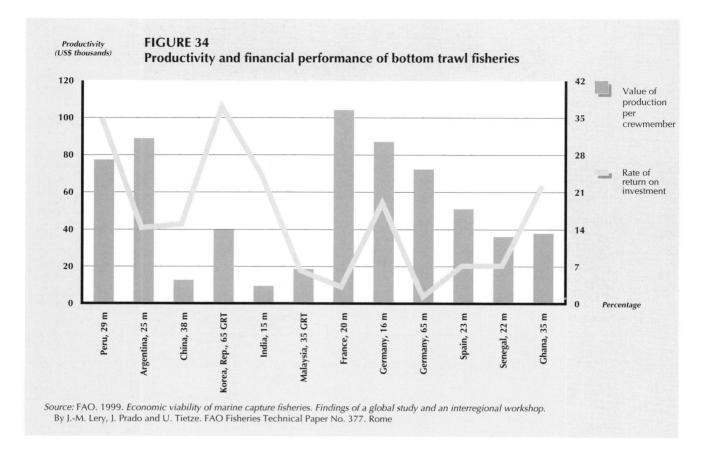

Productivity (US$ thousands)

**FIGURE 34**
**Productivity and financial performance of bottom trawl fisheries**

Value of production per crewmember

Rate of return on investment

Percentage

Peru, 29 m
Argentina, 25 m
China, 38 m
Korea, Rep., 65 GRT
India, 15 m
Malaysia, 35 GRT
France, 20 m
Germany, 16 m
Germany, 65 m
Spain, 23 m
Senegal, 22 m
Ghana, 35 m

Source: FAO. 1999. *Economic viability of marine capture fisheries. Findings of a global study and an interregional workshop.* By J.-M. Lery, J. Prado and U. Tietze. FAO Fisheries Technical Paper No. 377. Rome

(22 percent) and China (15 percent). The higher levels of productivity found in the OECD countries studied can probably be attributed to a higher degree of mechanization and sophistication of equipment for fish detection, capture and on-board handling. The higher profitability of trawl fisheries in the developing countries studied can be explained by these countries' lower cost of operation in relation to gross earnings and their lower cost of investment/higher depreciation because of the use of older fishing vessels.

As labour costs increase in the course of the overall economic development of developing countries and as old fishing vessels are replaced by new ones, it can be expected that the difference in profitability of fishing operations compared with those of developing countries might gradually disappear.

In the case of small-scale fishing vessels, the differences between productivity, on the one hand, and financial performance, on the other, are even more pronounced. As can be seen from Figure 35, productivity is highest, by far, on handliners and gillnetters in France. This is owing to extremely small crew sizes and a relatively high degree of mechanization and catch efficiency.

At 15 percent for handliners and only 1 percent for gillnetters, the rates of return on investment, however, are far lower than those of most of the small-scale fishing units studied in developing countries.

The financial performance of the small-scale fishing units studied in developing countries is better because of the lower costs of investments and operation. An outstanding example is the smallest and most traditional of the small-scale fishing vessels included in Figure 35 – the Indian sailing log-raft trammel netter, locally called the *kattumaram* or *teppa*. This fishing craft has an annual rate of return on investment that is as high as 388 percent because of the extremely low investment and operation costs and the use of a selective fishing method that targets high-value species.

## OUTLOOK: SUSTAINABILITY AND ECONOMIC VIABILITY

The findings of the study suggest that, with the exception of some small-scale fishing units in Indonesia, India and Senegal, some of the large-scale industrial trawlers in France and one type of pair-trawler and a stow netter in China, marine capture fisheries in the Latin American, African, European and Asian

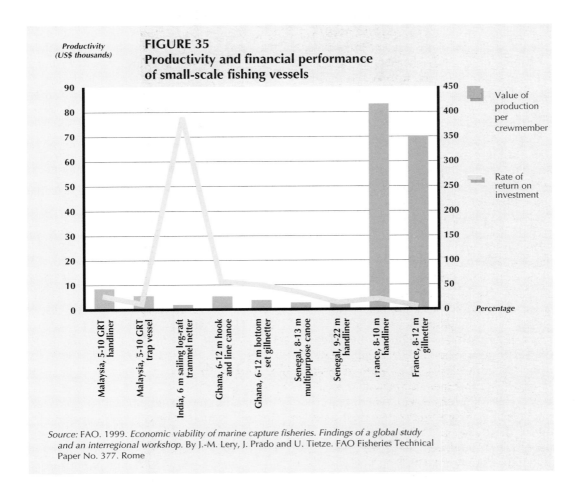

Productivity
(US$ thousands)

**FIGURE 35**
**Productivity and financial performance of small-scale fishing vessels**

Value of production per crewmember

Rate of return on investment

Percentage

*Source:* FAO. 1999. *Economic viability of marine capture fisheries. Findings of a global study and an interregional workshop.* By J.-M. Lery, J. Prado and U. Tietze. FAO Fisheries Technical Paper No. 377. Rome

countries studied usually generate sufficient revenues to cover their operating costs and also supply funds for reinvestment.

The findings of this study seem to contradict earlier FAO studies that concluded that, when all the world's fishing vessels are considered as one fleet, that fleet is losing money. There are two plausible explanations for this discrepancy.

The first concerns active versus non-active vessels. In the earlier global studies, all vessels – whether active or not – were included, while the more recent study includes only active vessels. The second factor is related to subsidies or "financial transfers". The global studies included pro forma estimates of income and costs, developed by FAO on the basis of the average known costs of the major factors of production and the longevity of physical assets. They therefore did not include any country-specific financial transfers from government to fisheries sectors. The more recent study uses a different approach. The costs and incomes derived for the various fleets are based on expenditures and income over time, and do not consider

individual financial transfers. The present study includes any financial transfers, while the global studies excluded most of them.

The degree to which either of these factors can explain the difference between the two studies is difficult to assess, although those familiar with both studies regard the first factor as being particularly significant.

The more recent study also shows that marine capture fisheries provide employment and income, as well as contributing much-needed export earnings in many developing countries. They also play important roles in meeting the nutritional needs of the population and in food security, particularly in developing countries. However, the generally positive economic performance of marine capture fisheries is being achieved in an environment where fisheries resources are fully exploited, and in many cases overexploited; so how long can it last?

The fishing industry, both small- and large-scale, and the general public have a vital interest in safeguarding and sustaining the beneficial economic and nutritional role of fisheries. If sustainability and viability are to be ensured, there is an urgent need to strengthen and put in place efficient measures to limit fishing effort and rehabilitate coastal areas and aquatic resources. In order to be successful, these measures must be designed and implemented in close cooperation with fishers and fisheries industry associations.

The impact of fisheries management measures on the economic performance of the fisheries industry and its various sectors needs to be closely monitored through studies similar to the one described in this article so that benefits can be maximized and negative impacts minimized. Another important area for monitoring in the future is the impact of subsidies, economic incentives and fiscal policies and measures on the profitability and sustainability of fishing operations.

In order to safeguard the important economic and social role of the small-scale fisheries sector as a provider of employment, income and food, particularly in rural areas of developing countries, special efforts are needed to protect that sector. The findings of the study suggest that the sector's economic performance has already been negatively effected by the overexploitation of coastal fisheries resources and competition with more catch-efficient commercial fishing vessels, such as purse seiners and trawlers.

Government and private sector support to the fishing industry, both small- and large-scale, in the form of technical advice and guidance, training and investment and credit support, is essential for successful adaptation to the changes accompanying the introduction of responsible and sustainable fishing practices and related management measures and regulations.

## TRENDS IN WORLD FISHERIES AND THEIR RESOURCES: 1974-1999[6]

### INTRODUCTION
Following the publication of its first global review of marine fish stocks,[7] FAO's Fisheries

Department has been monitoring the state of these stocks. The results have been published intermittently in *The state of world fishery resources, marine fisheries*, a document that describes and comments on trends in the state and use of these resources. This article presents a summary of the knowledge available, building on status reports accumulated between 1974 and 1999, the last year for which information is available. The analysis considers:

- the production level for the most recent year (1998), relative to historical levels;
- the state of stocks, globally;
- the state of stocks, by region;
- trends in the state of stocks since 1974, globally and by region.

### RELATIVE PRODUCTION LEVELS
The available data for 1998 from the 16 FAO statistical regions (see Box 16), considering the Antarctic Ocean as one region, indicate that four ocean regions – the Eastern Indian Ocean and the Northwest, Southwest and Western Central Pacific Oceans – were at their maximum historical level of production in 1998.[8] All the other ocean regions are at lower levels (Figure 36). While this might result, at least in part, from natural oscillations in productivity (e.g. resulting from the El Niño phenomenon of 1997 in the Southeast Pacific Ocean), the lowest values observed may indicate that a high proportion of the resources are overfished (e.g. in the Antarctic and the Southeast and Northwest Atlantic Oceans).

### GLOBAL LEVELS OF EXPLOITATION
The data available to FAO at the end of 1999 identified 590 "stock" items. For 441 (or 75 percent) of these, there is some information on the state of the stocks and, although not all of this is recent, it is the best that is available. The stock items are classified as underexploited (U), moderately exploited (M), fully exploited (F), overexploited (O), depleted (D) or recovering (R), depending on how far they are – in terms of biomass and fishing pressure – from the levels corresponding to full exploitation. Full exploitation is taken as being loosely equivalent to maximum sustainable yield (MSY) or maximum long-term average yield (MLTAY). The following are some of the features of stocks in each of the different classifications:

[6] The basic data used in this section are updates of the data published in FAO. 1997. *Review of the state of world fishery resources: marine fisheries.* FAO Fisheries Circular No. 920. Rome. 173 pp. (An updated version is in preparation.)

[7] FAO. 1970. *The state of world resources,* by J.A. Gulland. FAO Fisheries Technical Paper No. 97. Rome. 425 pp. and J.A. Gulland. 1971. *The fish resources of the ocean.* UK, Fishing News Books (International). 255 pp.

[8] Fishstat Plus (2.3), FAO 1996-2000.

BOX 16
**FAO statistical areas**

In order to help organize its data, FAO has
broken down the world's fishing areas into
statistical regions, identified by a two-digit
number (21 to 88). The abbreviations are used
in Figures 36, 38 and 39.

| | |
|---|---|
| AEC | Atlantic, Eastern Central (34) |
| ACW | Atlantic, Western Central (31) |
| ANE | Atlantic, Northeast (27) |
| ANT | Antarctic, total (48, 58, 88) |
| ANW | Atlantic, Northwest (21) |
| ASE | Atlantic, Southeast (47) |
| ASW | Atlantic, Southwest (41) |
| IE | Indian Ocean, Eastern (57) |
| IW | Indian Ocean, Western (51) |
| MBS | Mediterranean and Black Sea (37) |
| PEC | Pacific, Eastern Central (77) |
| PCW | Pacific, Western Central (71) |
| PNE | Pacific, Northeast (67) |
| PNW | Pacific, Northwest (61) |
| PSE | Pacific, Southeast (87) |
| PSW | Pacific, Southwest (81) |

*FAO Fishing Area*

**FIGURE 36**
**Ratio between recent (1998) and maximal production**

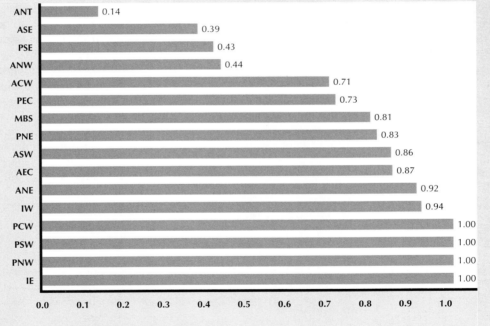

*Note:* The key to acronyms used for FAO Fishing Areas is given in Box 16, above

*Source:* FAO

Stocks tagged as U and M are believed to have the potential to produce more under increased fishing pressure, but this does not imply any recommendation to do so.

Stocks tagged as F are considered as being exploited at levels close to their MSY or MLTAY. They could be slightly under or above this level because of uncertainties in the data and stock assessments. These stocks are in need of (and in some cases already have) effective measures to control fishing capacity.

Stocks tagged as O or D are clearly exploited beyond their MSY level and are in need of effective strategies for capacity reduction and stock rebuilding.

Stocks tagged as R are usually very low compared with historical levels. Directed fishing pressure may have been reduced (by management or lack of profitability) but, depending on the specific situation, these stocks may still be under excessive fishing pressure. In some cases, their indirect exploitation as by-catch in another fishery might be enough to keep them in a depressed state, despite reduced direct fishing pressure.

Figure 37 shows that, in 1999, 4 percent of the stocks appeared to be underexploited, 21 percent were moderately exploited, 47 percent fully exploited, 18 percent overexploited, 9 percent depleted and 1 percent recovering. As MSY (modified by environmental and economic factors) is an important reference point for management that is enshrined in the United Nations Convention on the Law of the Sea, these data imply that 28 percent (O + D + R) of the world stocks for which data are available are below the level of abundance represented by MSY (or have a fishing capacity that is above this level) and require fisheries management action aimed at rebuilding them to at least the MSY level. Some of these stocks may already be under such a management scheme. As a further 47 percent of the stocks are exploited at about the MSY level, and they too require capacity control in order to avoid the overcapacity syndrome, it appears that 75 percent

(F + O + D + R) of the world stocks for which data are available require strict capacity and effort control if they are to be stabilized or rebuilt to the MSY biomass level, and possibly beyond.

Figure 37 indicates that 25 percent of the stocks (U + M) for which data are available are above the level of abundance that corresponds to the MSY level (or have a fishing capacity that is below this level). When the 47 percent of MSY-level stocks are taken into account, it emerges that 72 percent of stocks are at or above the level of abundance corresponding to MSY (i.e. they have a fishing capacity below this level) and should therefore be considered as being compliant with the basic requirements of the Convention on the Law of the Sea.

These two ways of looking at the data indicate that the "glass is half full and half empty" and are both equally correct depending on the viewpoint taken. From the "state of stocks" angle, it is comforting to see that 72 percent of the world's resources can still produce MSYs if required. From the management point of view, however, it should be noted that 75 percent of resources require stringent management of fishing capacity. Some stocks are already under some form of capacity management (mainly in a few developed countries), but most require urgent action to stabilize or improve their situation. For 28 percent of them, there is no doubt that forceful action is required for rebuilding.

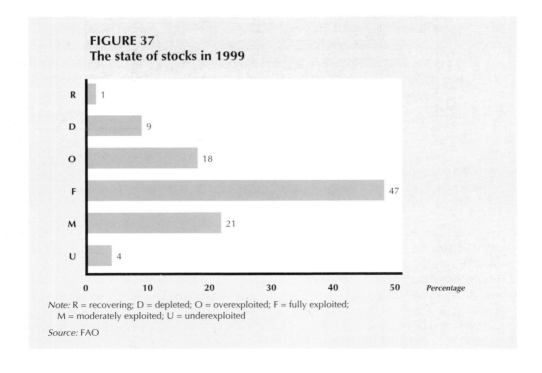

**FIGURE 37**
**The state of stocks in 1999**

*Note:* R = recovering; D = depleted; O = overexploited; F = fully exploited;
M = moderately exploited; U = underexploited

*Source:* FAO

## THE STATE OF STOCKS BY REGION

The data available on state of stocks can be examined by region and compared, keeping in mind that the quality of the data, the proportion of stocks for which information is available and the relative size of the stocks differ from case to case. Once again, a comparison can be made in terms of a stock's relation to the MSY.

The percentage of stocks exploited at or beyond MSY levels (F + O + D + R), and therefore reflecting a need for capacity control, ranges from 41 percent (in the Eastern Central Pacific) to 95 percent (in the Western Central Atlantic) (Figure 38). In most regions, at least 70 percent of the stocks are already fully or overfished. The percentage of stocks exploited at or below MSY levels (U + M + F) ranges from 43 percent (in the Southeast Pacific) to 100 percent (in the Southwest Pacific and Western Indian Ocean) (Figure 39). As a measure of management and development performance, the proportion of stocks that are exploited beyond the MSY level (O + D + R) ranges from 0 percent (in the Southwest Pacific and Western Indian Ocean) to 57 percent (in the Southeast Pacific).

## GLOBAL TRENDS

The following analysis considers trends in the proportions of stocks in each of the various states of exploitation. The years mentioned in the text and figures refer to the year of publication of the FAO Fisheries Circular *Review of the state of world fishery resources: marine fisheries.*

Figure 40 shows that the percentage of stocks maintained at MSY level (F) has slightly decreased since 1974, while underexploited stocks (U + M), offering the potential for expansion, have decreased steadily. As would be expected from these trends, Figure 40 also shows that the proportion of stocks exploited beyond MSY levels (O + D + R) has increased during the same period, from about 10 percent in the early 1970s to nearly 30 percent in the late 1990s. The number of stocks for which information is available has also increased during the same period, from 120 to 454.

The trend for stocks exploited beyond MSY levels can be decomposed according to major regions of the Atlantic and Pacific Oceans (Figures 41 and 42).

In the following analysis, distinctions are made between northern (mainly developed) areas of the oceans and central and southern areas (mainly tropical and developing). Data have been plotted together with their trend, as represented by a third-order polynomial. The results for the North Atlantic (FAO Fishing Areas 21 and 27) and the North Pacific (FAO Fishing Areas 61 and 67) (Figure 41) show an increasing proportion of stocks being exploited beyond MSY levels until the late 1980s or early 1990s. In the North Atlantic the situation seems to have improved and stabilized in the 1990s, while in the North Pacific the situation seems to have remained unstable.

Figure 42 shows a growing percentage of stocks exploited beyond MSY levels in both the tropical oceans studied. This increase might be reaching an asymptote in the tropical Atlantic (FAO Fishing Areas 31, 34, 41 and 47) but this does not seem to be the case in the tropical Pacific (FAO Fishing Areas 71, 77, 81 and 87). It can also be noted that the situation is more severe in the tropical Atlantic. In fact, a cross-comparison of Figures 41 and 42 shows that the magnitude of the problem is similar for the tropical and northern regions of the Atlantic, while, in the Pacific, the southern areas are less affected. For the southernmost areas of these oceans (the Antarctic) the situation appears to be more serious but improving.

## DISCUSSION

The overview of the state of world stocks obtained from the series of FAO biennial reviews clearly indicates a number of trends. Globally, between 1974 and 1999, there appears to have been an increase in the proportion of stocks classified as "exploited beyond the MSY limit", i.e. overfished, depleted or slowly recovering. When the information is stratified by large oceanic regions, the North Atlantic and North Pacific show a continuous worsening of the situation until the 1980s or early 1990s, with a possible stabilization afterwards – particularly in the North Atlantic. In the tropical and southern regions of these oceans the situation seems still to be deteriorating, with the possible exception of the tropical Atlantic, where stabilization might have started. These conclusions are in line with the findings of an earlier FAO study by Grainger and Garcia.[9]

These conclusions should be considered with caution because they are based on a sample of the world stocks and are severely constrained

---

[9] FAO. 1996. *Chronicles of marine fishery landings (1950-1994). Trend analysis and fisheries potential,* by R. Grainger and S.M. Garcia. FAO Fisheries Technical Paper No. 359. Rome. 51 pp.

*FAO Fishing Area*

**FIGURE 38**
**Percentage, by FAO Fishing Area, of stocks exploited at or beyond MSY levels (F+O+D+R) and below MSY levels (U+M)**

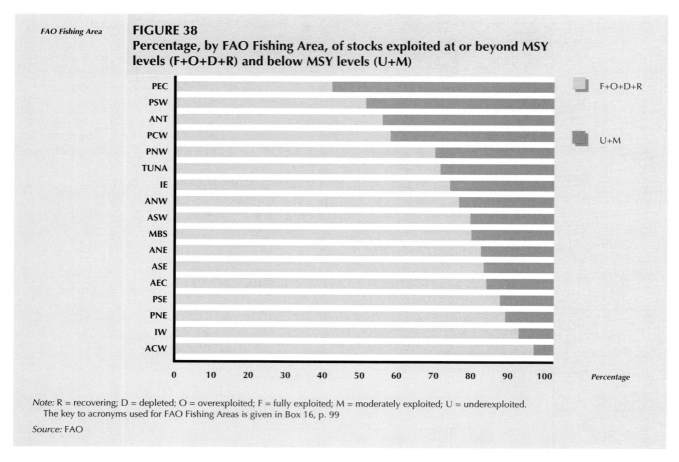

*Note:* R = recovering; D = depleted; O = overexploited; F = fully exploited; M = moderately exploited; U = underexploited.
The key to acronyms used for FAO Fishing Areas is given in Box 16, p. 99

*Source:* FAO

*FAO Fishing Area*

**FIGURE 39**
**Percentage, by FAO Fishing Area, of stocks exploited at or below MSY levels (U+M+F) and beyond MSY levels (O+D+R)**

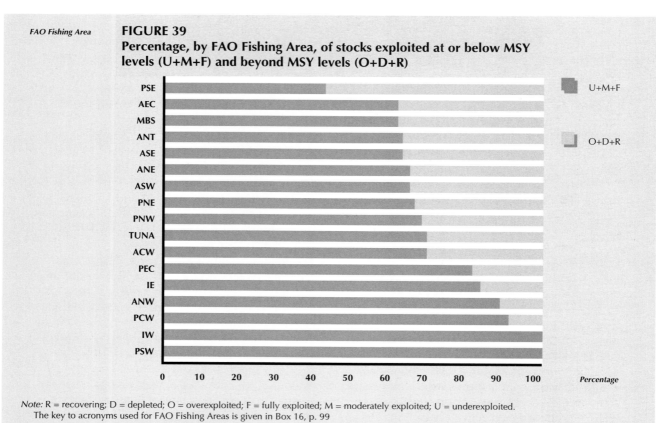

*Note:* R = recovering; D = depleted; O = overexploited; F = fully exploited; M = moderately exploited; U = underexploited.
The key to acronyms used for FAO Fishing Areas is given in Box 16, p. 99

*Source:* FAO

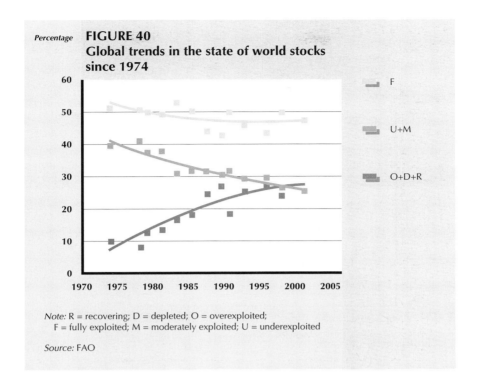

Percentage

**FIGURE 40**
**Global trends in the state of world stocks
since 1974**

*Note:* R = recovering; D = depleted; O = overexploited;
F = fully exploited; M = moderately exploited; U = underexploited

*Source:* FAO

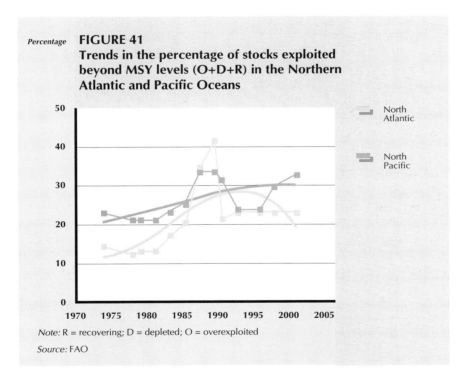

Percentage

**FIGURE 41**
**Trends in the percentage of stocks exploited
beyond MSY levels (O+D+R) in the Northern
Atlantic and Pacific Oceans**

*Note:* R = recovering; D = depleted; O = overexploited

*Source:* FAO

by the limited information that was available to FAO. The extent to which this information reflects reality is difficult to ascertain. There are many more stocks in the world than those referred to by FAO. In addition, some of the elements of world resources that FAO calls "stocks" are really conglomerates of stocks (and often of species) and it is not clear that a statement made about a conglomerate is valid for the individual stocks in that conglomerate.

However, in general, it is safe to assume that the global trends observed reflect trends in the monitored stocks, because the observations generally coincide with reports from studies

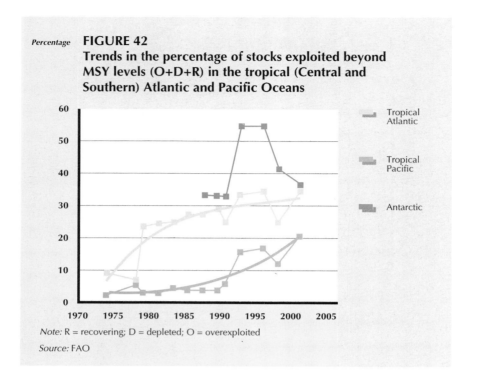

*Percentage* **FIGURE 42**
**Trends in the percentage of stocks exploited beyond MSY levels (O+D+R) in the tropical (Central and Southern) Atlantic and Pacific Oceans**

*Note:* R = recovering; D = depleted; O = overexploited

*Source:* FAO

conducted at a "lower" level, usually based on more insight and detailed data. For example, an analysis of Cuban fisheries was carried out for FAO by Baisre.[10] Using the same approach that Grainger and Garcia took for the whole world, Baisre's analysis led to surprisingly similar conclusions, based on less coarse aggregations and even longer time series, and with more possibility of double-checking the conclusions with conventional stock assessment results.

There is, of course, the possibility that stocks are "noticed" and appear in the FAO information base as "new" stocks only when they start to face problems. When this happens, scientists accumulate enough data to start dealing with the problems, thereby generating reports that FAO has access to. This

[10] FAO. 2000. *Chronicles of Cuban marine fisheries (1935-1995): Trend analysis and fisheries potential*, by J.A. Baisre. FAO Fisheries Technical Paper No. 394. 26 pp.

could explain the increase in the percentage of stocks exploited beyond MSY levels since 1974, although this seems an unlikely hypothesis for the following reasons:

- The number of stocks that have been identified by FAO but for which there is not enough information has also increased significantly over time, from 7 in 1974 to 149 in 1999, clearly showing that new entries in the system are not limited to "sick" fisheries.
- Since the 1980s, scientists have become more and more reluctant to classify stocks as definitely "overfished" because they recognize the uncertainties involved in identifying the MSY level and that declines can be the result of decadal natural fluctuations. The apparent plateauing of the proportion of stocks suffering from excessive exploitation in the northern regions of the world's oceans may, in part, be due to this new trend. ◆

# PART 4
## Outlook

# Outlook

## OVERVIEW

At the end of the 1990s, humankind's need for food and income was still the dominant determinant of the nature and magnitude of fish consumption and production. The desire to reserve access to fish for pleasure – including non-consumptive uses – was growing, and in many instances was respected, although such uses were still limited to a small number of countries and, from a global perspective, had only a minor impact on those who fished or cultured fish to earn a living. In recent decades, however, the conditions determining the traditional use of fish have been slowly changing. One factor that has made an impact is the increasing size of the market, in terms of both the number of people and the geographical area covered. On the one hand, most consumers have had access to an expanding variety of food and fish products and a growing number of sellers. On the other, most primary producers have been able to choose from among a larger number of buyers. Thus, there has been an expanding range of possibilities both to satisfy food needs and to generate income. The resulting increase in the number of trading possibilities has had, and will continue to have, repercussions on the fisheries and aquaculture sector.

Fisheries governance has been affected by the deliberations of the United Nations Conference on the Environment and Development (UNCED), held in 1992 in Rio de Janeiro, Brazil. Since that conference, the ecosystems dimensions of management issues have received increasing attention from governments, the UN system and the fishing industry. All are now more ready to recognize that fish are an integrated part of an aquatic ecosystem, a system in which modifications in one area have the potential to affect other areas. Thus, it is increasingly regarded as necessary, first to monitor the state of the aquatic ecosystem, and then to manage human interventions within that ecosystem. Only within such a framework will it be possible for capture fisheries to continue to be a source of food and income for future generations. In the

coming years, humankind is likely to improve dramatically its understanding of the intricacies of aquatic ecosystems, and this will lead not only to more knowledge but also, and perhaps paradoxically, to growing uncertainties. As a result, there will be growing pressure for a strict application of the precautionary approach to all interventions, including those by fishers, in aquatic ecosystems. Both the aquaculture industry and the capture fisheries sector will realize that they must be seen by all concerned to respect this principle.

In many developing countries, fish grew in economic importance during the second half of the twentieth century and, by the end of the 1990s, the fisheries sector had become an important source of food, employment and foreign exchange – a situation that is likely to continue. A stable source of foreign currency is vital for countries, as increased participation in international trade is an essential condition for their economic growth, particularly for smaller countries with only limited or no mineral resources.

For many developing countries, fisheries are also a major vehicle for creating value added, thereby promoting economic growth. In some of the poorest, where fish is an indispensable part of food security for large sections of the community, including fishers, the ever-expanding possibilities of export markets have led to reduced quantities of fish being available in local markets. It is likely that the decision to sell fish in foreign rather than local markets, where it plays an important role in ensuring food security, will become problematic in some countries during the next decade. It also seems plausible that an increasing number of developing countries will develop national food security strategies and that fish will occupy a place in these strategies.

## FISH AS FOOD

During the past decades, per capita fish consumption has expanded globally along with economic growth and well-being. However, growth will not go on forever. There is a limit to how much food – including fish – each individual will consume, and long-term ceilings for consumption will be established.

It is clear that the limit will be reached first by wealthy economies, and fastest in those where fish has been a staple food since ancient times – in Japan for example.

In well-off *developed economies* – essentially OECD countries – the image of fish is changing. It is moving away from being the basic food it once was and is becoming a culinary speciality. There are two main reasons for this: the vast majority of the population in these countries has the means to purchase adequate food and retailers are realizing that, to attract consumers, they have to sell a product that is more than just a basic foodstuff. Marketing campaigns launched for some fish products tend to affirm that the consumption of fish is an appropriate means of satisfying the consumer's need for variety and for nutritious, tasty, healthy and fashionable foods. The retailing of fish in these countries is no longer a question of satisfying a hungry consumer at a competitive price.

The term "fish" here stands for a large category of groups of varied consumer products made available by retailers. These groups of products vary distinctly from country to country and only a small proportion of them are traded internationally. In volume terms, fish trade is still dominated by intermediate products, mostly in frozen form with a few standard categories of cured and canned products. However, a portion of what are essentially national food specialities is finding its way on to the international market, and there are now a large number of such products. Fish has the potential to satisfy most desires for a variety of tasty, healthy and exotic products. International trade is likely to continue to grow rapidly and its composition to be altered in favour of more high-value finished products and fewer raw materials.

In OECD countries, economic growth has caused a growing proportion of fish to be consumed outside the home and in the form of ready-to-eat products. A recent study of fish consumption in Japan[1] showed that, in the period 1965 to 1998, the income elasticity of demand for fresh fish by Japanese households was -0.26. That is, for each 1 percent increase in average income, Japanese households demanded 0.26 percent less volume of fresh fish. However, consumption remained stable because the quantities consumed in restaurants or as ready-to-eat products increased.

There are signs that consumers in some other countries may also be approaching this voluntary limit to the quantity of fresh fish consumed. During the 1990s, changes in per capita consumption – expressed in live weight equivalent – did not seem to be explained by economic growth (see Box 17), at least in some of the wealthier countries where fish consumption was already above the world average in the late 1980s. There seems to be no way of telling with any precision at what level fish consumption in a particular country is likely to stabilize, but it would appear reasonable to assume that, for most countries, the figure would fall somewhere in the range of 20 to 40 kg/capita/year. Thus, countries where there is an extremely high consumption would see that consumption decrease, while those with a low consumption would see it rise. Argentina, where meat consumption is traditionally high, provides an example of such an increase. The consumption of fish in Argentina is reported[2] to have doubled in the 1990s, from about 4 to 9 kg per capita/year.

In the *developing countries*, fish is still very much an essential food. It contributes an important part of the animal protein in many people's diets. In the mid-1990s, fish provided more than 50 percent of the animal protein for the populations of 34 countries. Several Asian and some African countries fell into this category. Nevertheless, fish is generally not an important source of calories.

In LIFDCs, the apparent consumption of fish has also increased during the last decades (Figure 43). As noted in the Overview, this rapid increase largely reflects the rapid increase in the apparent consumption of China.

Figure 44 shows the apparent consumption of fish in Africa. For Africa as a whole, availability has declined, and in some countries (e.g. Ghana, Liberia, Malawi) the average diet contained less fish protein in the 1990s than it did during the 1970s.

In most developing countries, fish will continue to be an important source of protein, but there will still be the potential for exports of fish and strong macroeconomic arguments for permitting and even encouraging such

---

[1] FAO. *Prediction of demand for fish in Japan* (in preparation). By M. Tada. Rome.

[2] M.I. Bertolotti, E. Errazti, A. Pagani and J. Buono. *Sector pesquero Argentino.* 17 pp. Istituto Nacional de Desarrollo Pesquero/Universidad Nacional de Mar del Plata, Argentina. (mimeo.)

exports. Thus, countries will find that they need to promote schemes that make substitute foods, preferably other fish, available in local markets to replace what is being exported.

In Africa there are large stocks of small pelagic species off both the northwest and southwest coasts. These species can be harvested at a low cost and constitute an adequate replacement in local African diets for the exported high-value products. It seems plausible that countries along the Gulf of Guinea will want to develop joint strategies with countries in northwest and southwest Africa to exploit these stocks as a source of cheap and nutritious fish for local consumers. Existing regional fisheries management organizations would provide an institutional mechanism for coordinating national policies in this respect.

In some regions in Asia, cultured fish has the

---

*BOX 17*
## The relationship between fish consumption, wealth and economic growth

The world per capita fish consumption has been growing since the 1960s. Consumption has varied among continents and countries within each continent and, on average, has always been higher in richer than in poorer countries. Many studies forecast that per capita fish intake will continue to increase worldwide over the next three decades, and that most of this increase will result from economic prosperity. The existing positive income elasticity of fish demand, which generally ranges between 1 and 2, supports this finding, although the manner in which consumption responds to increases in wealth seems not only to depend on the level of wealth attained, but also on the quantities of fish that are currently eaten by the average consumer.

| 1988-97 fish consumption < 20 kg/capita | |
| --- | --- |
| Country | Correlation coefficient |
| Australia (18.4) | 0.284 |
| Austria (8.0) | 0.784 |
| Belgium (17.7) | 0.789 |
| China (9.7) | 0.998 |
| Germany (11.2) | 0.243 |
| Ireland (16.6) | -0.009 |
| United Kingdom (18.2) | 0.862 |

| 1988-97 fish consumption > 20 kg/capita | |
| --- | --- |
| Country | Correlation coefficient |
| Canada (22.6) | -0.574 |
| Chile (22.3) | -0.076 |
| France (27.9) | -0.257 |
| Italy (20.7) | +0.729 |
| Japan (72.1) | -0.626 |
| Norway (43.9) | +0.982 |
| Sweden (26.4) | -0.421 |
| United States (21.3) | +0.005 |

In order to investigate these relationships, 15 relatively wealthy countries that had experienced more or less steady economic growth between 1988 and 1997 were identified. These were divided into two arbitrary groups: low fish consumption countries, where annual per capita fish consumption was generally 20 kg or less for this period; and high fish consumption countries, where per capita annual fish consumption was more than 20 kg. Per capita fish consumption and per capita real GDP (used as proxy for income) were plotted against time. Correlation coefficients were also calculated.

The resulting correlation coefficients between per capita fish consumption and economic growth are given in the Table. The 1988-97 average volume of consumption per capita is given in parentheses, after the country name.

The results are not conclusive. On the one hand it appears that, for most of the high consumers, there is no clear relationship between changes in income and volume of consumption, although a clear exception is Norway, where fish still seems to be a much-preferred food. On the other hand, Germany seems to have reached stagnation at a very low level of consumption. In Japan, the picture is different. The negative correlation – although weak – between growth and volume of consumption could be taken to mean that increased incomes have given the Japanese the possibility of switching from their staple to other foods. The correlation between economic growth and fish consumption in China is very high, most likely reflecting the responsiveness of freshwater aquaculture to the stimulus of the market.

*Source:* N. Hishamunda, FAO Fisheries Department.

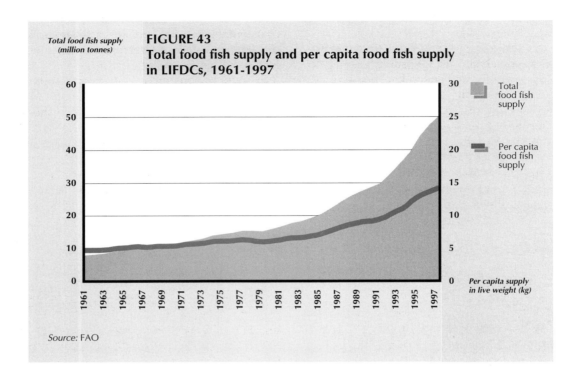

**Total food fish supply**
*(million tonnes)*

**FIGURE 43**
**Total food fish supply and per capita food fish supply in LIFDCs, 1961-1997**

Total food fish supply

Per capita food fish supply

*Per capita supply in live weight (kg)*

*Source:* FAO

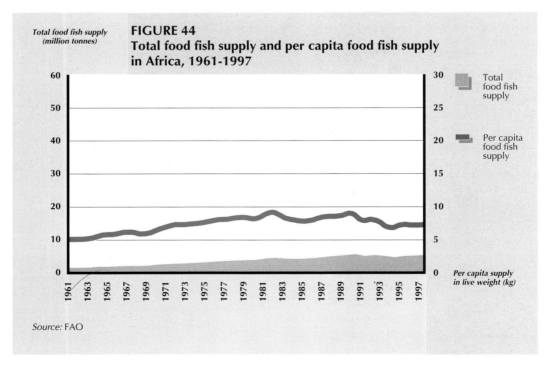

**Total food fish supply**
*(million tonnes)*

**FIGURE 44**
**Total food fish supply and per capita food fish supply in Africa, 1961-1997**

Total food fish supply

Per capita food fish supply

*Per capita supply in live weight (kg)*

*Source:* FAO

potential to replace exported high-value products in local markets. This is because fish farmers, with some exceptions such as those who culture shrimps and molluscs, already sell their produce in local markets. As a group, fish farmers have the ability to respond to increases in demand.

In South America, except for in the countries facing the Caribbean, fish consumption is generally low. The fish-dependent populations are coastal communities for whom fish supplies will not be a major problem.

As a result of the above trends in consumption, *international trade* will grow – possibly more rapidly in value than in volume terms. Trade will expand in two ways. First, in developing countries, fish processing for developed markets will become a very attractive employment-generating opportunity for governments that need to find alternative employment opportunities, particularly for displaced artisanal fishers and their families. In this context, the ready-to-eat segment of the industry is particularly attractive, as it is labour-intensive. However, most of the countries that depend on fish imports to satisfy demand also have fish processing industries and it is clear that these national industries will do their best to survive, even if it means opposing the abolition of existing trade barriers.

The second reason for an expansion in trade is that developing countries will become increasingly important markets for fish during the coming decades. As this happens, they will export more to neighbouring developing countries and other developing markets. For example, in South America, Brazil is likely to continue to be a major fish importer and its imports will come predominantly from other South American producers.

## FISH AS A SOURCE OF INCOME
Most individuals become fishers or fish farmers because they expect the activity to provide a means of livelihood for themselves and their families. During the early part of the twentieth century, as a rule, no one interfered with this choice and those who were not directly concerned paid little attention to the activities of fishers and aquaculturists. However, by the early 1990s the situation had changed and the activities of fishers and fish farmers were attracting the attention of civil society, particularly in developed economies. The concerns voiced by national and international NGOs centred on what they saw as the inability of governments and producers to prevent damage to the living aquatic resources being harvested and to the ecosystem at large.

As these concerns went beyond national borders they provided an impetus for government and industry representatives to discuss the issues in international fora. This led to the development of several international agreements, plans of action and guidelines (most of them voluntary) to restrict harmful practices in capture fisheries and aquaculture.

From a global perspective, the impact of these agreements has been marginal in terms of the volume of fish produced and employment generated. Simultaneously, technological developments have improved productivity in existing fisheries and opened the way for new ones. The resulting increases in production have more than offset any reduction brought about by international agreements that limit or restrict fishing practices. In capture fisheries the principal barriers to increased production continue to be the productivity of wild aquatic resources and the economic and technological possibility of harvesting them sustainably.

In recent decades, technological developments in capture fisheries have led to rapid increases in the volumes caught per fisher and per year, particularly in industrial fisheries. As fish resources are finite (and prices are under pressure – particularly in the high-value segment of the industry – as a result of the continuing expansion of aquaculture production), fish stocks have not been large or productive enough to permit all fishers to continue their activities.

As a result, the number of active full-time fishers is declining in most OECD countries. These trends will continue. As fishers are barred from entry to fisheries (as part of a successful policy to contain and reduce fishing effort), as technology improves and productivity (measured in volume of fish landed per fisher) increases, some of the people who work in the industry will have to leave it.

International discussions have drawn attention to the environmental harm caused by fisheries – and to some extent aquaculture – which many societies might consider a relatively minor problem; the major problem, in fact, is the continued loss of economic rent in capture fisheries (Box 18). In fisheries worldwide, very large amounts are lost yearly as a result of poor management.[3] It seems likely that this issue will attract increasing attention and civil society will demand that governments and industry capture these rents for the benefit of society as a whole. Governments are likely to have to confront this issue in the next decade. Optimal use of marine resources will become an agreed objective and access to fishing as a profession will be limited and reduced, but progress will be slow. There are substantial costs associated with the needed buy-out of industrial fishing vessels and, in small-scale fisheries, long-term funding will be needed to find alternative employment for fishers.

The practice of allocating tradable quotas is most likely to become more widespread, particularly in industrial monospecies fisheries. Most holders of such quotas will want their values to be high, and there are several strategies for assuring this, one of which is to ensure that there is a large number of buyers. In some countries, therefore, demands may emerge for the permission of international trading of quotas. If such permission becomes widespread in developed country fisheries, it seems plausible that entrepreneurs from developing countries with advanced fisheries will become buyers. They would be able to compete because of their lower labour costs and the availability of fishers who are still willing to face the risks linked to one of the world's most dangerous professions (see Fishers' safety, Part 2, p. 41). This could be the start of a reversal of the situation that emerged towards the end of the last half century, when developed countries purchased the right to fish in the EEZs of developing countries. Such developments would not alter the fact that the management of all "national" fisheries would remain with the states that have the exclusive rights to the extended economic zones, and the buyers of quotas would have to respect the national legislation applying to the waters in which the quotas were valid.

In advanced economies, this "internationalization" of national marine fisheries will be fuelled by the difficulty of recruiting sea-going personnel. The age pyramid of full-time fishers is changing. In Japan, fishers aged 60 years or more accounted for 35 percent of all full-time fishers in the mid-1990s, up from 14 percent in 1980.[4]

During the last part of the twentieth century, the fishing pressure on inshore resources in *developing countries* underwent a steady increase. The immediate reasons for this were growing populations, modernization of fishing methods, and access to an increasing number of buyers. The greater fishing effort was bringing more inshore fish stocks into a state of overexploitation and the situation was becoming serious for many communities. A few countries were beginning to deal with the problem. They did so by providing exclusive fishing rights for selected fish stocks to small-scale fishers' organizations (see Property rights and fisheries management, Part 2, p. 52) and by strengthening the enforcement of no-fishing zones for industrial vessels in inshore waters. It was becoming clear that, unless some power was given to local fishers' organizations, limiting participation in artisanal, small-scale tropical fishing would become a very difficult issue. As long as economies are depressed, the landless and the unemployed will see fishing as an opportunity for survival.

A strong reason for promoting improved management of small-scale fisheries and aquaculture is that these sectors provide employment in coastal (marine and inland) and rural areas that are often considered economically and socially marginal. Thus, fisheries activities are frequently one of the few employment alternatives, and sometimes the only one, available to local populations. Fisheries and aquaculture are seen as means to reinforce the food security of local populations; increase the geographical and economic integration of the countries concerned; mitigate the drift to urban areas; and create demand for goods and services that stimulate investment, decentralization of economic activities, regional economic growth and social welfare.

Over the last few years, the contribution of capture fisheries to food fish supplies has decreased, while that of *aquaculture* has increased. For the world as a whole, excluding mainland China, the supplies from aquaculture

---

[3] There are many reports of such losses. A bio-economic modelling of some demersal fisheries in the Gulf of Thailand, carried out in the middle of 2000, concluded that the losses for two of the fisheries involved could be about US$200 million a year. However, the reduction in effort needed to capture this foregone rent would be large and expensive to implement.

[4] Government of Japan. 1980 and 1997. *Fishery statistics of Japan.* Tokyo, Statistics and Information Department, Ministry of Agriculture, Forestry and Fisheries.

## BOX 18
## Rent and rent extraction

In economic theory, "rent" is the payment for use of a resource, whether it be land, labour, equipment, ideas or money. Originally derived for the use of land, in which the indestructibility of the resource was central, the term "economic rent" has come to denote a payment for the use of any resource whose supply is indestructible, non-augmentable and invariant to price, at least in the short term.

For resources to which private property rights are not applied, a question arises over whether the community at large should charge the users a portion of the economic rent. This can be done through taxation, royalties or other forms of payment for rents that have been realized by those who exploit the resource in question. The purpose would be to promote an equitable distribution of a "surplus" income that some consider, in principle, to belong to all members of the community.

In relation to fisheries, a rent is generally thought of as the difference between the total revenues obtained from the fishery and the total costs (estimated at their opportunity costs) of employing the various factors of production that make up the enterprises participating in the fishery. The total costs include charges for replacement of assets. The rent is often considered as a "surplus" profit over and above what is considered normal.

However, it would be extremely complex to design a system for the extraction of economic rent from fisheries, not least because, for most fisheries, effort must be significantly reduced before a rent is created. In addition, the question as to what is equitable is usually settled through negotiations among the parties concerned, some of whom are likely to argue that, as the right to fish has been rent-free for time immemorial – at least for coastal communities – it should remain so.

*Source:* A. Lem, FAO Fisheries Department.

---

grew from 1.6 kg/capita/year in 1991 to 2.12 kg in 1998. The same situation prevailed in mainland China where, over the same period, the per capita supply of aquaculture products reportedly rose from 6 kg to an astounding 17 kg.

There do not seem to be any insurmountable obstacles to the continued growth of aquaculture. The activity is increasingly recognized in law and, therefore, is able to compete on an equal footing for land, water, feed, labour, etc. Externalities linked to aquaculture have been identified, and a basic consensus seems to have been reached that externalities need to be dealt with by requiring producers to bear the major part of the costs that otherwise fall on third parties.

At the end of the 1990s, most of the countries that had small aquaculture sectors expected these to grow rapidly. While many attempts will fail, others will succeed, and a growing number of countries are likely to see a vigorously growing aquaculture sector. This will ensure growth but, relative to world production, the increases will appear small

and most are expected to be achieved by local entrepreneurs. Aquaculture is also likely to spread through experienced entrepreneurs bringing expertise, and sometimes species, from one country to another in their search for least-cost production sites for internationally traded products. This will ensure the expansion of production in Latin America and, increasingly, in Africa.

Asian production will continue to grow, but the rate of growth is likely to slow down in China when it becomes a member of WTO, and thus more open to food imports. China may become a market for cultured fish produced elsewhere in Asia.

## MEDIUM-TERM OUTLOOK: FISH CONSUMPTION IN 2010

In *The State of World Fisheries and Aquaculture 1998,* it was estimated that world demand for food fish in 2010 would be between 105 million and 110 million tonnes and available supplies about 105 million tonnes, with an additional 30 million tonnes being converted into animal feed. No great upward pressure on average prices for fish was foreseen. It was expected that increased supplies from capture fisheries would materialize only towards the end of the first decade of this century as a result of improved management. These estimates were based on, *inter alia*, UN population data from 1996.

In 1998, the UN revised its population projections downwards[5] and its medium projection is now for a world population of 6 795 million in 2010. This is 96 million fewer than the estimate for 2010 published by the UN in 1996.

In 1999, the World Bank predicted that the world economy as a whole would grow faster in the period 1999-2008 than it had done in the proceeding ten-year period. As a result, the world per capita growth in GDP for the period was projected to reach 1.9 percent; up from the 1.1 percent in the World Bank's earlier projections.[6]

Recent FAO projections for meat[7] show that worldwide per capita consumption is expected to grow at about 0.7 percent per year until 2015. This is lower than the growth rate projected for per capita GDP. Consumption in industrialized countries is expected to increase slightly, while it will grow in all developing country areas, fastest in East Asia and at a low level in sub-Saharan Africa and South Asia.

What are the implications of this for the projections made in *The State of World Fisheries and Aquaculture 1998*? Overall, not very many – possibly a slight downward revision of overall estimates of global demand. On the one hand, the reduction to the estimated population forecast for 2010 is minor, at about 1.4 percent. On the other hand, this smaller than previously forecast population is expected to be somewhat richer than was projected some years ago. In OECD countries, increased wealth is not expected to lead to any significant increases in the volume of production, but expenditures on fish are likely to grow and an increasing share will be directed towards imported finished products.

In developing countries in Asia, in general, the supply difficulties experienced by capture

fisheries will probably be counterbalanced by increased aquaculture production; even by the end of the 1990s, the great bulk of aquaculture production (in terms of volume) was already supplying local consumers, not OECD markets. Thus, consumption in these countries is likely to expand continuously during the next decade.

In the remaining developing countries, and particularly in Africa, local supplies of fish may continue to decline. The reasons for this are related to the time needed to institute effective effort controls in overexploited multispecies fisheries that are exploited by a large number of individuals from a large number of landing centres. In addition, aquaculture developments are likely to focus on high-value products and, therefore, concentrate mainly on export markets.

It is by no means certain that a general increase in wealth in LIFDCs outside Asia will actually lead to higher fish production and consumption in these countries. Production may stagnate in many countries and, as local fish processors are likely to continue to have access to lucrative overseas markets, local supplies may diminish. In fact, real price levels for fish may increase in developing countries, which will tend to cancel the effect that increased prosperity could have on demand. It seems unlikely that export barriers will be established in the name of food security.

However, this pessimistic scenario is unlikely to apply to those LIFDCs where the fisheries sector accounts for a significant proportion of the national economy (e.g. Namibia, Mauritania, Maldives). The importance of the fisheries sector should generate the need, the will and the means for its management.

There would therefore seem to be no reason to make major modifications to the 1998 prediction of consumption. However, as Asia is the centre of world fish consumption (accounting for some two-thirds of the total at the end of the 1990s), what happens there will determine global developments. As projected economic growth in Asia will stimulate both demand and production in that part of the world, it is possibly more realistic to expect consumption in 2010 to be at least 110 million tonnes. This would imply that, for the world as a whole, per capita consumption would be slightly higher, at 16.1 kg, than it was at the end of the 1990s. A breakthrough in aquaculture (e.g. an extremely rapid spread of

---

[5] United Nations Population Division. 1998. *World population prospects: the 1998 revision*. New York, UN.

[6] FAO. 2000. *Agriculture: towards 2015/30*, p. 27. Technical Interim Report. Rome.

[7] Ibid., p. 75.

### BOX 19
### Fish consumption and long-term income elasticities

Elasticities are measurements that economists use to analyse the price sensitivity of demand and supply. The demand for any given good is influenced, not only by the prices of the goods and substitutes but, above all, by buyers' incomes. Income elasticity measures the responsiveness of the quantity of the goods demanded to changes in the buyer's income.

Short-term income elasticities are calculated for finite time periods and product prices are held constant. They normally refer to one particular product but can also be calculated for a group of products. Income elasticities can also be calculated for longer periods of time, and for groups of products.

Most goods are normal goods with positive income elasticities, i.e. demand increases as income rises; negative income elasticities can be found for inferior goods. Thus, less expensive fish such as mackerel, suary and horse mackerel are considered inferior goods.

Long-term elasticities are lower in absolute value than short-term elasticities, perhaps because cheaper substitutes become available over time as technology changes and consumers' tastes and preferences for other products develop. When looking at international studies, it is clear that most historical income elasticities for fish products are rather low, showing a weak to moderate response of demand as income rises, although the relation is positive. However, there are large differences among countries.

Calculating historical income elasticities is a relatively simple matter; predicting income elasticities is far more complicated, and the complexity increases with the length of period considered. In attempting to predict the income elasticity to apply to a 30-year prediction for fish, it would be necessary to consider, *inter alia*, the following factors: food habits of the particular group of consumers concerned; the fact that prices will change (contrary to the normal assumption for elasticities); the fact that products are modified (and sometimes become different products); changes in patterns of consumption as disposable income increases throughout the period of consideration; the level of fish consumption already attained at the start of the period; and the fact that consumers will substitute less expensive products with more expensive ones.

*Source:* A. Lem, FAO Fisheries Department.

---

tilapia culture in Latin America and Africa) would be the only major reason for altering such a prediction. Another reason would be a faster than foreseen spread of good governance practices in small-scale fisheries – but this seems to be a remote possibility for the first decade of the new century.

### LONG-TERM OUTLOOK: SOME PLAUSIBLE STRUCTURAL CHANGES IN PRODUCTION AND DEMAND

By the year 2030, aquaculture will dominate fish supplies and less than half of the fish consumed is likely to originate in capture fisheries. The role of capture fisheries in the economies of the present OECD countries will have been reduced further as developing countries increase their share of both catches and subsequent processing. Their lower costs of labour will make these economies competitive both in the labour-intensive processing industry and as a source of seafaring fishers. In wealthy countries, an increasing share of the fish consumed will be imported and, as these countries will want to obtain fish as cheaply as possible, it is likely that most trade barriers will be removed in advanced economies.

Aquaculture will have expanded geographically, in terms of species cultured and technologies used. It is very unlikely that Asia will continue to dominate production to the extent that it did during the 1990s. Mariculture will account for a larger share of total production, particularly if offshore culture technology becomes viable.

Economic growth over the next 30 years will result in a larger number of individuals with established, steady patterns of fish consumption. A wide variety of products will be consumed – but the total quantity of products consumed per person and per year will not fluctuate greatly. By the end of the 1990s, it would seem that about 10 percent of the world's population had already reached this level of stability; that is, their consumption had stagnated in terms of the volumes of fish consumed. By 2030, the numbers of consumers in this category will have increased somewhat, mainly in Europe but also in some East Asian nations. However, as the growth of population in wealthy regions will be slower than in poor regions, the proportion of the world's population with stagnating volumes of consumption will not have increased substantially and is unlikely to be more than 20 percent in 2030.

Thus, over the coming decades, in most OECD countries the total volume of fish consumed will not change much, and the modifications that do take place are likely to be determined more by fluctuations in population size than by growing disposable real incomes. This does not mean that the value of per capita consumption will not increase – it most probably will as consumers increase the share of expensive fish products by buying more ready-to-eat products and substituting expensive for cheap fish products.

Consumption predictions for the 80 percent of the world's population who are still likely to increase the quantity of fish they consume are complicated. Although extrapolating the effect of population growth on the basis of UN projections and recorded apparent per capita consumption is straightforward, it is more difficult to make a reasonable prediction of how demand is influenced by rising incomes and the relative changes in real prices of substitutes.

For short-term predictions – over a year or two – recourse is usually made to calculating and applying elasticities of demand relative to growth in income and assuming prices to be stable. For a category that includes as wide a range of different products (and therefore substitution possibilities) as fish does, and for periods that are as long as 30 years, determination of the appropriate elasticity to use (Box 19) is a complicated issue. FAO is studying the development of long-term predictions in a two-pronged approach. In the first of these, during which the Organization worked in association with two CGIAR centres,[8] a computer-based modelling approach was developed. The second approach consists of a series of in-depth investigations of probable future fish consumption in major consuming countries. The results of both are scheduled to be published in the course of 2001. ◆

---

[8] The International Food Policy Research Institute (IFPRI), in Washington, DC, and the International Centre for Living Aquatic Resources Management (ICLARM), in Penang, Malaysia.

# PART 5
# Fisheries activities of country groupings

# ASSOCIATION OF SOUTHEAST ASIAN NATIONS

The Association of Southeast Asian Nations (ASEAN) was established on 8 August 1967, in Bangkok, with the signing of the Bangkok Declaration. At present, its members are Brunei Darussalam, Cambodia, Indonesia, the Lao People's Democratic Republic, Malaysia, Myanmar, the Philippines, Singapore, Thailand and Viet Nam.

The ASEAN Declaration states that the aims and purposes of the Association are: i) to accelerate economic growth, social progress and cultural development in the region, through joint endeavours and in the spirit of equality and partnership, in order to strengthen the foundations for a prosperous and peaceful community of Southeast Asian nations; and ii) to promote regional peace and stability, through maintaining respect for justice and the rule of law within the relationship among countries in the region and through adherence to the principles of the United Nations Charter.

## FISHERIES: PURPOSE AND ACTIVITIES

In consideration of the conceptual framework of the Hanoi Plan of Action to implement the ASEAN Vision 2020, the Senior Officers of the ASEAN Ministers of Agriculture and Forestry (SOM-AMAF) held a Special Meeting from 27 to 29 April

*TABLE 6*

### ASEAN: fisheries and aquaculture production, food balance and trade

|  | 1986 | 1990 | 1994 | 1998 |
|---|---|---|---|---|
| **Aquaculture production** | | | | |
| Inland production *('000 tonnes)* | 755 | 940 | 1 187 | 1 545 |
| Percentage of world total | 13.0 | 11.5 | 9.8 | 8.2 |
| Marine production *('000 tonnes)* | 212 | 469 | 736 | 802 |
| Percentage of world total | 6.2 | 9.5 | 8.5 | 6.6 |
| **Fisheries production** | | | | |
| Inland production *('000 tonnes)* | 1 003 | 999 | 1 045 | 984 |
| Percentage of world total | 16.8 | 15.5 | 15.6 | 12.3 |
| Marine production *('000 tonnes)* | 7 403 | 8 451 | 10 040 | 10 748 |
| Percentage of world total | 9.4 | 10.7 | 11.8 | 13.7 |
| **Fisheries and aquaculture production** | | | | |
| Combined total *('000 tonnes)* | 9 372 | 10 859 | 13 008 | 14 079 |
| Percentage of world total | 10.0 | 11.0 | 11.6 | 12.0 |
| **Food balance** | | | | |
| Total food supply *('000 tonnes)* | 7 640 | 8 597 | 10 334 | ... |
| Per capita supply *(kg)* | 18.7 | 19.5 | 21.9 | ... |
| Fish as share of animal protein *(%)* | 47.7 | 45.7 | 43.7 | ... |
| **Trade in fishery commodities** | | | | |
| Total imports *(US$ millions)* | 720 | 1 437 | 1 996 | 1 626 |
| Percentage of world total | 3.0 | 3.6 | 3.9 | 3.0 |
| Total exports *(US$ millions)* | 1 996 | 4 484 | 7 758 | 7 600 |
| Percentage of world total | 8.7 | 12.6 | 16.4 | 14.8 |

*Note:* ... = data not available.

1998 in Phuket, Thailand. At that meeting, it was decided that the Strategic Plan on ASEAN Cooperation in Food, Agriculture (including Fisheries) and Forestry (1999-2004) should cover overall cooperation in the three major sectors, with particular emphasis on strengthening food security arrangements in the region, enhancing the international competitiveness of food, agricultural and forest products and strengthening ASEAN's position in international fora.

Existing guidelines (priority areas and programmes), instruments and mechanisms for cooperation should also be taken into consideration and reviewed as part of the preparations for the Strategic Plan. The Plan's implementation will be coordinated by the ASEAN Secretariat. In the field of fisheries and aquaculture, the implementation will be carried out by the Sectoral Working Group on Fisheries. Cooperation in fisheries continues to focus on aquaculture development, the development and improvement of fisheries post-harvest technologies and the harmonization of quality assurance for fishery products.

*The manual on good shrimp farm management practices* was officially launched at the 20th Meeting of AMAF in Hanoi on 18 September 1998, and distributed to all member countries for use. A manual of guidelines for producing "high health" shrimp broodstock has been drafted. Member countries are implementing the HACCP training programme, which was developed as part of the completed ASEAN-Canada Project on Fisheries Post-harvest Technology: Phase 2. A survey of traditional fish products in the ASEAN region is being carried out and a framework for the compilation of fisheries sanitary measures to facilitate intra-ASEAN trade in fish and fishery products has been prepared. In its early stages, the harmonization effort will be confined to fish diseases and quarantine.

The Programme and Work Plan for ASEAN Sea Turtle Conservation and Protection, as stipulated in the Memorandum of Understanding on ASEAN Sea Turtle Conservation and Protection, was endorsed by the 20th Meeting of AMAF in Hanoi. A workshop was held in July 1999 in Malaysia, at which strategies were reviewed and a time frame set for the implementation of the action plan. Thailand has identified approximately 40 ha of land on the bank of the Mekong River in Chiang Mai Province for the building of a research centre for ASEAN-Mekong Basin Fisheries Development Cooperation, while Singapore has trained participants from Myanmar in fisheries post-harvest technology. A Fisheries Consultative Group Meeting has been established as a mechanism for collaboration between ASEAN's Fisheries Working Group and the Southeast Asian Fisheries Development Centre (SEAFDEC) on sustainable fisheries development in the Southeast Asia region. The Special Meeting of SOM-AMAF, held in April 2000 in Brunei, decided on the implementation of seven ASEAN-SEAFDEC collaborative programmes (all of which have already been started). The programmes cover: the upgrading of the traditional fish processing industry; promotion of mangrove-friendly aquaculture; conservation and management of the sea turtle; regionalization of the Code of Conduct for Responsible Fisheries; development of a fish disease diagnostical inspection mechanism; improvement of fisheries statistics; fish trade and environment. The Special Meeting also decided to organize an ASEAN-SEAFDEC Conference on Sustainable Fisheries for Food Security in the New Millennium (Fish for the People), to be held in October 2001 in collaboration with FAO.

## COOPERATION WITH FAO

There is no formal cooperation between ASEAN and FAO in the area of fisheries. However, member countries of ASEAN and its Fisheries Working Group do cooperate closely with FAO through the FAO Regional Office in Bangkok.

# CARIBBEAN COMMUNITY AND COMMON MARKET

The Caribbean Community and Common Market (CARICOM) was established by the Treaty of Chaguaramas on 4 July 1973 for the principal purpose of enhancing, through cooperation, the economic, social and cultural development of the populations of member countries. CARICOM's members are Antigua and Barbuda, Bahamas, Barbados, Belize, Dominica, Grenada, Guyana, Haiti, Jamaica, Montserrat, Saint Lucia, Saint Kitts and Nevis, Saint Vincent and the Grenadines, Suriname and Trinidad and Tobago.

## FISHERIES: PURPOSE AND ACTIVITIES

In fisheries, CARICOM aims to "promote the development of the fisheries subsector in member states with a view to optimal exploitation of their resources on a sustainable basis". It intends to do this by strengthening the legal and institutional framework, in part through the formulation and implementation of a common CARICOM Fisheries Policy and a CARICOM Regional Fisheries Mechanism.

The CARICOM Fisheries Unit, located in Belize, was established in 1991 to execute the CARICOM Fisheries Resource Assessment and Management Program (CFRAMP). This programme's goal is to promote sustainable development and conservation of the region's fish stocks in order to permit sustainable use of these

*TABLE 7*

| CARICOM: fisheries and aquaculture production, food balance and trade | | | | |
|---|---|---|---|---|
| | **1986** | **1990** | **1994** | **1998** |
| **Aquaculture production** | | | | |
| Inland production (*'000 tonnes*) | 2 | 3 | 3 | 4 |
| Percentage of world total | 0.0 | 0.0 | 0.0 | 0.0 |
| Marine production (*'000 tonnes*) | 0 | 0 | 1 | 2 |
| Percentage of world total | 0.0 | 0.0 | 0.0 | 0.0 |
| **Fisheries production** | | | | |
| Inland production (*'000 tonnes*) | 1 | 2 | 2 | 2 |
| Percentage of world total | 0.0 | 0.0 | 0.0 | 0.0 |
| Marine production (*'000 tonnes*) | 79 | 89 | 109 | 117 |
| Percentage of world total | 0.1 | 0.1 | 0.1 | 0.1 |
| **Fisheries and aquaculture production** | | | | |
| Combined total (*'000 tonnes*) | 82 | 94 | 115 | 124 |
| Percentage of world total | 0.1 | 0.1 | 0.1 | 0.1 |
| **Food balance** | | | | |
| Total food supply (*'000 tonnes*) | 154 | 143 | 155 | ... |
| Per capita supply (*kg*) | 12.7 | 11.1 | 11.4 | ... |
| Fish as share of animal protein *(%)* | 19.7 | 18.5 | 19.1 | ... |
| **Trade in fishery commodities** | | | | |
| Total imports (*US$ millions*) | 59 | 64 | 62 | 69 |
| Percentage of world total | 0.2 | 0.2 | 0.1 | 0.1 |
| Total exports (*US$ millions*) | 66 | 108 | 110 | 178 |
| Percentage of world total | 0.3 | 0.3 | 0.2 | 0.3 |

*Note:* ... = data not available.

resources by the peoples of 12 CARICOM Member States. It was created in 1991 and is funded jointly by the Canadian Government, through the Canadian International Development Agency (CIDA), and participating CARICOM countries. CFRAMP is being executed in two phases. Phase 1 was concluded in 1998, while Phase 2 is due for completion in December 2000. It is hoped that there will then be a transition to a more permanent regional fisheries mechanism.

The role of the CARICOM Fisheries Unit, as a leading regional executing agency for fisheries resource conservation and management, has been expanded to include:

- the ACP-EU Fisheries and Biodiversity Management Project: Caribbean Node, which was initiated in late 1997 with the participation of several ACP countries, including the Dominican Republic and CARICOM countries;
- the EU-funded fisheries component of the Lomé IV Integrated Caribbean Regional Agricultural and Fisheries Development Program (CARIFORUM Fisheries Project), which is intended to benefit several ACP countries in the Caribbean region, including CARICOM countries. This project started in August 1999;
- the Project on Multi-stakeholder Approaches to Coastal Zone Management in the Caribbean, supported by the International Development Research Centre.

## COOPERATION WITH FAO
CARICOM and FAO have cooperated closely over the past decades on various aspects of fisheries, including policy and legal matters. FAO has provided technical assistance to CFRAMP in specific areas since its inception in 1991 and, over the past two years, FAO and CFRAMP have collaborated in implementing joint technical activities through the Western Central Atlantic Fisheries Commission (WECAFC). Such activities have included training in stock assessment and the assessment of major fish stocks (e.g. spiny lobster, penaeid shrimp) in the WECAFC region.

# COMMONWEALTH OF INDEPENDENT STATES

The Commonwealth of Independent States (CIS) was established in December 1991. It is a voluntary association consisting of the following States: Armenia, Azerbaijan, Belarus, Georgia, Kazakhstan, Kyrgyzstan, the Republic of Moldova, the Russian Federation, Tajikistan, Turkmenistan, Ukraine and Uzbekistan. The main purpose of the Commonwealth is to develop and strengthen cooperation and to serve the cause of peace and security.

## FISHERIES: PURPOSE AND ACTIVITIES
To date, no common fisheries policy among countries of the CIS has been elaborated. Coordination is achieved through bilateral and multilateral agreements among the member countries, which can be divided into two groups:

i) states that have inland water fisheries and aquaculture activities only (Armenia, Azerbaijan, Belarus, Kazakhstan, Kyrgyzstan, the Republic of Moldova, Tajikistan, Turkmenistan and Uzbekistan); and

ii) states that have a well-developed distant-water fisheries sector (the Russian Federation, Ukraine and – to a certain extent – Georgia).

TABLE 8

| CIS: fisheries and aquaculture production, food balance and trade | | | | |
|---|---|---|---|---|
| | 1986 | 1990 | 1994 | 1998 |
| **Aquaculture production** | | | | |
| Inland production ('000 tonnes) | ... | 405 | 146 | 106 |
| Percentage of world total | ... | 5.0 | 1.2 | 0.6 |
| Marine production ('000 tonnes) | ... | 0 | 3 | 1 |
| Percentage of world total | ... | 0.0 | 0.0 | 0.0 |
| **Fisheries production** | | | | |
| Inland production ('000 tonnes) | ... | 565 | 319 | 316 |
| Percentage of world total | ... | 8.8 | 4.8 | 3.9 |
| Marine production ('000 tonnes) | ... | 8 233 | 3 747 | 4 644 |
| Percentage of world total | ... | 10.4 | 4.4 | 5.9 |
| **Fisheries and aquaculture production** | | | | |
| Combined total ('000 tonnes) | ... | 9 204 | 4 215 | 5 066 |
| Percentage of world total | ... | 9.3 | 3.8 | 4.3 |
| **Food balance** | | | | |
| Total food supply in ('000 tonnes) | ... | ... | 2 072 | ... |
| Per capita supply (kg) | ... | ... | 7.3 | ... |
| Fish as share of animal protein (%) | ... | ... | 6.6 | ... |
| **Trade in fishery commodities** | | | | |
| Total imports (US$ millions) | ... | ... | 287 | 375 |
| Percentage of world total | ... | ... | 0.6 | 0.7 |
| Total exports (US$ millions) | ... | ... | 1 797 | 1 268 |
| Percentage of world total | ... | ... | 3.8 | 2.5 |

Note: ... = data non available.

Most CIS countries have concentrated on the restructuring of their fleets and on the processing and marketing sectors.

## COOPERATION WITH FAO

To date there is no agreed policy within the CIS countries concerning their cooperation with FAO. Each state acts independently in fishery matters.

# ECONOMIC COMMUNITY OF WEST AFRICAN STATES

The Treaty of Lagos, which established the Economic Community of West African States (ECOWAS), was signed by representatives of 15 West African States in Lagos on 28 May 1975. At present, the following countries adhere to the treaty: Benin, Burkina Faso, Cape Verde, Côte d'Ivoire, the Gambia, Ghana, Guinea, Guinea-Bissau, Liberia, Mali, Mauritania, the Niger, Nigeria, Senegal, Sierra Leone and Togo.

The ECOWAS Treaty specifies the Community's objective, to be achieved in stages, as being the creation of economic and monetary union. Cooperation in the development of agriculture, forestry, animal husbandry and fisheries is one of its primary aims. The first stage in this cooperation entails the harmonization of internal and external policies; the second stage envisages the adoption of a common agricultural policy.

## FISHERIES: PURPOSE AND ACTIVITIES

Based on the recommendations of the Industry, Agriculture and Natural Resources Commission at its meeting in Cotonou, Benin, in April 1980, ECOWAS organized a conference of experts in Dakar, Senegal, to develop national policies to ensure

*TABLE 9*

### ECOWAS: fisheries and aquaculture production, food balance and trade

| | 1986 | 1990 | 1994 | 1998 |
|---|---|---|---|---|
| **Aquaculture production** | | | | |
| Inland production *('000 tonnes)* | 6 | 8 | 15 | 22 |
| Percentage of world total | 0.1 | 0.1 | 0.1 | 0.1 |
| Marine production *('000 tonnes)* | 0 | 0 | 1 | ... |
| Percentage of world total | 0.0 | 0.0 | 0.0 | ... |
| **Fisheries production** | | | | |
| Inland production *('000 tonnes)* | 334 | 341 | 344 | 420 |
| Percentage of world total | 5.6 | 5.3 | 5.1 | 5.2 |
| Marine production *('000 tonnes)* | 959 | 1 128 | 1 065 | 1 297 |
| Percentage of world total | 1.2 | 1.4 | 1.3 | 1.7 |
| **Fisheries and aquaculture production** | | | | |
| Combined total *('000 tonnes)* | 1 299 | 1 477 | 1 425 | 1 739 |
| Percentage of world total | 1.4 | 1.5 | 1.3 | 1.5 |
| **Food balance** | | | | |
| Total food supply *('000 tonnes)* | 1 517 | 2 191 | 1 652 | ... |
| Per capita supply *(kg)* | 9.9 | 12.8 | 8.7 | ... |
| Fish as share of animal protein *(%)* | 30.5 | 34.4 | 28.8 | ... |
| **Trade in fishery commodities** | | | | |
| Total imports *(US$ millions)* | 243 | 383 | 377 | 494 |
| Percentage of world total | 1.0 | 1.0 | 0.7 | 0.9 |
| Total exports *(US$ millions)* | 537 | 518 | 629 | 828 |
| Percentage of world total | 2.3 | 1.5 | 1.3 | 1.6 |

*Note:* ... = data not available.

better management and surveillance of waters under the jurisdiction of its Member States and also to ensure the conservation of fisheries resources in the region. Several recommendations were made concerning research, surveillance, the harmonization of fishing agreements and legislation, trade in fish and fishery products, data collection, etc. Since then, Members have made progress in implementing such recommendations.

## COOPERATION WITH FAO

ECOWAS's formal relationship with FAO is based on an exchange of letters between the Director-General of FAO and the Executive Secretary of ECOWAS. A Cooperation Agreement was established with FAO in December 1984, since which time FAO has been cooperating with the Community in various fields. However, as an organization, ECOWAS is not a member of any of FAO's statutory bodies.

In the mid-1990s, at the request of ECOWAS, FAO carried out a study entitled Economic development of fisheries, which made special reference to aspects of fisheries by foreign vessels off West Africa. In its conclusions, the study emphasized the necessity and the opportunities for regional cooperation in support of fisheries management and regional food security. Furthermore, FAO regional fishery projects have been cooperating with ECOWAS Member States, especially in promoting fisheries management in the artisanal subsector.

# EUROPEAN COMMUNITY

The Treaty of Rome established the European Economic Community (EEC) in 1957. In 1993, the Treaty of Maastricht established the European Union (EU) as a broader framework which retained the EEC, now the European Community (EC), as a legal entity. The aims of the EC include the abolition of restrictive trading practices and the free movement of capital and labour within the union. A single market with free movement of goods and capital was established in January 1993. The following countries are members of the EC: Austria, Belgium, Denmark, Finland, France, Germany, Greece, Ireland, Italy, Luxembourg, the Netherlands, Portugal, Spain, Sweden and the United Kingdom.

## FISHERIES: PURPOSE AND ACTIVITIES

The Common Fisheries Policy (CFP) is the EC's instrument for the conservation and management of fisheries and aquaculture. It was created with the aims of managing a common resource and meeting the obligation set out in the original Community Treaties. Wild fish are a natural and mobile resource that is considered common property. The treaties creating the Community stated that there should be a common policy in this area; that is, common rules adopted at the Community level and

*TABLE 10*

| EC: fisheries and aquaculture production, food balance and trade | | | | |
|---|---|---|---|---|
| | **1986** | **1990** | **1994** | **1998** |
| **Aquaculture production** | | | | |
| Inland production *('000 tonnes)* | 171 | 221 | 241 | 249 |
| Percentage of world total | 3.0 | 2.7 | 2.0 | 1.3 |
| Marine production *('000 tonnes)* | 699 | 717 | 796 | 1 085 |
| Percentage of world total | 20.6 | 14.5 | 9.2 | 8.9 |
| **Fisheries production** | | | | |
| Inland production *('000 tonnes)* | 113 | 107 | 104 | 120 |
| Percentage of world total | 1.9 | 1.7 | 1.6 | 1.5 |
| Marine production *('000 tonnes)* | 6 774 | 6 067 | 6 737 | 6 419 |
| Percentage of world total | 8.6 | 7.7 | 8.0 | 8.2 |
| **Fisheries and aquaculture production** | | | | |
| Combined total *('000 tonnes)* | 7 757 | 7 114 | 7 878 | 7 873 |
| Percentage of world total | 8.3 | 7.2 | 7.0 | 6.7 |
| **Food balance** | | | | |
| Total food supply *('000 tonnes)* | 7 466 | 8 236 | 8 547 | ... |
| Per capita supply *(kg)* | 20.2 | 21.9 | 22.4 | ... |
| Fish as share of animal protein *(%)* | 9.0 | 9.8 | 10.3 | ... |
| **Trade in fishery commodities** | | | | |
| Total imports *(US$ millions)* | 8 182 | 15 705 | 16 946 | 21 158 |
| Percentage of world total | 33.7 | 39.8 | 33.2 | 38.5 |
| Total exports *(US$ millions)* | 4 646 | 8 071 | 9 135 | 11 667 |
| Percentage of world total | 20.3 | 22.7 | 19.3 | 22.8 |

*Note: ... = data not available.*

implemented in all Member States. DG Fisheries is the Directorate-General responsible for the CFP, which is scheduled to be reviewed in 2002.

The CFP came into existence in 1983, although the first elements of this policy had already been introduced in 1970. Since then, it has been developed and adjusted continuously in accordance with international developments and changes within the EC itself. The CFP takes into account the biological, economic, social and environmental dimensions of fishing. Its implementation entails the following main issues and related measures.

*Conservation and responsible fishing.* The EC policy for the conservation of fishery resources focuses on:

- limiting fishing effort through a strict licensing system;
- restricting catch volumes by setting total allowable catches (TACs) and establishing technical measures to minimize the occurrence of discards;
- promoting more selective fisheries by establishing technical measures related to mesh sizes, selectivity devices, closed areas and seasons, minimum fish and shellfish landing sizes and limits of by-catch;
- reducing fishing capacity to a level compatible with fishery resources availability. Progress made in this crucial component of the CFP is monitored through the Multi-Annual Guidance Programme (MAGP IV – 1997-2001), which also establishes fleet reduction targets for each member country. DG Fisheries has already started to prepare proposals for MAGP V, to cover the 2002-2006 period;
- adapting management to fishing areas shared between the Community and third parties through active membership in the Northwest Atlantic Fisheries Organization (NAFO), the Commission for the Conservation of Antarctic Marine Living Resources (CCAMLR), the Northeast Atlantic Fisheries Commission (NEAFC), the Indian Ocean Tuna Commission (IOTC), the North Atlantic Salmon Conservation Organization (NASCO), the Fishery Committee for the Eastern Central Atlantic (CECAF), the International Baltic Sea Fishery Commission (IBSFC), the General Fisheries Commission for the Mediterranean (GFCM) and the International Commission for the Conservation of Atlantic Tunas (ICCAT).

*Fishing beyond Community waters.* The EC has exclusive competence in international relations in the domain of fisheries. It is empowered to undertake international commitments towards third countries or international organizations in matters relating to fisheries. The European Commission, on behalf of the Community, negotiates fisheries agreements with third countries and participates in various regional fisheries organizations. The EC has concluded 26 fishing agreements with third countries and is currently a member of nine regional and international fisheries organizations. The EC is also a member of FAO.

*Restructuring the fishing sector.* Restructuring of the EC fisheries sector relies heavily on the implementation of the structural policy, the purpose of which is to adapt and manage the development of structures (the equipment required to produce goods and the organization of production processes) in the fishing and aquaculture industry. EC assistance to the fisheries sector is provided under the Financial Instrument for Fisheries Guidance (FIFG). The FIFG aims to:

- contribute to the achievement of a lasting balance between fisheries resources and their exploitation;
- strengthen competitiveness and the development of economically viable businesses in the fishing industry;
- improve market supply and increase the value that can be added to fish and aquaculture products through processing;
- help revitalize areas that are dependent on fisheries and aquaculture.

The Council of the European Union agreed the detailed rules and arrangements regarding assistance under the FIFG on 17 December 1999. These rules replaced the Regulation, which came to an end on 31 December 1999, and cover the period 2000 to 2006. The EC was determined to ensure that public funds would not be used to increase fishing capacity because a number of commercial stocks are still overexploited. Measures regarding financial support linked to productive investment in the processing industry and aquaculture, such as building, enlarging or modernizing processing plants or fish farms, as well as those relating to fishing port facilities have been renewed. Others, such as supporting the creation of temporary joint ventures, have been cancelled, as they had not achieved their objective of contributing to the reduction of EC fleet capacity. Greater emphasis has been put on environmental aspects, and priority will be given to collective projects undertaken by the industry itself. The new rules contain substantial modifications to some previous rules which were shown to be insufficiently explicit or difficult to implement, including rules on fleet renewal and joint enterprises. In the case of the latter, a number of conditions have been attached to the eligibility and implementation of projects to ensure that they do not lead to overfishing in third countries and that the obligations attached to the granting of aid are fulfilled.

In addition, there are provisions relating to support for producers' organizations, which were previously implemented under the Common Organization of the Markets for Fisheries and Aquaculture Regulation. The measures aim to reinforce the competitiveness of the industry through reinforcement of the role of producers' organizations. The inclusion of these measures as well as those in favour of small-scale fisheries in the FIFG allows for a rationalization of its contents and increased coherence with other structural measures.

In conclusion, the new rules widen the range of socio-economic measures by, for example, granting aid to young fishers who are acquiring a fishing vessel for the first time and to individual fishers who are leaving the industry; redefining the current support mechanisms for fishers and vessel owners who are subject to a temporary cessation of activities; and updating the current premiums and scales.

***Common organization of the market.*** The EC set up a system for the common organization of the market for fisheries and aquaculture products almost 30 years ago. Since July 1996, the common market organization in fisheries and aquaculture products has been being adapted to recent changes in the market, including increased globalization of markets, greater dependence on imports, continued scarcity of resources, change in consumption patterns and concentration and vertical integration within the distribution chain. The common organization of the EC market has four components:

- common marketing standards for quality, grades, packaging and labelling of both EC and imported fishery products;
- producers' organizations, which are voluntary associations of fishers that are established to help stabilize markets (their role is to protect fishers from sudden changes in market demand);
- a price support system that sets minimum prices below which fish products cannot be sold. Financial support is available to producers' organizations if they have to take fish and shellfish off the market, store them for later use or process them;
- rules for trade with non-EC countries.

The regulation for the common organization of the market for fishery products was adopted on 12 December 1999 and is expected to be fully implemented by 1 January 2001.

***Enforcement of the law within the fishing sector.*** The 1992 review of the CFP stressed the need to make the policy more effective. A new control regulation, created in 1993, reinforced the role of surveillance and extended the CFP's domain of action from that of direct conservation measures to one that also included implementation of structural policy, marketing, transport and sale of fish and shellfish. The new regulation also encouraged harmonization of the proceedings and penalties against wrongdoers across the EC. Information technology was to be used to complement traditional monitoring methods. Fishing surveillance has also been substantially strengthened by the setting up of a Vessel Monitoring System (VMS). As from 1 January 2000, wherever they operate, all EC fishing vessels that exceed 24 m in length (or 20 m between perpendiculars) must be equipped with a satellite tracking device, as must the vessels of third countries operating in EC waters. The authorities will be able to use satellite tracking to optimize the use of their aircraft and patrol vessels and to compare satellite evidence with the information contained in vessels' log-books.

***Fishing and the wider environment.*** In 1997, a ministerial meeting on the integration of fisheries and environmental issues, held in Bergen, Norway, and attended by ministers from all North Sea States and by EC representatives, agreed on a so-called "ecosystem approach" to marine environments which included elements of the precautionary approach. Given the commitment demonstrated by various states and international organizations, including the EC, to integrating an environmental dimension into their policies, greater effort is now being made to promote the relevant research and data collection within the framework of the EC FAIR Programme. Related to this topic, the Community's DG Environment is implementing a project called Integrating biodiversity and European fisheries policy: rebuilding a healthy and productive ecosystem.

The international dimension of fisheries has acquired greater importance for the EC in recent years. Bilateral and multilateral negotiations with third countries have increased, as have negotiations within regional fisheries organizations and international bodies. International trade of fish and fishery products has also become more important for the Community, especially in relation to import trade as well as to environmental issues and health and safety standards of fish and fishery products.

## COOPERATION WITH FAO
The EC is a full member of FAO. The EC is also a member of most FAO regional fishery bodies and participates actively in the work of several of these.

The financial contribution of the EC makes it possible for FAO to implement its international agreements and plans of action for improved global management of fishing capacity, shark fisheries and incidental catch of seabirds in longline fisheries.

# LATIN AMERICAN ECONOMIC SYSTEM

The Latin American Economic System (LAES) is a regional intergovernmental organization that groups 28 Latin American and Caribbean countries: Argentina, the Bahamas, Barbados, Belize, Bolivia, Brazil, Chile, Colombia, Costa Rica, Cuba, the Dominican Republic, Ecuador, El Salvador, Grenada, Guatemala, Guyana, Haiti, Honduras, Jamaica, Mexico, Nicaragua, Panama, Paraguay, Peru, Suriname, Trinidad and Tobago, Uruguay and Venezuela. LAES was established on 17 October 1975 by the Panama Convention.

The objectives of LAES are to promote a system for consultation and coordination, aiming to achieve consensus in the form of joint positions and common strategies on economic issues for the Latin American and Caribbean region. The common strategies may be for individual countries or groups of countries. LAES also serves to promote cooperation and integration among the countries of the region.

## FISHERIES: PURPOSE AND ACTIVITIES

The Action Committees of LAES are flexible cooperation mechanisms and are set up when more than two Member States voice their interest in promoting joint programmes and projects in specific areas. These committees are dissolved once their objectives are fulfilled, otherwise they may become Permanent Bodies of the System.

*TABLE 11*

| LAES: fisheries and aquaculture production, food balance and trade | | | | |
|---|---|---|---|---|
| | **1986** | **1990** | **1994** | **1998** |
| **Aquaculture production** | | | | |
| Inland production *('000 tonnes)* | 45 | 74 | 101 | 203 |
| Percentage of world total | 0.8 | 0.9 | 0.8 | 1.1 |
| Marine production *('000 tonnes)* | 57 | 132 | 261 | 518 |
| Percentage of world total | 1.7 | 2.7 | 3.0 | 4.3 |
| **Fisheries production** | | | | |
| Inland production *('000 tonnes)* | 458 | 429 | 474 | 466 |
| Percentage of world total | 7.7 | 6.7 | 7.1 | 5.8 |
| Marine production *('000 tonnes)* | 15 382 | 15 601 | 23 485 | 11 841 |
| Percentage of world total | 19.6 | 19.7 | 27.7 | 15.1 |
| **Fisheries and aquaculture production** | | | | |
| Combined total *('000 tonnes)* | 15 941 | 16 236 | 24 322 | 13 028 |
| Percentage of world total | 17.0 | 16.5 | 21.7 | 11.1 |
| **Food balance** | | | | |
| Total food supply *('000 tonnes)* | 3 615 | 4 054 | 4 182 | ... |
| Per capita supply *(kg)* | 9.0 | 9.3 | 9.0 | ... |
| Fish as share of animal protein *(%)* | 8.0 | 8.3 | 7.5 | ... |
| **Trade in fishery commodities** | | | | |
| Total imports *(US$ millions)* | 353 | 477 | 805 | 1 113 |
| Percentage of world total | 1.5 | 1.2 | 1.6 | 2.0 |
| Total exports *(US$ millions)* | 2 737 | 3 220 | 5 461 | 6 596 |
| Percentage of world total | 11.9 | 9.1 | 11.5 | 12.9 |

*Note:* ... = data not available.

## COOPERATION WITH FAO

There is a long record of cooperation in technical activities between FAO and LAES. Initially the forum for this cooperation was the Action Committee of Sea and Freshwater Products. When this action committee was dissolved, the Latin American Organization for Fisheries Development (OLDEPESCA) was established, and this independent body has become the centre of cooperation. FAO usually attends the annual OLDEPESCA conferences of Fisheries Ministers.

# LEAGUE OF ARAB STATES

The League of Arab States, more generally known as the Arab League, was established on 22 March 22 1945. It comprises Algeria, Bahrain, the Comoros, Djibouti, Egypt, Iraq, Jordan, Kuwait, Lebanon, the Libyan Arab Jamahiriya, Mauritania, Morocco, Oman, Palestine, Qatar, Saudi Arabia, Somalia, the Sudan, the Syrian Arab Republic, Tunisia, the United Arab Emirates and Yemen.

The broad objectives of the Arab League are to develop cooperation and strengthen complementarity among the Member States in economic, cultural, scientific, social and military fields. To do so, the League has set up several specialized agencies. Those of interest to FAO are: the Arab Bank for Economic Development in Africa (Khartoum, the Sudan); the Arab Centre for the Study of Arid Zones and Dry Lands (Damascus, the Syrian Arab Republic); the Arab Fund for Economic and Social Development (Kuwait); the Arab League Educational, Cultural and Scientific Organization (Tunis, Tunisia); the Arab Organization for Agricultural Development (Khartoum, the Sudan); the Arab Academy for Science, and Maritime Transport (Alexandria, Egypt); and the Inter-Arab Investment Guarantee Corporation (Kuwait).

TABLE 12

## League of Arab States: fisheries and aquaculture production, food balance and trade

|  | 1986 | 1990 | 1994 | 1998 |
|---|---|---|---|---|
| **Aquaculture production** | | | | |
| Inland production *('000 tonnes)* | 53 | 69 | 65 | 139 |
| Percentage of world total | 0.9 | 0.8 | 0.5 | 0.7 |
| Marine production *('000 tonnes)* | 0 | 2 | 6 | 20 |
| Percentage of world total | 0.0 | 0.0 | 0.1 | 0.2 |
| **Fisheries production** | | | | |
| Inland production *('000 tonnes)* | 188 | 234 | 271 | 320 |
| Percentage of world total | 3.2 | 3.6 | 4.0 | 4.0 |
| Marine production *('000 tonnes)* | 1 244 | 1 315 | 1 596 | 1 574 |
| Percentage of world total | 1.6 | 1.7 | 1.9 | 2.0 |
| **Fisheries and aquaculture production** | | | | |
| Combined total *('000 tonnes)* | 1 486 | 1 620 | 1 939 | 2 052 |
| Percentage of world total | 1.6 | 1.6 | 1.7 | 1.8 |
| **Food balance** | | | | |
| Total food supply *('000 tonnes)* | 1 089 | 1 234 | 1 470 | ... |
| Per capita supply *(kg)* | 5.4 | 5.5 | 6.0 | ... |
| Fish as share of animal protein *(%)* | 8.1 | 8.6 | 9.7 | ... |
| **Trade in fishery commodities** | | | | |
| Total imports *(US$ millions)* | 244 | 213 | 323 | 457 |
| Percentage of world total | 1.0 | 0.5 | 0.6 | 0.8 |
| Total exports *(US$ millions)* | 612 | 878 | 985 | 1 124 |
| Percentage of world total | 2.7 | 2.5 | 2.1 | 2.2 |

*Note:* ... = data not available.

## FISHERIES: PURPOSE AND ACTIVITIES

The League of Arab States has no subsidiary body or institution that deals exclusively with fisheries matters.

## COOPERATION WITH FAO

FAO has participated in several meetings organized by subsidiary bodies of the Arab League. The Organization has attended and partly sponsored meetings of the Arab Federation of Fish Producers (AFFP), which is a subsidiary of the Council for Arab Economic Union. In 1998, FAO was represented at the Conference on the Development of Marine Fisheries in the Arab World, organized by the Council.

# NORTH AMERICAN FREE TRADE AGREEMENT

Canada, Mexico and the United States of America are members of the North American Free Trade Agreement (NAFTA), which came into effect on 1 January 1994. NAFTA's main aims are to contribute to the expansion of world trade; create, expand and secure markets for the goods produced in their territories; reduce distortions to trade; create new employment opportunities and improve working conditions and living standards in their respective territories; and address related environmental and conservation issues.

NAFTA is a trading block of global reach. It is innovative, as it establishes linkages between economies with different levels of economic development. Current discussions envisage the linking of existing subregional integration schemes, of which NAFTA is one, into a Free Trade Area of the Americas.

## FISHERIES: PURPOSE AND ACTIVITIES
NAFTA does not have any particular activities concerned with fisheries.

## COOPERATION WITH FAO
To date, there is no cooperation between NAFTA and FAO on fisheries matters. NAFTA member countries deal individually with FAO in this field.

*TABLE 13*

### NAFTA: fisheries and aquaculture production, food balance and trade

|  | 1986 | 1990 | 1994 | 1998 |
|---|---|---|---|---|
| **Aquaculture production** | | | | |
| Inland production *('000 tonnes)* | 248 | 254 | 287 | 342 |
| Percentage of world total | 4.3 | 3.1 | 2.4 | 1.8 |
| Marine production *('000 tonnes)* | 148 | 120 | 189 | 235 |
| Percentage of world total | 4.4 | 2.4 | 2.2 | 1.9 |
| **Fisheries production** | | | | |
| Inland production *('000 tonnes)* | 218 | 197 | 190 | 197 |
| Percentage of world total | 3.7 | 3.1 | 2.8 | 2,5 |
| Marine production *('000 tonnes)* | 7 405 | 8 356 | 7 565 | 6 688 |
| Percentage of world total | 9.4 | 10.6 | 8.9 | 8.5 |
| **Fisheries and aquaculture production** | | | | |
| Combined total *('000 tonnes)* | 8 020 | 8 927 | 8 231 | 7 462 |
| Percentage of world total | 8.5 | 9.1 | 7.3 | 6.4 |
| **Food balance** | | | | |
| Total food supply *('000 tonnes)* | 5 995 | 7 056 | 7 768 | ... |
| Per capita supply *(kg)* | 17.3 | 19.3 | 20.3 | ... |
| Fish as share of animal protein *(%)* | 6.4 | 7.5 | 7.5 | ... |
| **Trade in fishery commodities** | | | | |
| Total imports *(US$ millions)* | 5 188 | 6 257 | 8 115 | 9 872 |
| Percentage of world total | 21.4 | 15.8 | 15.9 | 18.0 |
| Total exports *(US$ millions)* | 3 690 | 5 649 | 5 893 | 5 382 |
| Percentage of world total | 16.1 | 15.9 | 12.4 | 10.5 |

*Note: ... = data not available.*

# SOUTH ASIAN ASSOCIATION
# FOR REGIONAL COOPERATION

The South Asian Association for Regional Cooperation (SAARC) was established in 1985 by the Heads of State and Government of Bangladesh, Bhutan, India, Maldives, Nepal, Pakistan and Sri Lanka. SAARC's main goal is to accelerate economic and social development in Member States through joint action in certain agreed areas of cooperation. To achieve this objective SAARC seeks to:

* promote the welfare of the peoples of South Asia and improve their quality of life;
* accelerate economic growth, social progress and cultural development in the region, and provide all individuals the opportunity to live in dignity and realize their full potential;
* promote and strengthen collective self-reliance among the countries of South Asia;
* promote active collaboration and mutual assistance in economic, social, cultural, technical and scientific fields;
* strengthen cooperation with other developing countries;
* strengthen cooperation among Member States in other international fora on matters of common interest, and cooperate with international and regional organizations with similar aims and purposes.

TABLE 14

## SAARC: fisheries and aquaculture production, food balance and trade

|  | 1986 | 1990 | 1994 | 1998 |
|---|---|---|---|---|
| **Aquaculture production** | | | | |
| Inland production (*'000 tonnes*) | 823 | 1 182 | 1 755 | 2 502 |
| Percentage of world total | 14.2 | 14.5 | 14.5 | 13.4 |
| Marine production (*'000 tonnes*) | 29 | 50 | 123 | 156 |
| Percentage of world total | 0.9 | 1.0 | 1.4 | 1.3 |
| **Fisheries production** | | | | |
| Inland production (*'000 tonnes*) | 1 088 | 1 128 | 1 221 | 1 395 |
| Percentage of world total | 18.3 | 17.5 | 18.2 | 17.4 |
| Marine production (*'000 tonnes*) | 2 462 | 3 022 | 3 630 | 3 653 |
| Percentage of world total | 3.1 | 3.8 | 4.3 | 4.7 |
| **Fisheries and aquaculture production** | | | | |
| Combined total (*'000 tonnes*) | 4 401 | 5 382 | 6 729 | 7 705 |
| Percentage of world total | 4.7 | 5.5 | 6.0 | 6.6 |
| **Food balance** | | | | |
| Total food supply (*'000 tonnes*) | 3 772 | 4 566 | 5 555 | … |
| Per capita supply (*kg*) | 3.7 | 4.1 | 4.6 | … |
| Fish as share of animal protein (*%*) | 12.1 | 12.6 | 13.4 | … |
| **Trade in fishery commodities** | | | | |
| Total imports (*US$ millions*) | 31 | 46 | 39 | 92 |
| Percentage of world total | 0.1 | 0.1 | 0.1 | 0.2 |
| Total exports (*US$ millions*) | 616 | 790 | 1 641 | 1 695 |
| Percentage of world total | 2.7 | 2.2 | 3.5 | 3.3 |

*Note:* … = data not available.

## FISHERIES: PURPOSES AND OBJECTIVES

The Integrated Programme of Action is the key component of SAARC's activities. It now includes 11 areas of cooperation, each covered by a Technical Committee: Agriculture; Communications; Education; Culture and Sports; Environment and Meteorology; Health and Population Activities; Prevention of Drug Trafficking and Drug Abuse; Rural Development, Science and Technology; Tourism; Transport; and Women in Development. Regular meetings of counterpart scientists are a very important feature of the Technical Committee on Agriculture, and a list of fisheries counterpart scientists has also been prepared and made available.

## COOPERATION WITH FAO

SAARC does not cooperate formally with FAO in fisheries or aquaculture.

# SOUTHERN AFRICAN DEVELOPMENT COMMUNITY

The Declaration and Treaty establishing the Southern African Development Community (SADC) was signed at the Summit of Heads of Government in Windhoek, Namibia, in August 1992. Its member countries are Angola, Botswana, the Democratic Republic of the Congo, Lesotho, Malawi, Mauritius, Mozambique, Namibia, Seychelles, South Africa, Swaziland, the United Republic of Tanzania, Zambia and Zimbabwe. The objectives of SADC are to:

- achieve development and economic growth, alleviate poverty, enhance the standard and quality of life of the peoples of southern Africa and support the socially disadvantaged through regional integration;
- evolve common political values, systems and institutions;
- promote and defend peace and security;
- promote self-sustaining development on the basis of collective self-reliance and the interdependence of Member States;
- achieve complementarity among national and regional strategies and programmes;
- promote and maximize productive employment and utilization of the resources of the region;
- achieve sustainable utilization of natural resources and effective protection of the environment;
- strengthen and consolidate long-standing historical, social and cultural affinities and links among the peoples of the region.

## FISHERIES: PURPOSES AND ACTIVITIES

SADC's work related to specific sectors is handled by Sector Coordinating Units (SCUs). These are allocated to individual Member States, who provide coordination, leadership and guidance on the formulation, implementation and management of sector-specific policies, programmes and projects. A Sectoral Committee of Ministers, chaired by the coordinating country's minister for the sector, supervises the sectoral activities. There are currently 21 such SCUs. Responsibility for marine fisheries and resources was allocated to Namibia following a decision by the Council of Ministers in 1991. The Sector Coordinator is Namibia's Permanent Secretary of the Ministry of Fisheries and Marine Resources, with the Minister of Fisheries and Marine Resources chairing the Sectoral Committee of Ministers. Sector contact points are allocated by each of the eight Member States, and these form the grassroots level of cooperation between the SCU and the region. Matters concerning marine and fisheries resources are also coordinated by SADC's overall Sector Coordinator for Food, Agriculture and Natural Resources, as one of the eight subsectors it oversees.

The task of guiding and leading SADC's fisheries sector is based on the policy objectives and strategy document that direct the Programme of Action for the sector. One of the most important elements of the Programme of Action is finalization of the Protocol on Fisheries that is currently being drawn up and is expected to be a key policy instrument in the fulfilment of SADC objectives in the field of marine and inland fisheries sustainable development. The SCU of marine and fisheries resources is coordinating the implementation of seven projects that focus on the priority areas for the sector: the Regional Fisheries Information System; SADC monitoring, control and surveillance (MCS) of fishing activities; support to the SADC Marine Fisheries SCU; assessment of the marine fisheries resources of the SADC region; the Benguela Current Large Marine Ecosystem; and harmonization of marine fisheries policy and marine fisheries training. In addition, the SCU is formulating three project proposals, as directed by the Annual Marine Fisheries Ministers Meeting (May 1999, United Republic of Tanzania). These are: cooperation with research on the east coast large marine ecosystem; a policy study for mariculture development; and language training.

The SADC fisheries programme has raised a total of US$9 million to support SCU-driven marine fisheries initiatives during 2000. Funding of US$35 million, for the next five years, has been committed from a wide range of donors.

## COOPERATION WITH FAO

SADC and FAO cooperate closely in relation to fisheries matters. FAO is providing technical and financial assistance to two of the projects currently being implemented by the SCU for marine and fisheries resources.

*TABLE 15*

### SADC: fisheries and aquaculture production, food balance and trade

|  | 1986 | 1990 | 1994 | 1998 |
|---|---|---|---|---|
| **Aquaculture production** | | | | |
| Inland production *('000 tonnes)* | 2 | 5 | 7 | 8 |
| Percentage of world total | 0.0 | 0.1 | 0.1 | 0.0 |
| Marine production *('000 tonnes)* | 0 | 2 | 4 | 4 |
| Percentage of world total | 0.0 | 0.0 | 0.0 | 0.0 |
| **Fisheries production** | | | | |
| Inland production *('000 tonnes)* | 594 | 694 | 560 | 619 |
| Percentage of world total | 10.0 | 10.8 | 8.3 | 7.7 |
| Marine production *('000 tonnes)* | 1 013 | 1 032 | 1 038 | 1 158 |
| Percentage of world total | 1.3 | 1.3 | 1.2 | 1.5 |
| **Fisheries and aquaculture production** | | | | |
| Combined total *('000 tonnes)* | 1 609 | 1 733 | 1 609 | 1 789 |
| Percentage of world total | 1.7 | 1.8 | 1.4 | 1.5 |
| **Food balance** | | | | |
| Total food supply *('000 tonnes)* | 1 364 | 1 511 | 1 085 | ... |
| Per capita supply *(kg)* | 10.0 | 9.9 | 6.3 | ... |
| Fish as share of animal protein *(%)* | 21.8 | 21.8 | 17.2 | ... |
| **Trade in fishery commodities** | | | | |
| Total imports *(US$ millions)* | 223 | 264 | 249 | 256 |
| Percentage of world total | 0.9 | 0.7 | 0.5 | 0.5 |
| Total exports *(US$ millions)* | 165 | 203 | 665 | 843 |
| Percentage of world total | 0.7 | 0.6 | 1.4 | 1.6 |

*Note:* ... = data not available.

# SOUTH PACIFIC FORUM

The South Pacific Forum (SPF), consisting of Heads of Government, was established in 1971. It provides an opportunity to discuss a wide variety of South Pacific and international concerns and issues common to members, including the promotion of a free trade area in the South Pacific region. In 1998, the members of the SPF and its affiliated agencies were: Australia, Cook Islands, Federated States of Micronesia, Fiji, Kiribati, Marshall Islands, Nauru, New Zealand, Niue, Palau, Papua New Guinea, Samoa, Solomon Islands, Tonga, Tuvalu and Vanuatu. The SPF has a Secretariat (Forum Secretariat) which promotes regional cooperation among members on important economic issues.

## FISHERIES: PURPOSE AND ACTIVITIES

The South Pacific Forum Fisheries Agency (FFA) was established as a specialized agency by the SPF in 1979. The FFA Convention reflects the common concerns of member countries regarding conservation, optimum utilization and coastal states' sovereign rights over the region's living marine resources. The functions of FFA include accumulating detailed and up-to-date information on aspects of living marine resources in the region; evaluating and analysing data to provide clear, timely, concise, complete and accurate advice to member countries; developing and maintaining a communication network for the dissemination of information to member countries, and implementing policies and programmes that have been approved by the Forum Fisheries Committee. The following are the main functions and objectives of FFA, which are reviewed periodically.

*Economics and marketing.* Assistance is given to member countries in the formulation of policies and identification of projects for the sustained use of their tuna resources (the main areas covered are tuna management, industry, marketing, fisheries access, training and linkages).

*Legal services.* Support is provided to strengthen member countries in the understanding of their legal responsibilities and rights and ability to fulfil responsibilities and take advantage of rights. This support includes the provision of advice in the fields of international law, national legislation, illegal fishing, access negotiations and of training for responsible lawyers and officers within member countries. FFA is simultaneously assisting members in achieving full and independent legislative control of their fisheries resources and ensuring the necessary regional compatibility and cohesion.

*Monitoring, control and surveillance.* MCS activities aim at reinforcing the capacity of fishing operators in member countries to comply with national regulations and regional licence conditions. This function includes such actions as: assistance to member countries in developing and coordinating national MCS plans; coordination of regional observer programmes and assistance to the development of national observer programmes; coordination of regional surveillance operations; collection and dissemination of data in support of national MCS operations; assistance to FFA members in determining their maritime boundaries; and provision of training, advice and regional exchanges on enforcement and technological developments. FFA's achievements in this field include:

- participation in the coordination and planning of aerial surveillance flights covering members' EEZs;
- the successful development and implementation of a regional observer programme for the South Pacific;
- the research, design and implementation of a satellite-based VMS;

• the establishment of a Maritime Surveillance Communications Network, which will integrate other information systems, including the VMS.

FFA also undertakes *corporate and treaty services*, including the establishment and maintenance of administrative systems that meet the requirements of treaties and agreements for which FFA is responsible. In the field of *information technology and communication*, FFA has developed an innovative and sophisticated computer system that provides support in the reception, processing and transfer of information to facilitate the monitoring and control of foreign fishing fleets as well as to increase the speed, efficiency and cost-effectiveness with which FFA conducts its work.

FFA has brought important economic and social benefits to its members. Small island developing states have benefited, in particular through regional cooperation and the adoption of regional minimum standards. Regionally agreed measures to limit fishing effort (e.g. in the purse seine tuna fishery) have also been of tangible benefit to FFA member countries.

## COOPERATION WITH FAO

FFA has formal relations with FAO, which cooperates with the agency on a range of technical issues, including such matters as joint training exercises and exchanges of technical information. FAO participates in the annual FFC meeting as an observer.

FAO also participates as an observer in the Multilateral High-Level Conference on the Conservation and Management of Highly Migratory Fish Stocks in the Central

TABLE 16

### SPF: fisheries and aquaculture production, food balance and trade

|  | 1986 | 1990 | 1994 | 1998 |
|---|---|---|---|---|
| **Aquaculture production** | | | | |
| Inland production *('000 tonnes)* | 1 | 2 | 3 | 3 |
| Percentage of world total | 0.0 | 0.0 | 0.0 | 0.0 |
| Marine production *('000 tonnes)* | 25 | 40 | 68 | 119 |
| Percentage of world total | 0.7 | 0.8 | 0.8 | 1.0 |
| **Fisheries production** | | | | |
| Inland production *('000 tonnes)* | 20 | 22 | 19 | 22 |
| Percentage of world total | 0.3 | 0.3 | 0.3 | 0.3 |
| Marine production *('000 tonnes)* | 505 | 505 | 793 | 1 074 |
| Percentage of world total | 0.6 | 0.8 | 0.9 | 1.4 |
| **Fisheries and aquaculture production** | | | | |
| Combined total *('000 tonnes)* | 551 | 734 | 882 | 1 219 |
| Percentage of world total | 0.6 | 0.7 | 0.8 | 1.0 |
| **Food balance** | | | | |
| Total food supply *('000 tonnes)* | 500 | 541 | 550 | ... |
| Per capita supply *(kg)* | 20.6 | 21.0 | 20.1 | ... |
| Fish as share of animal protein *(%)* | 8.7 | 8.7 | 8.5 | ... |
| **Trade in fishery commodities** | | | | |
| Total imports *(US$ millions)* | 320 | 444 | 534 | 575 |
| Percentage of world total | 1.3 | 1.1 | 1.0 | 1.0 |
| Total exports *(US$ millions)* | 749 | 1 036 | 1 538 | 1 543 |
| Percentage of world total | 3.3 | 2.9 | 3.2 | 3.0 |

*Note:* ... = data not available.

and Western Pacific (MHLC), in close cooperation with FFA and its members, as well as with the Distant Water Fishing Nations.

The FAO Subregional Office for the Pacific is expected to participate in the Marine Sector Working Group of the South Pacific Organizations' Coordinating Committee, which is being convened by the Forum Secretariat and its members. The Working Group was established to facilitate the coordination of regional activities in the development of a regional strategy for the marine sector, and its membership comprises relevant Pacific regional organizations. ◆

Sales and Marketing Group, Information Division, FAO
Viale delle Terme di Caracalla, 00100 Rome, Italy
Tel.: +39 06 57051 – Fax: +39 06 5705 3360
E-mail: publications-sales@fao.org

أمـاكـن بيـع مطبوعـات المنظمـة
当地何处可以购买粮农组织出版物
**WHERE TO PURCHASE FAO PUBLICATIONS LOCALLY**
**POINTS DE VENTE DES PUBLICATIONS DE LA FAO**
**PUNTOS DE VENTA DE PUBLICACIONES DE LA FAO**

**ANGOLA**
mpresa Nacional do Disco e de
ublicações, ENDIPU-U.E.E.
ua Cirilo da Conceição Silva, N° 7
.P. N° 1314-C, Luanda

**ARGENTINA**
brería Agropecuaria
asteur 743, 1028 Buenos Aires
orld Publications S.A.
v. Córdoba 1877, 1120 Buenos Aires
el./Fax: +54 11 48158156
orreo eléctronico:
obooks@infovia.com.ar

**AUSTRALIA**
unter Publications
O Box 404, Abbotsford, Vic. 3067
el.: 61 3 9417 5361
ax: 61 3 9419 7154
mail: jpdavies@ozemail.com.au

**AUSTRIA**
erold Buch & Co.
eihburggasse 26, 1010 Vienna

**BANGLADESH**
ssociation of Development
gencies in Bangladesh
ouse No. 1/3, Block F
lmatia, Dhaka 1207

**BELGIQUE**
. De Lannoy
2, avenue du Roi, B-1060 Bruxelles
CP: 000-0808993-13
él.: jean.de.lannoy@infoboard.be

**BOLIVIA**
s Amigos del Libro
Heroínas 311, Casilla 450
ochabamba;
ercado 1315, La Paz

**BOTSWANA**
tsalo Books (Pty) Ltd
O Box 1532, Gaborone

**BRAZIL**
ndação Getúlio Vargas
aia do Botafogo 190, C.P. 9052
o de Janeiro
cleo Editora da Universidade
deral Fluminense
a Miguel de Frias 9
araí-Niterói 24
0-000 Rio de Janeiro
ndação da Universidade
deral do Paraná - FUNPAR
a Alfredo Bufrem 140, 30° andar
020-240 Curitiba

**CAMEROUN**
DDES
entre Africain de Diffusion et
eveloppement Social
.P. 7317, Douala Bassa
l.:+237 43 37 83
lécopie: +237 42 77 03

**CANADA**
nouf Publishing
69 chemin Canotek Road, Unit 1
tawa, Ontario K1J 9J3
l.: +1 613 745 2665
x:+1 613 745 7660
mail: renouf@fox.nstn.ca
ebsite: www.renoufbooks.com

**CHILE**
brería - Oficina Regional, FAO
FAO, Oficina Regional para América
tina y el Caribe (RLC)
da. Dag Hammarskjold, 3241
acura, Santiago
l.: +56 2 33 72 314
rreo eléctronico:
rman.rojas@field.fao.org
iversitaria Textolibros Ltda.
da. L. Bernardo O'Higgins 1050
ntiago

• **CHINA**
**China National Publications
Import & Export Corporation**
16 Gongti East Road, Beijing 100020
Tel.: +86 10 6506 3070
Fax: +86 10 6506 3101
E-mail: serials@cnpiec.com.cn

• **COLOMBIA**
**INFOENLACE LTDA.**
Calle 72 N° 13-23 Piso 3
Edificio Nueva Granada
Santafé de Bogotá
Tel.: +57 1 2558783-2557969
Fax: +57 1 2480808-2176435
Correo eléctronico:
infoenlace@gaitana.interred.net.co

• **CONGO**
**Office national des librairies
populaires**
B.P. 577, Brazzaville

• **COSTA RICA**
**Librería Lehmann S.A.**
Av. Central, Apartado 10011
1000 San José
**CINDE**
Coalición Costarricense de Iniciativas
de Desarrollo
Apartado 7170, 1000 San José
Correo eléctronico:
rtacinde@sol.rassa.co.cr

• **CÔTE D'IVOIRE**
**CEDA**
04 B.P. 541, Abidjan 04
Tél.: +225 22 20 55
Télécopie: +225 21 72 62

• **CUBA**
**Ediciones Cubanas
Empresa de Comercio Exterior
de Publicaciones**
Obispo 461, Apartado 605, La Habana

• **CZECH REPUBLIC**
**Artia Pegas Press Ltd
Import of Periodicals**
Palác Metro, PO Box 825
Národní 25, 111 21 Praha 1

• **DENMARK**
**Munksgaard, Direct**
Ostergate 26 A - Postbox 173
DK - 1005 Copenhagen K.
Tel.: +45 77 33 33 33
Fax:+45 77 33 33 77
E-mail: direct@munksgaarddirect.dk
URL: www.munksgaardirect.dk

• **ECUADOR**
**Libri Mundi, Librería Internacional**
Juan León Mera 851
Apartado Postal 3029, Quito
Correo eléctronico:
librimul@librimundi.com.ec
**Universidad Agraria del Ecuador
Centro de Información Agraria**
Av. 23 de julio, Apartado 09-01-1248
Guayaquil
**Librería Española**
Murgeón 364 y Ulloa, Quito

• **EGYPT**
**MERIC
The Middle East Readers' Information
Centre**
2 Baghat Aly Street, Appt. 24
El Masry Tower D
Cairo/Zamalek
Tel.:+202 3413824/34038818
Fax:+202 3419355
E-mail: mafouda@meric-co.com

• **ESPAÑA**
**Librería Agrícola**
Fernando VI 2, 28004 Madrid
**Librería de la Generalitat
de Catalunya**
Rambla dels Estudis 118 (Palau Moja)
08002 Barcelona
Tel.:+34 93 302 6462
Fax:+34 93 302 1299

**Mundi Prensa Libros S.A.**
Castelló 37, 28001 Madrid
Tel.: +34 91 436 37 00
Fax: +34 91 575 39 98
Sitio Web: www.mundiprensa.com
Correo eléctronico:
libreria@mundiprensa.es
**Mundi Prensa - Barcelona**
Consejo de Ciento 391
08009 Barcelona
Tel.: +34 93 488 34 92
Fax: +34 93 487 76 59

• **FINLAND**
**Akateeminen Kirjakauppa Subscription
Services**
PO Box 23, FIN-00371 Helsinki
Tel.: +358 9 121 4416
Fax: +358 9 121 4450

• **FRANCE**
**Editions A. Pedone**
13, rue Soufflot, 75005 Paris
**Lavoisier Tec & Doc**
14, rue de Provigny
94236 Cachan Cedex
Mél.: livres@lavoisier.fr
Site Web: www.lavoisier.fr
**Librairie du commerce international**
10, avenue d'Iéna
75783 Paris Cedex 16
Mél.: pl@net-export.fr
Site Web: www.cfce.fr
**WORLD DATA**
10, rue Nicolas Flamand
75004 Paris
Tél.: +33 1 4278 0578
Télécopie: +33 1 4278 1472

• **GERMANY**
**Alexander Horn Internationale
Buchhandlung**
Friedrichstrasse 34
D-65185 Wiesbaden
Tel.: +49 611 9923540/9923541
Fax: +49 611 9923543
E-mail: alexhorn1@aol.com
**S. Toeche-Mittler GmbH
Versandbuchhandlung**
Hindenburgstrasse 33
D-64295 Darmstadt
Tel.: +49 6151 336 65
Fax: +49 6151 314 043
E-mail: triops@booksell.com
Website: www.booksell.com/triops
**Uno Verlag**
Poppelsdorfer Allee 55
D-53115 Bonn 1
Tel.: +49 228 94 90 20
Fax: +49 228 21 74 92
E-mail: unoverlag@aol.com
Website: www.uno-verlag.de

• **GHANA**
**SEDCO Publishing Ltd**
Sedco House, Tabon Street
Off Ring Road Central, North Ridge
PO Box 2051, Accra
**Readwide Bookshop Ltd**
PO Box 0600 Osu, Accra
Tel.: +233 21 22 1387
Fax: +233 21 66 3347
E-mail: readwide@africaonline.cpm.gh

• **GREECE**
**Papasotiriou S.A.**
35 Stournara Str., 10682 Athens
Tel.: +30 1 3302 980
Fax: +30 1 3648254

• **GUYANA**
**Guyana National Trading
Corporation Ltd**
45-47 Water Street, PO Box 308
Georgetown

• **HONDURAS**
**Escuela Agrícola Panamericana
Librería RTAC**
El Zamorano, Apartado 93, Tegucigalpa
**Oficina de la Escuela Agrícola
Panamericana en Tegucigalpa**
Blvd. Morazán, Apts. Glapson
Apartado 93, Tegucigalpa

• **HUNGARY**
**Librotrade Kft.**
PO Box 126, H-1656 Budapest
Tel.: +36 1 256 1672
Fax:+36 1 256 8727

• **INDIA**
**Allied Publisher Ltd**
751 Mount Road
Chennai 600 002
Tel.: +91 44 8523938/8523984
Fax: +91 44 8520649
E-mail:
allied.mds@smb.sprintrpg.ems.vsnl.net.in
**EWP Affiliated East-West
Press PVT, Ltd**
G-I/16, Ansari Road, Darya Gany
New Delhi 110 002
Tel.: +91 11 3264 180
Fax:+91 11 3260 358
E-mail: affiliat@nda.vsnl.net.in
**Oxford Book and Stationery Co.**
Scindia House
New Delhi 110001
Tel.: +91 11 3315310
Fax: +91 11 3713275
E-mail: oxford@vsnl.com
**Periodical Expert Book Agency**
G-56, 2nd Floor, Laxmi Nagar
Vikas Marg, Delhi 110092
Tel: +91 11 2215045/2150534
Fax: +91 11 2418599
E-mail: oriental@nde.vsnl.net.in
**Bookwell**
Head Office:
2/72, Nirankari Colony, New Delhi - 110009
Tel.: +91 11 725 1283
Fax:+91 11 328 13 15
Sales Office:
24/4800, Ansari Road
Darya Ganj, New Delhi - 110002
Tel.: +91 11 326 8786
E-mail: bkwell@nde.vsnl.net.in

• **IRAN**
**The FAO Bureau, International
and Regional Specialized
Organizations Affairs**
Ministry of Agriculture of the Islamic
Republic of Iran
Keshavarz Bld, M.O.A., 17th floor
Teheran

• **ITALY**
**FAO Bookshop**
Viale delle Terme di Caracalla
00100 Roma
Tel.: +39 06 5705 2313
Fax:+39 06 5705 3360
E-mail: publications-sales@fao.org
**Libreria Commissionaria Sansoni
S.p.A. - Licosa**
Via Duca di Calabria 1/1
50125 Firenze
Tel.: +39 55 64 8 31
Fax:+39 55 64 12 57
E-mail: licosa@ftbcc.it
**Libreria Scientifica Dott. Lucio de Biasio
"Aeiou"**
Via Coronelli 6, 20146 Milano

• **JAPAN**
**Far Eastern Booksellers
(Kyokuto Shoten Ltd)**
12 Kanda-Jimbocho 2 chome
Chiyoda-ku - PO Box 72
Tokyo 101-91
Tel.: +81 3 3265 7531
Fax:+81 3 3265 4656
**Maruzen Company Ltd**
PO Box 5050
Tokyo International 100-31
Tel.: +81 3 3275 8585
Fax:+81 3 3275 0656
E-mail: h_sugiyama@maruzen.co.jp

ساكن بيع مطبوعـات المنظمـة

当地何处可以购买粮农组织出版

**WHERE TO PURCHASE FAO PUBLICATIONS LOCALL**
**POINTS DE VENTE DES PUBLICATIONS DE LA FA**
**PUNTOS DE VENTA DE PUBLICACIONES DE LA FA**

• **KENYA**
**Text Book Centre Ltd**
Kijabe Street
PO Box 47540, Nairobi
Tel.: +254 2 330 342
Fax: +254 2 22 57 79
**Inter Africa Book Distribution**
Kencom House, Moi Avenue
PO Box 73580, Nairobi
Tel.: +254 2 211 184
Fax: +254 2 22 3 5 70
**Legacy Books**
Mezzanine 1, Loita House, Loita Street
Nairobi, PO Box 68077
Tel.: +254 2 303853
Fax: +254 2 330854

• **LUXEMBOURG**
**M.J. De Lannoy**
202, avenue du Roi
B-1060, Bruxelles (Belgique)
Mél.: jean.de.lannoy@infoboard.be

• **MADAGASCAR**
**Centre d'Information et de
Documentation Scientifique et
Technique**
Ministère de la recherche appliquée
au développement
B.P. 6224, Tsimbazaza, Antananarivo

• **MALAYSIA**
**Southbound**
Suite 20F Northam House
55 Jalan Sultan Ahmad Shah
10050 Penang
Tel.: +60 4 2282169
Fax: +60 4 2281758
E-mail: chin@south.pc.my
Website: www.southbound.com.my

• **MALI**
**Librairie Traore**
Rue Soundiata Keita X 115
B.P. 3243, Bamako

• **MAROC**
**La Librairie Internationale**
70, rue T'ssoule
B.P. 302 (RP), Rabat
Tél./Télécopie: +212 7 75 01 83

• **MÉXICO**
**Librería, Universidad Autónoma de
Chapingo**
56230 Chapingo
**Libros y Editoriales S.A.**
Av. Progreso Nº 202-1º Piso A
Apartado Postal 18922
Col. Escandón, 11800 México D.F.
**Mundi Prensa Mexico, S.A.**
Río Pánuco, 141 Col. Cuauhtémoc
C.P. 06500, México, DF
Tel.: +52 5 533 56 58
Fax: +52 5 514 67 99
Correo electrónico:
1015452361@compuserve.com

• **NETHERLANDS**
**Roodveldt Import b.v.**
Brouwersgracht 288
1013 HG Amsterdam
Tel.: +31 20 622 80 35
Fax: +31 20 625 54 93
E-mail: roodboek@euronet.nl
**Swets & Zeitlinger b.v.**
PO Box 830, 2160 Lisse
Heereweg 347 B, 2161 CA Lisse
E-mail: infono@swets.nl
Website: www.swets.nl

• **NEW ZEALAND**
**Legislation Services**
PO Box 12418
Thorndon, Wellington
E-mail: gppmjxf@gp.co.nz
**Oasis Official**
PO Box 3627, Wellington
Tel.: +64 4 499 1551
Fax: +64 4 499 1972
E-mail: oasis@clear.net.nz
Website: www.oasisbooks.co.nzl

• **NICARAGUA**
**Librería HISPAMER**
Costado Este Univ. Centroamericana
Apartado Postal A-221, Managua

• **NIGERIA**
**University Bookshop (Nigeria) Ltd**
University of Ibadan, Ibadan

• **PAKISTAN**
**Mirza Book Agency**
65 Shahrah-e-Quaid-e-Azam
PO Box 729, Lahore 3

• **PARAGUAY**
**Librería Intercontinental
Editora e Impresora S.R.L.**
Caballero 270 c/Mcal Estigarribia
Asunción

• **PHILIPPINES**
**International Booksource Center, Inc.**
1127-A Antipolo St, Barangay Valenzuela
Makati City
Tel.: +63 2 8966501/8966505/8966507
Fax: +63 2 8966497
E-mail: ibcdina@webquest.com

• **POLAND**
**Ars Polona**
Krakowskie Przedmiescie 7
00-950 Warsaw

• **PORTUGAL**
**Livraria Portugal, Dias e Andrade
Ltda.**
Rua do Carmo, 70-74
Apartado 2681, 1200 Lisboa Codex

• **REPÚBLICA DOMINICANA**
**CUESTA - Centro del libro**
Av. 27 de Febrero, esq. A. Lincoln
Centro Comercial Nacional
Apartado 1241, Santo Domingo
**CEDAF - Centro para el Desarrollo
Agropecuario y Forestal, Inc.**
Calle José Amado Soler, 50 - Urban.
Paraíso
Apartado Postal, 567-2, Santo Domingo
Tel.: +001 809 544-0616/544-0634/
565-5603
Fax: +001 809 544-4727/567-6989
Correo electrónico: fda@Codetel.net.do

• **SINGAPORE**
**Select Books Pte Ltd**
03-15 Tanglin Shopping Centre
19 Tanglin Road, Singapore 1024
Tel.: +65 732 1515
Fax: +65 736 0855

• **SLOVAK REPUBLIC**
**Institute of Scientific and Technical
Information for Agriculture**
Samova 9, 950 10 Nitra
Tel.: +421 87 522 185
Fax: +421 87 525 275
E-mail: uvtip@nr.sanet.sk

• **SOMALIA**
**Samater**
PO Box 936, Mogadishu

• **SOUTH AFRICA**
**David Philip Publishers (Pty) Ltd**
PO Box 23408, Claremont 7735
Tel.: Cape Town +27 21 64 4136
Fax: Cape Town +27 21 64 3358
E-mail: dpp@iafrica.com
Website: www.twisted.co.za

• **SRI LANKA**
**M.D. Gunasena & Co. Ltd**
217 Olcott Mawatha, PO Box 246
Colombo 11

• **SUISSE**
**UN Bookshop**
Palais des Nations
CH-1211 Genève 1
Site Web: www.un.org
**Van Diermen Editions Techniques
ADECO**
41 Lacuez, CH-1807 Blonzy

• **SURINAME**
**Vaco n.v. in Suriname**
Domineestraat 26, PO Box 1841
Paramaribo

• **SWEDEN**
**Wennergren Williams AB**
PO Box 1305, S-171 25 Solna
Tel.: +46 8 705 9750
Fax: +46 8 27 00 71
E-mail: mail@wwi.se
**Bokdistributören**
c/o Longus Books Import
PO Box 610, S-151 27 Södertälje
Tel.: +46 8 55 09 49 70
Fax: +46 8 55 01 76 10; E-mail:
lis.ledin@hk.akademibokhandeln.se

• **THAILAND**
**Suksapan Panit**
Mansion 9, Rajdamnern Avenue,
Bangkok

• **TOGO**
**Librairie du Bon Pasteur**
B.P. 1164, Lomé

• **TURKEY**
**DUNYA INFOTEL**
100.Yil Mahallesi
34440 Bagcilar, Istanbul
Tel.: +90 212 629 0808
Fax: +90 212 629 4689
E-mail: dunya@dunya-gazete.com.tr
Website: www.dunya.com

• **UGANDA**
**Fountain Publishers Ltd**
PO Box 488, Kampala
Tel.: +256 41 259 163
Fax: +256 41 251 160

• **UNITED ARAB EMIRATES**
**Al Rawdha Bookshop**
PO Box 5027, Sharjah
Tel.: +971 6 734687
Fax: +971 6 384473
E-mail: alrawdha@hotmail.com

• **UNITED KINGDOM**
**The Stationery Office**
51 Nine Elms Lane
London SW8 5DR
Tel.: +44 20 7873 9090 (orders)
+44 20 7873 0011 (inquiries)
Fax: +44 20 7873 8463
**and through The Stationery Office
Bookshops**
E-mail: postmaster@theso.co.uk
Website: www.the-stationery-
office.co.uk
*Electronic products only:*
**Microinfo Ltd**
PO Box 3, Omega Road
Alton, Hampshire GU34 2PG
Tel.: +44 1420 86 848
Fax: +44 1420 89 889
E-mail: emedia@microinfo.co.uk
Website: www.microinfo.co.uk
**Intermediate Technology Bookshop**
103-105 Southampton Row
London WC1B 4HH
Tel.: +44 20 7436 9761
Fax: +44 20 7436 2013
E-mail: orders@itpubs.org.uk
Website: www.oneworld.org/itdg/
publications.html

• **UNITED STATES**
*Publications:*
**BERNAN Associates (ex UNIPUB)**
4611/F Assembly Drive
Lanham, MD 20706-4391
Toll-free: +1 800 274 4447
Fax: +1 800 865 3450
E-mail: query@bernan.com
Website: www.bernan.com
**United Nations Publications**
Two UN Plaza, Room DC2-853
New York, NY 10017
Tel.: +1 212 963 8302/800 253 9646
Fax: +1 212 963 3489
E-mail: publications@un.org
Website: www.unog.ch
**UN Bookshop** (direct sales)
The United Nations Bookshop
General Assembly Building Room 32
New York, NY 10017
Tel.: +1 212 963 7680
Fax: +1 212 963 4910
E-mail: bookshop@un.org
Website: www.un.org
*Periodicals:*
**Ebsco Subscription Services**
PO Box 1943
Birmingham, AL 35201-1943
Tel.: +1 205 991 6600
Fax: +1 205 991 1449
**The Faxon Company Inc.**
15 Southwest Park
Westwood, MA 02090
Tel.: +1 617 329 3350
Telex: 95 1980
Cable: FW Faxon Wood

• **URUGUAY**
**Librería Agropecuaria S.R.L.**
Buenos Aires 335, Casilla 1755
Montevideo C.P. 11000

• **VENEZUELA**
**Tecni-Ciencia Libros**
CCCT Nivel C-2
Caracas
Tel.: +58 2 959 4747
Fax: +58 2 959 5636
Correo electrónico:
tclibros@attglobal.net
**Fudeco, Librería**
Avenida Libertador-Este
Ed. Fudeco, Apartado 254
Barquisimeto C.P. 3002, Ed. Lara
Tel.: +58 51 538 022
Fax: +58 51 544 394
**Librería FAGRO**
Universidad Central de Venezuela (UC
Maracay

• **ZIMBABWE**
**Grassroots Books**
The Book Café
Fife Avenue, Harare;
61a Fort Street, Bulawayo
Tel.: +263 4 79 31 82
Fax: +263 4 72 62 43